the BANKRUPTCY KIT

Third Edition

John Ventura

Dearborn™
Trade Publishing
A **Kaplan Professional** Company

This publication is designed to provide accurate and authoritative information in regard to the subject matter covered. It is sold with the understanding that the publisher is not engaged in rendering legal, accounting, or other professional service. If legal advice or other expert assistance is required, the services of a competent professional person should be sought.

Vice President and Publisher: Cynthia A. Zigmund
Acquisitions Editor: Mary B. Good
Senior Managing Editor: Jack Kiburz
Interior Design: Lucy Jenkins
Cover Design: KTK Design Associates
Typesetting: the dotted i

Published by Dearborn Trade Publishing
A Kaplan Professional Company

Printed in the United States of America

04   05   06   07   10 9 8 7 6 5 4 3 2 1

Library of Congress Cataloging-in-Publication Data

Ventura, John.
    The bankruptcy kit / John Ventura.— 3rd ed.
        p.   cm.
    Includes index.
    ISBN 0-7931-3551-6 (pbk.)
    1. Bankruptcy—United States—Popular works.   I. Title.
    KF1524.6.V46 2004
    346.7307′8—dc22

                                                    2004009129

Dearborn Trade books are available at special quantity discounts to use for sales promotions, employee premiums, or educational purposes. Please call our Special Sales Department to order or for more information at 800-245-2665, e-mail trade@ dearborn.com, or write to Dearborn Trade Publishing, 30 South Wacker Drive, Suite 2500, Chicago, IL 60606-7481.

Dedicated to my wife, Mary Ellen

Contents

Preface

In my 26 years of work as a bankruptcy attorney, countless financially troubled consumers have come to my office full of anxiety, depression, and fear about the prospect of filing for bankruptcy. In nearly every case, I found that if I took the time to explain the bankruptcy process to them and to describe the roles of lawyers, the court, and other players in the process, they usually left my office feeling a lot better.

In 1990, with bankruptcies at record levels and even greater numbers predicted for the coming years, I decided to write a book about bankruptcy for consumers and small business people. Avoiding legal mumbo jumbo, I wanted this book to provide readers with much of the same information I give my clients, guiding them through the bankruptcy process and telling them what their lawyers should be doing for them. The result was the first edition of *The Bankruptcy Kit*. A second edition of the book was published in 1996, after Congress passed important amendments to the Bankruptcy Code in 1994.

Since then, millions of new bankruptcies have been filed in the United States, and new records for the number of consumer filings have become commonplace. Sadly, there is a greater need than ever for the information and advice in this book.

The need for bankruptcy-related guidance and advice is particularly critical since the little-known Bankruptcy Civil Enforcement Initiative was implemented by John Ashcroft, who is the attorney general in the Bush administration. The initiative has put into effect many of the new changes to the bankruptcy law that Congress has been trying to pass in recent years. Because the new legislation has not been enacted, the Justice Department implemented much of it administratively. As a result, most consumers who are considering bankruptcy or who have already filed are unaware of the Bankruptcy Civil Enforcement Initiative and how it may affect them. Among other things, when consumers file for bankruptcy they are more apt to be treated with suspicion and distrust by the courts. There is an assumption that a high percentage of those consumers don't really need to take that step and just want to get out of paying their debts. Another assumption of the initiative is that most consumers who file for bankruptcy can afford to pay more on their debts than they are willing to admit.

As a result of these and other assumptions, bankruptcy has become much more adversarial than it used to be, and consumers now must provide the court with a lot more documentation to prove how much they owe, how much they make, and what their assets are worth. Furthermore, it has become more difficult to file a Chapter 7 liquidation bankruptcy as a result of the initiative. Instead, consumers are being forced into Chapter 13 reorganization of debt bankruptcies, even if their attorneys believe that they would be better off filing a Chapter 7.

Therefore, to ensure that this book continues to be a valuable resource for those who are contemplating bankruptcy as well as for those who have already filed, I have written this third edition of *The Bankruptcy Kit.* In it I explain how the Bankruptcy Civil Enforcement Initiative affects consumers, and I provide up-to-date information about bankruptcy in general.

I know that filing for bankruptcy is never easy, but sometimes it's the best decision. I hope that the information and advice in *The Bank-*

WARNING

The information in this book reflects the state of the law at the time of publication. Please note that laws change, and the reader is therefore urged to seek legal counsel on any important issue.

ruptcy Kit will help make that important decision an easier one for anyone who is experiencing serious financial trouble. And I hope that knowing what to expect when they file for bankruptcy will ease the anxiety and fear they are probably feeling.

John Ventura
March, 2004

"I would like to amend this bill, if it were legal to do, by putting in a provision making it a capital offense for any of you retailers to seduce these people into installment purchasing beyond their means."

—Congressman Hobbs, in hearings before the Subcommittee on the Judiciary on H.R. 8046, 75th Congress, First Session, page 13, 1937

"It's too damned easy to file bankruptcy. These people just don't suffer enough."

—Comment overheard at a meeting of the Seattle Consumer Credit Association, 1981

1

Introducing You to Bankruptcy

Things Have Changed

During my 26 years practicing bankruptcy law, I have seen a lot of changes, many of which directly affected the consumer bankruptcy process and how much debt consumers can get rid of through bankruptcy. For example, in the last edition of this book, I wrote about the Bankruptcy Reform Act of 1994, which made the most sweeping revisions to bankruptcy law since the federal Bankruptcy Code was enacted in 1978. Although many of its changes benefited consumers who filed for bankruptcy, many others harmed them.

I wrote this new edition of *The Bankruptcy Kit,* not because Congress had passed still more changes to the Bankruptcy Code, but because in the fall of 2001, Attorney General John Ashcroft ordered all federal bankruptcy courts in this country to change many of the ways they handle consumer bankruptcies. Many of these changes, the result of the *Bankruptcy Civil Enforcement Initiative,* are very harmful to consumers. The stated goal of the initiative is to "more aggressively use existing civil enforcement methods to curb abuse of the bankruptcy system."

Although no one can disagree that consumers should not be allowed to abuse the system, in practice the initiative assumes that abuse is rampant and that consumers who file for bankruptcy cannot be trusted and will lie and cheat the system to get out of paying their debts. My experience and the experience of other consumer bankruptcy attorneys across the country, however, is that abuse of the bankruptcy system is rare and that most consumers do not file for bankruptcy unless they absolutely have to because it is an emotionally difficult step for them to take. Certainly, consumers sometimes provide their bankruptcy attorneys with inaccurate information about their finances and do not always keep good financial records prior to filing for bankruptcy, but they don't do that with a criminal intent, but rather because they are disorganized or confused, or because they are stressed out by the problems in their financial lives. Now, however, as a result of the Bankruptcy Civil Enforcement Initiative, most bankruptcy trustees take the attitude that the information on consumers' schedules of assets and debts—information that they must provide the court when they file for bankruptcy—is inaccurate. The trustees assume that most consumers who file for bankruptcy are dishonest and can spend less and pay more on their debts than what their schedules indicate. They also assume that the consumers who file for Chapter 7 bankruptcy to get most of their debts wiped out because they owe too much relative to their income can actually pay what they owe over time and, therefore, should file a Chapter 13 reorganization bankruptcy instead. Since the initiative was implemented, the court seems to care less about which kind of bankruptcy consumers' attorneys believe is most appropriate for their clients based on their financial situations and assumes that consumers who file for bankruptcy are out to cheat the system. As a result, although the aggressiveness with which the initiative is enforced varies somewhat by area of the country, generally speaking, getting through bank-

WARNING

At the time this book was written, Congress was considering amendments to the Bankruptcy Code that would make it more difficult for consumers to get rid of debt through bankruptcy and would provide unsecured creditors, such as credit card companies, greater rights in bankruptcy.

ruptcy has become more stressful than ever for consumers, primarily because it's now a confrontational process that calls into question their honesty and intentions. Furthermore, because the initiative has made the process more complicated and time-consuming, bankruptcy attorneys are charging their clients higher fees.

As you read this book, you will learn much more about the effects of the Bankruptcy Civil Enforcement Initiative on the bankruptcy process, but here are some highlights:

- It has become much more difficult for consumers to file a Chapter 7 liquidation bankruptcy, the type of bankruptcy that extremely cash-strapped consumers have traditionally used to wipe out most of their debts to get a financial fresh start. Now, the initiative is forcing consumers who can afford to pay anything at all on their debts, no matter how small an amount, into a Chapter 13 reorganization bankruptcy even if it means that those consumers will be burdened by debt for the next three to five years—the number of years that a Chapter 13 bankruptcy can last.
- Bankruptcy trustees used to assume that consumers were honest when they provided their attorneys with information about their finances. That has changed, however, although the degree to which this is true varies from court to court. As a result,

WARNING

As a result of the Bankruptcy Civil Enforcement Initiative, some trustees now hire Realtors to conduct "drive-by appraisals" of consumers' homes. Often, these Realtors overvalue homes. As a result, the trustees may require these consumers to pay more money to their creditors. Other trustees now question the budgets that consumers file with the court to show how much they will spend while they are in bankruptcy. Although the consumers' budgets tend to be quite minimal, the trustees often require that they reduce certain spending items even more so that they can pay their creditors more money. As a result, consumers' families often suffer.

trustees often require consumers to prove that the information on the forms that their bankruptcy attorney filed with the court is complete and accurate. In many instances, this means that consumers have to dig through boxes of financial records from years past or call numerous offices to obtain the information they need. Sometimes, not being able to find the information can have a negative effect on the outcome of their bankruptcy.

- The personal and private decisions of consumers are being questioned. For example, trustees have demanded that the "unemployment" of a full-time career homemaker be explained. The unstated message in their demand is that the woman should get a job so that the couple can pay more on its debts. Yet, it may be that the marriages of these consumers succeed because one spouse works and the other one manages the home life. Is the bankruptcy court entitled to tell married couples how to structure their relationship with one another, especially considering that most bankruptcies are not filed because the couples wildly overspent? In reality, most consumers end up in bankruptcy because they are saddled with thousands of dollars in unpaid medical bills, because they lost their jobs and haven't been able to find new ones that paid them as much as their old jobs did, because they suffered a financial setback as a result of a divorce, and so on.

- Bankruptcy has become much more adversarial. Previously, consumers who filed for bankruptcy could expect to spend very little time in court. Now, however, emboldened by the Bankruptcy Civil Enforcement Initiative, creditors involved in a consumer's bankruptcy are more apt to request court hearings to resolve issues related to the bankruptcy, and a trustee is much more likely to file multiple adversary motions against the consumer, which must also be resolved through hearings. During the hearings, attorneys for all sides will argue before the bankruptcy judge and the judge will decide what to do.

- It has become much more difficult for consumers who file Chapter 13 and who are having trouble completing their bankruptcy to convert to a Chapter 7 liquidation. Although bankruptcy law gives consumers the right to convert, the Bankruptcy Civil Enforcement Initiative has made converting more difficult and more expensive, even if the conversion is necessary. Reasons why a consumer may need to convert include: The consumer has a serious medical condition that affects his or her ability to earn an income, the consumer's spouse has died and so the consumer's household income has decreased, the consumer lost his or her job and cannot find a new one or the consumer has taken a job that pays a lot less, and so on. Also, when consumers want to convert, their financial information is now being carefully scrutinized for a second time to find any inconsistencies or other problems that might indicate that they committed fraud.

The changes that have occurred as a result of the Bankruptcy Civil Enforcement Initiative were made quietly, without debate by Congress, with little discussion by consumer groups and policymakers, and with virtually no media attention. Therefore, most consumers who file for bankruptcy are unaware of them and totally unprepared for what their bankruptcy will be like. I hope that this new edition of *The Bankruptcy Kit* will help prepare financially strapped consumers for bankruptcy by shining the light on the changes and explaining how those changes will affect them.

What Is Bankruptcy?

Bankruptcy is a constitutional right of protection against creditors. It allows consumers and businesses to make a fresh start when they owe so much money relative to their income that they cannot afford to pay their debts. Depending on the specific type of bankruptcy that is filed, most of the debts owed by a consumer or a business will be wiped out or the debts will be reorganized so that the consumer or business can afford to pay them. In exchange for the financial fresh start that bankruptcy provides, however, the consumer or business may have to give some of their assets back to their creditors. Furthermore, the bankruptcy will remain in the consumer's credit history for up to ten years and during that time, if the consumer is approved for new credit, the cost of that credit will be high.

If you are like most consumers who are struggling to pay their bills, even though you know that filing for bankruptcy will help you deal with your financial situation, you may not be sure that you want to take that step. After all, you have worked hard throughout your life and you have been willing to make sacrifices to pay your bills. As a case in point, when your financial troubles began, you probably tried everything you could think of to turn your financial situation around. But if you are like countless others in the same situation, despite your efforts, you still cannot meet all your financial obligations. As a result, debt collectors may be hounding you, your creditors may be sending you threatening letters, or maybe they are about to take your home or your car. Meanwhile, your financial situation is creating a tremendous amount of stress in your life. Therefore, you may be reading this book because you have concluded that filing for bankruptcy is probably the best thing you can do to resolve your financial problems and you want to learn more about how bankruptcy works. Or, you may be reading *The Bankruptcy Kit* because you have already filed and you want to know more about what to expect during your bankruptcy.

If you have filed for bankruptcy, you must understand what your attorney will do for you during each stage of the bankruptcy process and what decisions you will have to make. If you are considering bankruptcy but have not filed yet, you should become familiar with the protections you will get from bankruptcy, what you will have to give up to get those protections, and what you should and should not do before you file.

I don't know anyone who plans to have a financial crisis. Based on my experience counseling consumers who are having serious financial problems, their problems are the result of events beyond their control—a sudden job loss, high medical bills, or divorce. Regardless of why you are reading this book, it's important to make informed decisions about the best way to resolve your problems so that you can begin to rebuild your financial life as soon as possible and so that if you decide to file, you will get the most benefit from bankruptcy. *The Bankruptcy Kit* helps you do that.

HOT TIP

Your attorney must make sure that you understand all the legal terms you will encounter when you file for bankruptcy. If your attorney does not automatically explain a term that you do not understand, ask him or her to tell you what it means.

How to Locate a Good Bankruptcy Attorney

Bankruptcy is a complicated legal process that requires special expertise. This is particularly true since the implementation of the Bankruptcy Civil Enforcement Initiative. Therefore, to gain the maximum benefit from your bankruptcy, be sure to hire an experienced bankruptcy attorney. Don't try to handle your own bankruptcy.

When you are looking for a good attorney, you want to find one who:

- Has handled many consumer bankruptcies before.
- Is comfortable in the courtroom.
- Is a good negotiator for he or she may have to negotiate with your creditors.
- Charges reasonable fees that you can afford.
- Understands your problems and provides you with clear solutions to them.
- Really cares about helping you and is sensitive to your concerns.

You should also look for an attorney who makes you feel comfortable. For example, it should be easy for you to talk to the attorney, and you should feel that the attorney listens to you and provides you with complete answers to your questions.

Meet with several bankruptcy attorneys to find the right one. Your "getting-to-know-you meetings" should not cost you anything.

Here are several resources you can use to find some attorneys to meet with.

- *The yellow pages of your local phone directory.* When you look in the attorneys section of the yellow pages stay alert for attorneys who are board certified in bankruptcy. Certification signifies that an attorney has a special interest in bankruptcy and has passed a state bankruptcy law exam. Board certification usually also means that the attorney has practiced bankruptcy law for a number of years and has personally handled a substantial number of cases.
- *Ads in the media.* Lawyers may advertise their services on television or radio, in the newspaper, or on the Internet. Sometimes, lawyers who advertise price their services more reasonably than do other attorneys. If you can find an attorney who is board certified and has reasonable fees, you've got a winning combination.

```
┌─────────────────────────────────────────────────────┐
│  ┌─────────────────────────────────────────────────┐  │
│  │                  H O T   T I P                   │  │
│  └─────────────────────────────────────────────────┘  │
│                                                         │
│  Before you hire an attorney on the basis of his or    │
│  her advertising, whether a yellow pages ad or a       │
│  television, radio, or newspaper ad, conduct a little  │
│  research into the attorney's reputation and           │
│  experience. Use the Internet, ask any attorneys you   │
│  may know about the bankruptcy attorney's reputation,  │
│  and/or call your state bar organization to find out   │
│  if the attorney has ever been disciplined for         │
│  misconduct.                                           │
└─────────────────────────────────────────────────────┘
```

- *Attorney referrals.* If you have worked with an attorney in the past—the attorney who helped with your real estate closing, prepared your estate plan, or handled your divorce, for example—ask him or her for a referral to a bankruptcy attorney. That attorney will know who the good bankruptcy attorneys are in your community.

- *The bankruptcy trustees in your area.* These people work in the bankruptcy system every day and, therefore, they know which attorneys do the best work. Most of them will be willing to recommend several attorneys for you to contact. Contact your local bankruptcy court for the names and phone numbers of the trustees in your area.

- *The American Bankruptcy Board of Certification (ABBC).* This national organization certifies consumer bankruptcy attorneys. To become certified by the ABBC, an attorney must pass a daylong exam, complete at least 60 hours of continuing education over a three-year period, and prove that a substantial portion of his or her legal practice is devoted to bankruptcy. To get a referral to an ABBC-certified attorney, go to the organization's Web site at http://www.abcworld.org or call the organization at 703-739-1023 in Alexandria, Virginia.

- *The National Association of Consumer Bankruptcy Attorneys (NACBA).* Go to the organization's Web site at http://www.nacba.com for a referral to a member attorney in your area.

What Your Attorney Should Warn You about before You File

The attorney you hire should warn you against taking certain actions before you file for bankruptcy. For example, the attorney should tell you:

1. Don't do anything that will cause you to give up an asset that you truly need or that will give a creditor undue power over you. If you do not voluntarily relinquish something you own, the creditor may obtain a court order to make you give it up or may try to repossess it. Your bankruptcy attorney may be able to prevent that from happening.

2. Don't give one of your creditors a postdated check. If your check bounces, you may face criminal charges. This could be a problem because the protections of the bankruptcy court do not extend to criminal problems.

3. Don't transfer property out of your name and into the names of your friends or relatives thinking that if you do the assets won't be included in your bankruptcy. If you do, the court may treat the transfer as a fraudulent act. Usually, the court will be concerned about any transfers that may have occurred during the year prior to the start of your bankruptcy, and, in fact, the schedules of your assets, which list all your assets and that your bankruptcy attorney will fill out for the court, will specifically ask if you have transferred any of them to someone else. (See Appendixes A and B for copies of bankruptcy forms.) If you answer "Yes," the trustee may void the transfer. The trustee is appointed by the court to supervise your bankruptcy and to make sure that you abide by all the bankruptcy rules, among other things.

4. Don't charge up your credit cards or obtain cash advances using your credit cards immediately before you file for bankruptcy. Bankruptcy law states that if you run up more than "$1,100 worth of debt for luxury goods or services" with a single creditor "within 60 days" of filing for bankruptcy, that debt may not be wiped out by your bankruptcy. Instead, you will have to pay the creditor what you owe. This provision of the law also applies to credit card cash advances of more than $1,100 that you may have obtained during the 60 days prior to the start of your bankruptcy. By the way, these rules apply to luxury goods and services. Therefore, they probably won't

apply if you have to use one of your credit cards to pay for a necessity such as essential medical care or prescription drugs.

5. Don't pay one of your unsecured creditors at the expense of others during the 90 days prior to the start of your bankruptcy hoping that the creditor will treat you better after your bankruptcy. The court will view your payment as *preferential* and the bankruptcy trustee will probably cancel it and try to recover the money from the creditor you paid so that the funds can be distributed to your creditors according to the rules of bankruptcy.

H O T   T I P

The sooner you consult with an attorney prior to filing for bankruptcy, the more helpful your attorney's warnings can be.

H O T   T I P

If a debt collector contacts you about a debt you owe and tries to scare you into paying it with a postdated check, don't! The debt collector is violating the federal Fair Debt Collection Practices Act. For an explanation of your debt collection rights and a discussion of what to do if a debt collector contacts you, go to http://www.StopDebtCollectorsCold.com.

The attorneys you meet with should also explain how the bankruptcy process works and how the Bankruptcy Civil Enforcement Initiative will affect you. Among other things, the attorneys should explain what kinds of information you will have to provide so they can complete all the forms related to your bankruptcy and comply with the ini-

```
W A R N I N G
```

If you have transferred any of the assets you own to a friend or relative, don't do anything about the transfers until you have talked to a bankruptcy attorney.

tiative. As already indicated in this chapter, as a result of the initiative, you must be prepared to provide the court with a lot more information than in the past. For example, you must be prepared to prove the amount of every debt your attorney lists on your Schedules of Debts and the value of every asset on your Schedules of Assets, and you should be prepared to justify all the dollar amounts in your budget.

There Are Alternatives to Bankruptcy

Any competent bankruptcy attorney will tell you that you should treat bankruptcy as a remedy of last resort. In other words, you should pursue it only after you have exhausted all other realistic means of resolving your financial problems. In fact, during your first meeting, the attorney should make certain that you have pursued other options and should suggest any viable alternatives that you may have overlooked.

How to Avoid Bankruptcy

Short of winning the lottery or being left a windfall by a proverbial rich uncle, the most common ways to avoid bankruptcy are:

Spend less. If you don't have a budget that shows exactly where your family's money goes each month, prepare one. Then examine it carefully for expenses you can reduce or eliminate. Apply the money you save toward paying your debts. However, spending less may not be an option if you barely have enough money to pay for necessities such as housing, food, utilities, and gasoline for your car.

Earn more. Taking a second job may help end your financial crisis. You can take a night job, work on weekends, or consult on the side. If your spouse does not work outside the home, he or she could get a paying job for a while to help pay your family's bills. Also, if you have teenagers, consider asking them to get work part-time, assuming that having a job will not jeopardize their grades or create other problems in their lives. For example, if you have been paying for their car insurance and gasoline, make paying for those expenses their responsibility. Letting your older children know that your family is going through some tough times and that you need their help may not only improve your financial situation but may bring you closer together as a family.

Give up something. Are you buying something on time that you are willing to part with to ease your financial situation? The monthly payments on a second car, a boat, a second home, etc., may have helped create your financial problems. Therefore, if you are paying on an asset that you don't need, sell it and pay off the debt or give the asset back to the creditor that financed its purchase. However, don't give back a necessity.

It may be difficult for you to come to terms with the idea of giving up an asset for you have probably worked hard to make the payments on it. Giving it up may even make you feel like a failure. Try to be realistic and fair to yourself if you begin having such thoughts. Tell yourself that you are *not* a failure. You are simply going through tough times just like millions of other consumers in this country. Also, remember that just because you give up an asset that you cannot afford to keep right now, when your finances improve you can purchase it again if it is something that you still really want. Although self-denial is not a popular concept in this country, it makes sense when you are short on money.

Make a deal. Contact your creditors to ask them to lower the interest rate you are paying on your debts or to let you make smaller, more affordable payments on your debts. With a little old-fashioned horse trading, you may get enough of a break from some of them that you will be able to weather your financial hard times without having to file for bankruptcy, especially if, until recently, you always paid your bills on time and maintained a good credit history.

You can do your own negotiating or you can get help from the Consumer Credit Counseling Services (CCCS) office in your area. CCCS is a creditor-supported national nonprofit organization that helps people who are having financial problems develop household budgets and negotiate new debt payment arrangements with their creditors. To locate a CCCS office in your area, go to http://www.nfcc.org or call 800-388-2227.

HOT TIP

If you want to negotiate lower debt payments with your creditors, be sure you know how much you can realistically afford to pay each month before you contact them. You need a budget to do that.

HOT TIP

A good resource for learning about your debt collection legal rights and what you should do if a debt collector violates those rights is http://www.stopdebtcollectorscold.com.

Should You Consolidate Your Debts? Borrow from Relatives?

Don't get a bank loan, transfer all your credit card debts to another credit card, or use a credit card cash advance to consolidate your debts unless the interest rate on the new debt is lower than the rate on the debts you would be paying off and you clearly understand the terms of the new debt. For example, it is possible that if you consolidate your credit card debts by transferring them to a new low-interest credit card, the interest rate on that card could increase dramatically if you are just a day late with a payment. Also, the low, low rates on some credit cards often last for just a few months. Therefore, unless you pay off the transferred balances while the low rate is in effect, you may be worse off financially when the rate increases if the new rate is higher than the rates on the cards you transferred the balances from. To figure out if a balance transfer offer is truly a good deal, read the fine print in the offer.

WARNING

Think twice before you borrow against the equity in your home and use that money to pay off your credit card debts. You risk losing your home if you cannot pay the new debt.

Also, it is almost always a bad idea to borrow from friends or relatives. Sure, they may want to help you, but they may not really be able to afford to and they may suffer financially as a result. Furthermore, if you fall behind on your payments, you may put them in a difficult financial situation and you could even jeopardize your relationship with them. Save the relationship and find another way to solve your financial problems.

What You Keep and What You Give Up When You File for Bankruptcy

In bankruptcy, the court refers to the property you are entitled to keep as *exempt property*. You won't have to give up your exempt property if you file a Chapter 7 liquidation bankruptcy, although you will have to give up your nonexempt property. Your nonexempt property also determines the minimum amount of money you will have to pay to your creditors if you file a Chapter 13 reorganization of debt bankruptcy instead. Also, in a Chapter 13, you may not have to give up your nonexempt assets. Chapter 2 explains how Chapters 7 and 13 bankruptcy work.

The concept of exemptions is derived from the belief that debtors should be able to hold on to some of their assets when they file for bankruptcy even if they owe so much that they must liquidate their assets to pay their creditors. Being able to keep some of their assets will help them start over.

WARNING

If you borrow money from a friend or relative, protect that lender by securing the loan with an asset that you own. Also, do what is necessary in your state to ensure that your friend or relative will have a legal claim to the asset if you default on the loan. Taking these steps will make your relative or friend a secured creditor, which means that if you file for bankruptcy in the future, he or she will be more apt than your unsecured creditors to get at least some of the money you owe to that person.

State and Federal Exemptions

Each state has its own property exemption law. These laws allow consumers to protect a limited amount of assets from the collection actions of their creditors. The total value of property that consumers can exempt varies from state to state; Florida and Texas have the most generous exemptions. The federal government also has its own exemptions. If you live in one of the following states, you must use your state's exemptions when you file for bankruptcy: Alabama, Alaska, Arizona, Arkansas, California, Colorado, Delaware, Florida, Georgia, Idaho, Illinois, Indiana, Iowa, Kansas, Kentucky, Louisiana, Maine, Maryland, Mississippi, Missouri, Montana, Nebraska, Nevada, New Hampshire, New York, North Carolina, North Dakota, Ohio, Oklahoma, Oregon, South Carolina, South Dakota, Tennessee, Utah, Virginia, West Virginia, and Wyoming. If you live in any other state, you can choose whether to claim your state's exemptions or the federal ones. Your attorney will help you make this decision and will help you decide which specific assets to exempt.

Appendix C lists the federal exemptions. Appendix D highlights some of the exemptions offered by each state. Ask your attorney for a copy of the exemptions you can claim in your particular state and be sure that you claim every exemption you are entitled to.

An Exception to Exemption Laws

One exception to the exemption laws relates to secured assets. When you finance the purchase of an asset and use the asset to collateralize the debt, that asset is secured. Homes and vehicles are common examples of secured assets. If you do not pay a secured debt, the creditor can take the asset you used as collateral. If you exempt a secured asset, you must pay the creditor who financed the asset what you owe to the creditor or you risk losing that asset.

How to Keep Your Nonexempt Property

If you are going to file a Chapter 7 liquidation bankruptcy and you own nonexempt property—assets that you could lose in the bankruptcy—your attorney will tell you that:

- If your nonexempt property has little value, the bankruptcy trustee may decide that the cost of liquidating it would not be offset by any profit the court might realize from the sale. In that case, the trustee might "abandon" the property, which would mean that you could keep it.
- You may be able to purchase your nonexempt assets from the bankruptcy trustee if you can afford to pay a fair price for them. However, the trustee is less likely to let you do that now that the Bankruptcy Civil Enforcement Initiative is in effect. The trustee will want you to put the money toward your debts instead, unless the money you use to purchase the nonexempt assets comes from a friend or relative.
- If you cannot come up with the money you need to buy back the nonexempt assets you want to keep and if the trustee does not intend to abandon them, you may qualify for a Chapter 13 reorganization. In this kind of bankruptcy, you can keep your nonexempt property, but at a minimum, you must pay your unsecured creditors the value of that property. For example, if you own a nonexempt tract of land that is worth $15,000, you will have to pay a minimum of $15,000 to your unsecured creditors over the term of your debt reorganization plan.

WARNING

If you are confused about anything related to your bankruptcy, ask your attorney. If your attorney does not answer your questions or if you don't understand any of your attorney's answers, ask your question again. Remember, attorneys are human, so they may assume that you know what they are talking about or they may not provide you with clear and complete answers all the time.

2

The Different Types of Bankruptcy

There are four basic types of bankruptcy:

1. Chapter 13—a court-supervised reorganization of debts. When you file this kind of bankruptcy, the court will expect you to pay as much as you can on your debts. To help you do that, it will allow you to reduce your debt payments and will give you three to five years to pay what you owe.

2. Chapter 7—a liquidation of debts. This type of bankruptcy wipes out most but not all of your debts. However, you may have to give up some of the assets you own when you file this kind of bankruptcy. When you file for Chapter 7, you will have to decide which of your assets you want to keep or exempt from the bankruptcy and you will have to give up the assets you do not exempt. They will be sold and the proceeds will go to your creditors. There is a set of federal exemptions and a set of state exemptions. In some states you can choose between the two, but in the others you must use the exemptions offered by your state.

3. Chapter 11—a reorganization of debts. Partnerships and corporations must use this type of bankruptcy to pay off as much of their debts as possible. Also, individuals who owe too much to qualify for Chapter 13 must also use Chapter 11 if they want to reorganize their debts. Because this book focuses on Chap-

ter 13 reorganizations rather than on Chapter 11s, you should read my book, *The Business Turnaround and Bankruptcy Kit* (Dearborn Trade, 2003), if you want information about how the Chapter 11 bankruptcy process works.

4. Chapter 12—a reorganization for family farmers. This book does not discuss this kind of bankruptcy.

Your attorney will help you choose the kind of bankruptcy that is best for you given your particular financial situation. However, as a result of the Bankruptcy Civil Enforcement Initiative, you now have a lot less discretion over whether you file for Chapter 7 or Chapter 13. The bankruptcy court will expect you to file for Chapter 13 unless there is absolutely no way that you can pay anything on your debts.

Chapter 13 Reorganization of Debt

A Chapter 13 bankruptcy lets you reduce the amount that you must pay on your debts and gives you three to five years to pay them. It also helps you hold on to assets you might lose otherwise, and it protects you from your creditors while you are paying on your debts.

Do You Qualify for Chapter 13?

Only individuals and small businesses that are operated as sole proprietorships can file for Chapter 13. To be eligible, however, you cannot owe more than $922,975 in secured debts and more than $307,675 in unsecured debts. If you do and you want to reorganize your debts, you must file a Chapter 11 bankruptcy, which is more expensive, more time-consuming, and more difficult to complete than a Chapter 13 is.

The Chapter 13 Process in Brief

Your debt reorganization plan is central to the Chapter 13 bankruptcy process. This plan shows exactly how you intend to repay your debts over a three- to five-year period. Your attorney will prepare a plan for you based on the information you provide to him or her, and then the court must approve it. However, you must begin paying your creditors according to the terms of your plan 30 days after you file a bankruptcy petition with the court to begin your bankruptcy. In other words, you will begin paying on your reorganization plan before it has been approved by the court.

You will probably make payments on your plan through payroll deductions. In other words, your employer will be required to deduct your Chapter 13 debt payments directly from your paychecks and send them to the federal trustee in charge of your bankruptcy. In turn, the trustee will distribute your payments to your creditors according to the terms of your plan. If this arrangement will create difficulties in your life, however, the court may allow you to pay the trustee directly. Of course, if you are in business for yourself as a sole proprietor, you will send your debt payments directly to the trustee.

HOT TIP

If it is not practical for you to make monthly payments to the trustee, you can propose an alternative way to meet the terms of your reorganization plan. For example, if you are a seasonal worker whose income goes up and down according to the time of the year, a monthly payment plan might not be practical.

Your Luxury Items Are in Jeopardy

If you have luxury items that you owe money on, such as a vacation home, an extra car, or a boat, your attorney will warn you that the bankruptcy court may not be willing to approve your plan if you want

HOT TIP

If you want to keep your luxury items, a third person, a relative or close friend for example, may be willing to make the payments on them while you are in bankruptcy.

to keep them because the trustee will expect you to pay as much as possible on your debts. Therefore, you might be asked to sell your luxury items or give them up and use the proceeds to pay the creditors who loaned you money to purchase them.

You can keep luxury items that you do not owe money on; if you cannot claim them as exempt, however, you may have to pay at least their market or current value to your creditors to get your plan confirmed, which is another word for approved by the judge. Whether or not you can keep them will depend on the philosophy of the judge in the district where you file your bankruptcy and on how tough the trustee is. The philosophy of some judges is that if you are going to pay less than the full amount that you owe on your debts, you should not be able to keep any luxury items at all because that would be unfair to your creditors for they would end up with less than if you did not hold on to the items. These judges will consider that you did not present your plan in "good faith."

WARNING

The concept of good faith is somewhat vague in bankruptcy law. However, if a judge decides that you are not eligible for the benefits of a Chapter 13 and cannot find any other reason to deny your reorganization plan, the judge may use the good faith test to deny it.

HOT TIP

Never try to hold onto a car that is more expensive than the car the trustee or judge owns.

Chapter 13 for Small, Individually Owned Businesses

If you run your business as a sole proprietorship, you can use Chapter 13 to stay in business and pay off its debts.

Chapter 13 versus Chapter 11 for Small Businesses

Before 1978, if your small or middle-size business was having money troubles, you had few alternatives for dealing with them. Unless you were able to find new sources of operating capital or unless your creditors were willing to restructure your debts so that your business could afford to pay them, you would either have to shut your business down (usually through bankruptcy) or try to reorganize your business debts through a Chapter 11 bankruptcy. Because Chapter 11 tends to be complicated, expensive, and time-consuming, only relatively strong companies were able to reorganize successfully.

Therefore, in 1978 Congress created Chapter 13 to give small and medium-size businesses as well as consumers a new alternative for dealing with their debts. As a result, assuming your business qualifies for Chapter 13, it can benefit from this kind of bankruptcy just like consumers can and it will have a better chance of reorganizing successfully so it can continue to operate.

Qualifying for Chapter 13—Small Business

Your business must meet a couple of key criteria to qualify for Chapter 13. First, you must operate it as a sole proprietorship. If your business is structured as a partnership, it won't qualify unless you and your spouse own it. Also, your business won't qualify for Chapter 13 if it is incorporated and you are its only shareholder. Therefore, if your business is currently organized as a corporation or a partnership and it is having financial problems, you might want to consider dissolving it and making your business a sole proprietorship. Then, if later you need to reorganize your business's debts so it can survive, your business can file a Chapter 13 rather than a Chapter 11.

> ## WARNING
>
> Many businesspeople are urged to incorporate immediately when they start a new business. Their advisors do not consider the fact that most new businesses experience serious financial problems and that being incorporated will limit their options for dealing with those problems. New small business owners might be better served if they were told to wait to incorporate until their business survives the initial start-up period.
>
> Also, your business cannot owe more than $307,675 in unsecured debts and more than $992,975 in secured debts. If it does, your business will have to file for Chapter 11 if it wants to try to continue operating.

The Benefits of Chapter 13 for a Small Business

There are many advantages to filing for Chapter 13 rather than for Chapter 11. One key advantage is that it costs a lot less to file a Chapter 13 bankruptcy compared to a Chapter 11.

Also, compared to a Chapter 11, it is usually easier to get your reorganization plan approved by the court in a Chapter 13. The main reason is that Chapter 13 creditors have a lot less power than do Chapter 11 creditors. In fact, many businesses who try to reorganize through

> ## WARNING
>
> If you want to use Chapter 13 to reorganize your small business, be sure that your current suppliers will continue to do business with you after you file or line up other suppliers first. If you cannot obtain the supplies, inventory, or products you need to operate, you are out of business.

Chapter 11 end up having to close down by filing Chapter 7 because their creditors created so many problems and so many delays that the businesses' finances deteriorated to the point that they could not afford to continue trying to reorganize. At that point, a liquidation bankruptcy becomes the only realistic option they have left. The next section explains how a Chapter 7 liquidation bankruptcy works.

Chapter 7—Straight Liquidation Bankruptcy

You can use Chapter 7 bankruptcy to wipe out most of your debts; you will never have to pay them. However, once your debts are discharged, you won't be able to file another Chapter 7 bankruptcy for six years.

Filing for Chapter 7 is a good option if you owe so much to your creditors relative to your income that it is impossible for you to pay what you owe. It is also a good option if you do not own a lot of property for you will lose much of your nonexempt assets through the Chapter 7 liquidation process.

A Chapter 7 begins in the same way that a Chapter 13 does—by filing a bankruptcy petition with the court, by providing the court with lists or schedules of all your debts and all your assets, and by answering questions about your finances.

Your attorney should make sure that you claim whatever property exemptions you are entitled to so that you can keep as many of the assets you own as possible. The trustee will have the right to sell the assets that you do not exempt and will apply the sale proceeds to your debts.

W A R N I N G

If any of the assets you want to exempt are securing a debt, you must continue paying on that debt according to the terms of your contract with the creditor. For example, if you want to keep your home, you must continue making your mortgage payments.

Some Debts Survive Chapter 7

A Chapter 7 bankruptcy will eliminate most of your debts. However, certain types of debts will survive the bankruptcy that you will have to pay once it is over. These nondischargeable debts include:

- Any debts that you incurred through fraud. For example, if the court decides that you obtained credit by providing false information on a credit application, even if the error was unintentional, the debt you incurred as a result of the false information will not be included in your bankruptcy, which means that it will not be discharged and you will still have to pay it. For that to happen, however, the creditor who gave you the credit will have to file a complaint with the court and prove to the bankruptcy judge that you committed fraud.

- Any past-due alimony and child support payments you may owe. You will be expected to continue making your alimony, maintenance, and child support payments while you are in bankruptcy.

- Any debts you incurred because you willfully or maliciously injured someone.

- Noncompensatory (punitive) fines. For instance, you were convicted of a crime and the judge ordered you to make restitution by paying a fine.

- Certain educational loans. The only way to get rid of federal student loans is to file a motion with the court claiming a hardship. If the judge agrees that having to pay those debts would create a financial hardship in your life, he or she can agree to discharge them. But it's tough to prove a hardship and if you can afford to pay anything at all on your federal student loans, the judge will not discharge those debts.

- Any debts that you may still owe from a previous bankruptcy.

- Most types of taxes.

- A consumer debt for more than $1,100 that you owe a single creditor for the purchase of luxury goods or services that you incurred during the 60 days prior to filing your bankruptcy petition. Also, cash advances for more than $1,100 that you obtained during that same 60-day period. These exceptions are intended to prevent consumers from running up the balances on their credit cards just before they file for bankruptcy. For debts related to the purchase of luxury items to be nondischargeable, your creditors will have to file complaints with the court and prove that the charges were for luxury items and that they were over the allowable dollar amounts within the 60-day period.

- Debts that arise from damages you caused as a result of operating a motor vehicle while you were legally intoxicated or while you were under the influence of drugs.
- A bank loan or credit card debt you incurred to pay off a past-due tax debt.

The Positive and Negative Aspects of Bankruptcy

Your attorney should not only discuss the different types of bankruptcy you can file but should also explain their positive and negative aspects. You need this information to make an informed decision about which kind of bankruptcy is best for you and whether you should file in the first place. Figure 2.1 compares some of the positive and negative aspects of Chapter 13 and Chapter 7 bankruptcy.

 FIGURE 2.1
Advantages and Disadvantages of Filing Chapter 13 and Chapter 7

The Positive Aspects of Chapter 13 Are:

- *The automatic stay will keep your creditors off your back.* Once the court invokes the stay, your creditors will be prohibited from trying to collect from you.

- *You can reduce your debt payments and you can modify the rights of most of your secured creditors.*

- *You can keep all your property, including your nonexempt assets.* Remember, however, the bankruptcy judge won't let you keep any nonexempt assets that he or she considers luxury items if you still owe money on them, unless you will pay 100 percent of *all* your debts.

- *Wipes out more debts than a Chapter 7 does.*

- *Gives you up to five years to pay any money you owe to the IRS or to another taxing authority.*

- *Gives you up to five years to catch up on your past-due mortgage payments.*

(continued)

FIGURE 2.1
Advantages and Disadvantages of Filing Chapter 13 and Chapter 7
Continued

- *A percentage of your unsecured debt may be forgiven.* However, the court will not approve your reorganization plan if it believes that you can afford to pay more on your unsecured debts than your plan says you will pay.

- *Lets you pay your unsecured creditors only what you can afford to pay over the three to five years of your bankruptcy.* However, you cannot pay these creditors less than what they would have received if you had filed for Chapter 7.

- *Helps you hold on to your secured assets, such as your house, car, and any furniture you may have financed.* If you are having trouble paying for these assets, you may be able to lower your debt payments on everything but your home so that you can keep your secured assets. You cannot use bankruptcy to modify the amount of your house payments.

The Negative Aspects of Chapter 13 Are:

- *Filing for Chapter 13 will hurt your credit history and your credit score, but they were probably already damaged by the financial troubles that led up to your needing to file for bankruptcy.* The three national credit bureaus (Equifax, Experian, and TransUnion) will report your Chapter 13 bankruptcy for just seven years in contrast to the 10 years they will report a Chapter 7.

- *You will be involved with the bankruptcy court for three to five years, which is the period of time that your reorganization plan can last.*

The Positive Aspects of Chapter 7 Are:

- *An automatic stay will take effect as soon as your bankruptcy petition is filed with the court at which point most of your creditors must cease their efforts to collect from you.* In other words, they will not be able to call you about your debts, write to you, or try to repossess or foreclose on your property. In addition, the automatic stay will stop any lawsuits that may have been filed against you.

- *With some exceptions, most of your debts will be wiped out, or discharged, by your Chapter 7 bankruptcy.*

- *Completing a Chapter 7 bankruptcy does not take long. From the time that you file for bankruptcy the process will probably take about 120 days to complete.* At the end of that time, you will be out of bankruptcy.

FIGURE 2.1
Advantages and Disadvantages of Filing Chapter 13 and Chapter 7
Continued

The Negative Aspects of Chapter 7 Are:

- *Filing for Chapter 7 will damage your credit record and your credit score, but, most likely, they will already be damaged by the financial problems that caused you to file for bankruptcy in the first place.* The fact that you filed for Chapter 7 bankruptcy will be a part of your credit record for ten years.

- *Chapter 7 does not discharge all your debts.* Once your Chapter 7 is over, you will be obligated to pay any debts that are not dischargeable.

- *You cannot modify the rights of your secured creditors if you want to keep an asset that you used as collateral.* When you file for Chapter 7, your only options if you want to keep a secured asset are to:

  1. Continue paying on the debt that the asset secures according to your original agreement with the creditor.

  2. Reaffirm the debt with different terms, or with the same terms, and get caught up on your past-due payments. If you are behind on your payments, however, your creditor is not legally obligated to agree to a reaffirmation.

  3. Redeem the asset by paying the creditor the asset's market value. The market value is the asset's current value and it may be less than what you owe on it. You must pay the market value in a lump sum.

  If you cannot do any of these things, then you will have to give the secured asset back to your creditor to satisfy your debt.

- *You could lose some of your nonexempt assets.*

3

The Procedures of Bankruptcy

This chapter outlines the procedures for the two types of bankruptcy discussed in this book—Chapter 7 and Chapter 13. During your initial meetings with your bankruptcy attorney, these procedures should be explained to you.

Chapter 7—Straight Liquidation Bankruptcy

Chronologically, the steps in a typical Chapter 7 case are:

1. Your attorney will assess your financial situation based on the financial information you provide to him or her, including information about all your assets and debts as well as your income. Your attorney will tell you if there is another way, short of bankruptcy, for you to deal with your debts. Otherwise, the attorney will decide whether you should file for a Chapter 7 or a Chapter 13 bankruptcy. If it is possible for you to pay anything at all on your debts, your attorney will advise you to file a Chapter 13 reorganization. As a result of the Bankruptcy Civil Enforcement Initiative, bankruptcy trustees are under pressure to make as many debtors as possible reorganize their debts, not liquidate them.

2. Your attorney will complete your *Statement of Financial Affairs* and will prepare your *Schedules of Debts* and *Schedules of Assets* based on the information you provide (see Appendixes A and B for sample forms). Your Schedules of Assets will list each of your assets and its market value. Your Schedules of Debts will itemize each of your debts and its amount. When the attorney reviews your asset information, he or she will make certain that you claim every exemption you are entitled to so that you can hold on to as many of your assets as possible. If some of your assets cannot be exempted, the attorney will find out if you care that you will lose them. If you do care, your attorney will advise you that you may be able to buy the assets back from the trustee. The attorney will also explain that you can keep them if you file a Chapter 13.

3. Your attorney will file your bankruptcy petition with the court together with your debts and assets schedules, your Statement of Financial Affairs, and the other forms that must be filed in a Chapter 7 bankruptcy. Then, the court will invoke the automatic stay, which will protect you from your creditors' collection actions. Although the court will notify your creditors about the automatic stay, your attorney should contact them, too, because the court won't notify them right away and you will want your creditors to cease all collection actions against you as soon as possible.

4. After your bankruptcy starts, your attorney will try to work out any problems your creditors may have related to it. For example, although some of your creditors may decide to wait and see what will happen, your secured creditors may file motions to lift the automatic stay. When they do, they will be asking the court to let them take back their collateral or they will also be putting pressure on you to pay them for the asset so that you can keep it.

5. About six to eight weeks after your bankruptcy has begun, you and your attorney will attend a creditors' meeting. The meeting will take place at the courthouse, and the trustee appointed by the court to oversee your case will preside over the meeting. Your creditors may attend as well.

    Your attorney should prepare you ahead of time for the questions you will be asked at this meeting. For example, the trustee will ask you questions to determine whether you have any nonexempt property that can be sold to help pay your debts. The trustee will also want to make sure that you have not transferred any of your assets to someone else in the months just prior to filing for bankruptcy or paid certain creditors at the expense of others during that same time period. For instance, during the 60-day period prior to the date that you filed, you may have transferred an asset that you want to keep to your brother, or you may have paid a favorite creditor or a relative.

Your creditors may also ask you questions at the meeting. Your secured creditors, for example, will want to know if you intend to keep any of the assets you used to collateralize the debts you owe them. If you do, they will tell you whether they want you to continue paying your debts according to the contracts you signed with them (including any past-due or missed payment you may owe) or whether they are willing to renegotiate the terms of your debts to make your payments more affordable. In bankruptcy, when you keep a secured asset that you still owe money on, you are *reaffirming* the debt that is associated with that asset. Your unsecured creditors will want to know how much they are going to receive in your bankruptcy, if anything. Only the trustee can answer this question.

During this meeting, the trustee will also make sure that you fully understand the implications of filing for Chapter 7, including how it will affect your credit history and credit score. The trustee will also make sure that you realize that you can file for a Chapter 13 rather than a Chapter 7, that in a Chapter 7 you have the right to reaffirm debt, and will explain what it means to have your debts discharged. Your bankruptcy attorney should explain all these things to you prior to the meeting.

6. At the creditors' meeting, the trustee will review the other legal documents that your attorney filed on your behalf and

---

HOT TIP

When you are asked a question by the trustee, don't worry about what the "right answer" is because there are no "right answers." Just be honest.

will ask you questions about the information in those documents. The trustee may also ask you to provide the court with additional information related to your past financial affairs. And the trustee may require you to provide the court with additional written information regarding your finances. Here is some of the additional information you may have to provide as a result of the Bankruptcy Civil Enforcement Initiative:

- Tax returns from past years with W-2s attached
- Canceled checks and bank statements for the past 90 days
- Your check registers
- Documentation proving that you have been paying certain bills
- Stock certificates
- Stockbroker statements
- Titles to your vehicles
- Your lease if you are a renter
- Finance contracts. For example, you financed the purchase of your furniture
- Your mortgage paperwork
- An appraisal of your home
- Your life insurance policies

If you can't provide all the additional information that the trustee asks for, the trustee may ask the court to dismiss your case.

7. One or more of your creditors may file motions against you with the bankruptcy court to try to take back their collateral or they may file complaints against you because of something you did or did not do in your bankruptcy. Whenever a motion is filed, there will be a court hearing. Although your attorney will represent you at the hearing, you will probably have to be there, too.

8. During the 60 days following the creditors' meeting, your creditors can object to the discharge of the debts you owe to them, although they must give the court a reason for objecting. Your attorney will explain which of the debts you owe will survive your bankruptcy. You will have to pay them once your bankruptcy is over. Chapter 2 explains which debts survive a bankruptcy.

9. You may or may not have to attend a discharge hearing at the end of your Chapter 7 bankruptcy, depending on how the bankruptcy court in your district operates. If there is a hearing, it will take place 60 to 120 days after the date of your creditors' meet-

ing. At the hearing, the judge will officially discharge your debts except for the ones that cannot be discharged, or the ones that you have reaffirmed or agreed to continue paying. In some districts you will have to attend a discharge hearing only if you are reaffirming any of your debts. However, you won't have to attend if your attorney files an affidavit on your behalf stating that the consequences of a reaffirmation have been explained to you.

Chapter 13—Adjustment of Debts for Individuals

Now let's look at the steps in a typical Chapter 13 reorganization of debt bankruptcy:

1. Just as in a Chapter 7 bankruptcy, you will have to provide your attorney with information about all your assets, all your debts, and about your income. Your attorney will use this and other financial information to prepare your debt reorganization plan, which the court will have to approve.

2. You will meet with your attorney to discuss your reorganization plan. The plan will explain which debts you intend to pay during the three to five years that your Chapter 13 bankruptcy will be in effect, and how much you intend to pay on those debts during that time, among other things. Your attorney's goal in creating your plan should be to make your debt payments as low as possible and to ensure at the same time that you can keep all the assets you want to hold on to. Your attorney should explain that in bankruptcy certain kinds of debts are more important than others and that they will have to be paid before other kinds of debts.

3. Your attorney will prepare the various assets and debts schedules that must be filed with the bankruptcy court and will finalize your reorganization plan after discussing it with you. Be sure that you understand what is in your plan and what you are agreeing to do before the plan is filed with the court. Don't agree to anything in the plan that you are not sure you can live up to.

4. Once your attorney has filed your bankruptcy petition and Schedules of Assets and Schedules of Debts, the court will issue an automatic stay. When that happens, all your creditors must

stop trying to collect from you. The court will notify them of the automatic stay, but your attorney should do that, too, for it may take the court a while to notify your creditors.

5. Your attorney may not file your reorganization plan at the same time as your bankruptcy petition. If so, your attorney will have 15 more days to file it. Thirty days after your proposed plan of reorganization has been filed with the court, you must begin paying your debts according to the terms of your plan. Most likely, your payments will be deducted from your paychecks and then sent to the trustee who, in turn, will pay your creditors.

6. Before the date of your creditors' meeting, which will take place 40 to 60 days after your petition has been filed, your attorney will contact your creditors to try to resolve any problems they may have with your plan of reorganization so that they will not file formal objections to it with the court. However, some of your creditors may file objections anyway. For example, your secured creditors may decide to file motions with the court to take back their collateral or motions objecting to the confirmation of your plan. They may file these motions if they do not think you have treated them fairly in your reorganization plan or if they are unwilling to accept the amount of money you are offering to pay them on your debts.

7. At the creditors' meeting your attorney will try to resolve any objections to your plan that were not worked out before the meeting. Although any of your creditors can attend this meeting to find out what you intend to do about the money that you owe to them, your secured creditors are most apt to show up for they will be concerned about their collateral. However, if your attorney resolves all your creditors' objections prior to the meeting, then it's likely that none of them will attend.

8. The trustee will run the meeting and will ask questions to determine if your plan is feasible. Then the trustee will either recommend that the bankruptcy judge confirm your plan or suggest changes that you must make to the plan before he or she will agree to recommend confirmation.

9. After the creditors' meeting, a confirmation hearing will be held before the bankruptcy judge. In some districts, this hearing occurs on the same day as the creditors' meeting; in other districts, it is held three to four weeks later; and in still other districts, the confirmation hearing does not occur for up to three months after the creditors' meeting. If none of your creditors

files any objections to the approval of your plan, the judge will confirm it. If any of them formally object, the judge will hear their objections and then decide whether or not to confirm your plan. It is possible that the judge will order you to make certain changes to the plan to get it confirmed. If your plan is not confirmed, the court will probably give you time to revise it and try to get the new plan approved.

10. Once your reorganization plan has been confirmed, you will be expected to continue sending your payments to the trustee according to the terms of the plan for a specific period of time, between three and five years. Your payments will include money for your creditors and the trustee's fees as well. If you have problems making your payments while your plan is in effect, you can ask the court for permission to modify your plan or to convert your Chapter 13 reorganization bankruptcy to a Chapter 7 liquidation bankruptcy.

11. If you complete your plan, the court will give you a discharge and any unsecured debts that you still owe will be wiped out at that time.

WARNING

Before attending any court hearing related to your bankruptcy, ask your attorney exactly what to expect and how to dress. Expensive jewelry and designer clothes are not appropriate.

The Cost of Filing Bankruptcy

"How much will my bankruptcy cost?" If you are considering bankruptcy, this may be your first concern. Other than the fee you will have to pay when your bankruptcy petition is filed, the cost of your bankruptcy will vary depending on what part of the country you are filing in, the amount of your attorney's fee, and the number of motions your creditors file during your bankruptcy.

Some Attorneys Charge a Flat Rate

Most bankruptcies are complicated cases but an experienced bankruptcy attorney will handle it as smoothly as possible. Also, an experienced bankruptcy attorney may be willing to charge you a flat fee for handling your bankruptcy because he or she will have a good idea of exactly what services you need and how long it will take to provide them. The flat fee for an uncomplicated bankruptcy whether you file a Chapter 13 or a Chapter 7 bankruptcy typically ranges from $750 to $3,000. You will also have to pay a filing fee. A Chapter 7 usually costs between $750 and $2,500, and if you file a Chapter 13, you will probably have to pay between $1,300 and $3,000.

W A R N I N G

Even if an attorney agrees to handle your bankruptcy for a flat fee, he or she will probably tell you that if problems develop with your case, you will be charged more. Since the passing of the Bankruptcy Civil Enforcement Initiative, problems are increasingly common.

Some attorneys will expect to be paid their full fee before they will do any work on your bankruptcy case, but others will ask you to make a down payment and let you pay the balance over time. If you are filing a Chapter 7, it's unlikely that you will get more than four months to pay the balance, which is the length of time that it usually takes the court to process a Chapter 7 bankruptcy. If you file a Chapter 13, after you pay your attorney a down payment, the balance you owe the attorney will be incorporated into your plan and some of the money that you pay to the trustee each month will go to your attorney.

Some Attorneys Charge by the Hour

Some attorneys will charge you an hourly rate to handle your bankruptcy and will bill you based on the amount of time they spend on

WARNING

More and more bankruptcy attorneys now require their clients to pay them the full amount of their fee up front. (Generally, the lawyers who advertise charge the lowest flat fees and, usually, they are good enough to get you through the bankruptcy process; some, in fact, are better than average and even specialize in bankruptcy law.) However, if your case is at all complicated, make sure that your attorney has a lot of experience handling bankruptcies. Ideally, bankruptcy cases should make up most if not all of his or her practice.

your case. The hourly rates for bankruptcy attorneys tend to range from $50 an hour to $350 an hour, depending on the area of the country where they practice law and their level of expertise and experience. On average, you won't spend more if you hire an attorney who bills by the hour than if you work with one who charges a flat fee, but that is not always the case.

If you hire an attorney who charges by the hour, the lawyer will probably expect you to pay him or her a retainer of $200 to $700 or even more depending on the complexity of your case. A retainer is an up-front fee that covers the immediate costs of handling a case. If your attorney expects to be paid a retainer, he or she will not begin work on your case until you have paid it.

If your bankruptcy is relatively uncomplicated, your attorney should be able to complete most of the work related to it within 120 days of filing your bankruptcy petition. Things will move slower after that.

Fees Reviewed by the Court

The bankruptcy court will monitor what your attorney charges you to handle your case. In fact, bankruptcy is the only area of the law that requires an attorney's fee to be court-monitored. Your attorney will have to file a disclosure statement with the court that explains the fee arrangement he or she has with you and where you are getting the

WARNING

Before you pay an attorney any money, be sure to get a written statement from the attorney that describes the services the attorney will provide and what you will be charged for those services.

funds that you will use to pay the attorney. If the court decides that your attorney is charging too much, it can require him or her to refund all or part of what you paid.

Filing Fees

To begin your bankruptcy you must pay the bankruptcy court a filing fee. The amount of the filing fee will depend on the kind of bankruptcy you file. Although filing fees change periodically, at the time this book was revised, they were:

- Chapter 7, liquidation bankruptcy: $209
- Chapter 13, adjustment of debts for individuals: $194
- Chapter 11, reorganization: $844
- Chapter 12, adjustment of debts for farmers: $209

4

Filing a Chapter 7
Bankruptcy

When you file a Chapter 7 liquidation bankruptcy, your goals are to get rid of as much of your debt as possible and to hold on to all the assets you are entitled to keep so that you can make a fresh start. This chapter reviews how Chapter 7 can help you do that.

Gathering Information on Your Debts and Assets

Your lawyer will prepare your assets and debts schedules and the other legal paperwork you must file with the court. The attorney will also make sure that you exempt all the assets you are entitled to so that you can keep them. To help him or her prepare your assets and debts schedules, your attorney will probably ask you to fill out some worksheets.

Be Careful When Listing Your Debts

When your attorney reviews the information on your worksheets, he or she will warn you that any debt that is not listed on your Schedules of Debts and any debt that is listed but provides an incorrect address for the creditor may not be discharged by your Chapter 7 bankruptcy. Therefore, be sure that you list every debt you can think of, not just the obvious ones, and also list the names of everyone who *might* have a claim against you—an ex-business partner or a former customer, if you are a small business owner, or someone who was injured in a car accident that you caused, for example. Also, you should list anyone who has not made a claim against you but who might do so in the near future. Sometimes, just listing a possible claim on your debts schedules is enough to get it discharged.

HOT TIP

Review the information on your Schedules of Debts once your attorney has filled them out to make sure that the information is accurate and complete.

Priority Claims, Secured Claims, and Unsecured Claims

Bankruptcy law places debts into three different categories, making some debts more important than others, and requiring that you treat each category of debt in a very specific way. Therefore, when your attorney is preparing your debts schedules, he or she will categorize your debts as priority claims, secured claims, or unsecured claims. Figure 4.1 explains how each type of debt must be treated.

When your attorney is listing your *priority debts* on your debts schedules, he or she will note whether you owe any back taxes. In most cases, taxes are not dischargeable through bankruptcy, although under certain circumstances, past-due federal income taxes can be discharged. For example, if you have a federal income tax debt, you may be able to get the past-due taxes discharged if they became due more than three years before you began your bankruptcy.

Even if you can't discharge your past-due tax debt, while you are in bankruptcy, the taxing authority you owe the money to cannot try to collect from you. However, it can begin trying to collect from you as soon as your bankruptcy is over.

When your attorney lists all your *secured debts,* it is important that your collateral (the assets you used to secure or guarantee payment of those debts) be described accurately and be given an accurate fair market value. *Fair market value* is the amount that you would get for an asset if you sold it today, not what you paid for it. Placing an accurate value on a secured asset is important because the more equity you have in an asset, the more likely it is that you will use up your exemptions, which means that you will have to let the trustee take some of your assets so they can be sold to help pay your debts. *Equity* is the difference between what an asset is worth today and the balance on the loan that financed the purchase of the asset.

If you want to keep an asset that you used as loan collateral, such as your home, car, or furniture, you will have to continue making payments on it while you are in bankruptcy. If you decide not to keep one of your secured assets, like a second car or a vacation home, you can return it and the balance of the debt that you owe to the creditor will be discharged.

If you want to keep a secured asset but you are behind on your loan payments, the creditor may agree to renegotiate the terms of the loan so that you can afford to make them. However, as a condition of agreeing to this, the creditor may require that you get caught up on your past-due payments first.

When your attorney lists all your *unsecured debts* on your Schedules of Debts, he or she will check to be certain that you have provided a complete address for each of those creditors. If you don't, those debts may not get discharged. The attorney will also pay close attention to when you incurred each debt because if any of them were incurred during the 60 days just prior to your filing for bankruptcy, you may not be able to get them discharged. This would happen if a creditor feels that the debts are fraudulent or that you incurred them in "bad faith" and files a *complaint* with the court asking that they not be discharged. If no complaints are filed, however, those debts will be discharged.

Listing Your Assets and Claiming Your Exemptions

After your attorney has listed all your debts and all your assets on your schedules, he or she will elect the exemptions you are taking. Your exemptions are important because they will determine which assets you will keep in your Chapter 7 bankruptcy. Your attorney should let you know which assets are not exempt because you will have to give them to the bankruptcy trustee. However, if you want to keep any of your nonexempt assets, you may be able to buy them back from the trustee, assuming you can afford to. Usually your attorney will negotiate a purchase price with the trustee.

W A R N I N G

If your attorney lets the trustee know that you want to buy back an asset, the trustee may want to know where you are getting the money to do that. If it appears as though you hid money from the court when you completed your Schedules of Assets, you may get in trouble. Usually, however, when a consumer wants to buy back one of his or her nonexempt assets, a relative or close friend buys it and then the consumer buys it from the relative or friend later.

   If you cannot afford to buy back an asset that you want to keep, your attorney should talk to you about filing for Chapter 13 rather than Chapter 7, because in a Chapter 13 you can keep your nonexempt property.

W A R N I N G

If you have a tax refund coming, try not to file for bankruptcy until you have received and spent the refund. That way, you won't risk losing it in bankruptcy. However, it's possible that the refund will be exempt, in which case you won't need to worry about when you file your tax return and how soon you spend your refund. Ask your bankruptcy attorney if the refund will be exempt.

Reviewing the Statement of Financial Affairs

The last document your attorney will prepare for your bankruptcy is your Statement of Financial Affairs.

Trap for the Unwary

The questions in the Statement of Financial Affairs (see Appendixes A and B for sample forms) are intended to help the court determine if you have made any inappropriate financial transactions prior to the start of your bankruptcy and to identify any assets that you may not have listed on your schedules. Therefore, your attorney will go over the statement questions with you, review your answers to each of them, and discuss any potential problems related to your answers.

Why Certain Questions Are Asked

Before your Statement of Financial Affairs is filled out, it is helpful to know why certain questions are asked and what kinds of answers are likely to create problems with the trustee. Therefore, here is information about the most important questions on that document:

- *Questions 1 and 2* ask how much income you received from your trade or profession and from other sources during each of the two calendar years immediately preceding the date that you filed your bankruptcy petition.

The trustee will compare your past income to the value of your current debts and assets, looking for anything that seems suspicious. For example, if you have earned a lot of money but your schedules do not show many debts or assets, the trustee may wonder what happened to all that money. The trustee may think that you used it to buy assets that you did not list on your schedules.

- *Question 3* asks what debt payments you made during the 90 days immediately preceding the filing of your bankruptcy petition.

The trustee will be interested in determining whether you paid one creditor at the expense of others. If you did, the trustee may try to get that payment back so that the money can be distributed among your creditors according to the rules of bankruptcy that govern which creditors must be paid first.

- *Question 4* asks if you were a party to any lawsuits that were pending at the time that your bankruptcy petition was filed. If you filed a lawsuit against someone and it has not been concluded by the start of your bankruptcy, the trustee could settle the lawsuit on your behalf and use the settlement money to pay your creditors, unless you can exempt the money.

- *Question 6* asks if you have assigned any of your property to your creditors, or reached a general settlement with any of your creditors during the 120 days immediately preceding the date of your original bankruptcy petition. The trustee may think that assigning property or paying creditors to settle a claim before you file for bankruptcy is evidence that you gave preferential treatment to the creditors at the expense of other creditors and may try to recover the money or property.

- *Question 7* asks if you gave any of your assets to relatives or anyone else you know during the year immediately preceding the start of your bankruptcy. From your answers to this question, the trustee will decide whether or not you gave away the assets so that your creditors could not get them. If the trustee believes that was your motivation, he or she will try to recover the assets. Therefore, if you transferred any property to others during the year prior to the start of your bankruptcy, make sure that you let your attorney know.

- *Question 11* asks you to list all your financial accounts, certificates of deposit, and safe deposit boxes. The trustee will use this information to figure out how you spent your money during the year prior to filing for bankruptcy. For example, the trustee may

---

WARNING

Under the Bankruptcy Civil Enforcement Initiative, the trustee overseeing your bankruptcy is entitled to ask to see your bank statements, check registers, tax returns, contracts, and other financial documents. If you think there is anything in these documents that could create problems for you, discuss them with your bankruptcy attorney.

notice that your financial statement indicates that you purchased assets that are not listed on your Schedules of Assets, that large amounts of money have disappeared, or that you made payments to your relatives or friends. Any of these discrepancies could spell trouble for it is illegal to knowingly conceal assets from your creditors and from the bankruptcy court.

Your attorney should also look for evidence that you gave any of your creditors preferential treatment before you filed for bankruptcy. The trustee will scrutinize any payments you made to your creditors before your bankruptcy began to determine if you did. For example, before you filed for bankruptcy, you may have paid your next-door neighbor the money you owed him, but did not pay any of your other debts using the last $1,000 in your bank account.

If your bankruptcy attorney believes that the trustee will question any of your answers on your Statement of Financial Affairs, he or she will discuss those answers with you. Your attorney should also caution you about trying to hide information from the trustee. Therefore, if you have done something you were not supposed to do prior to filing for bankruptcy, be sure to tell your attorney so that it can be described on your schedules. Otherwise, if the trustee finds out what you did, you may be accused of fraud and face criminal charges as a result. I am sure you agree that it would be better to lose property than to spend time in prison.

W A R N I N G

Not only will incomplete schedules cause problems with the bankruptcy trustee, but they will also increase the cost of your bankruptcy for you will have to pay the attorney extra money to correct the schedules.

Notifying Your Creditors When You File a Chapter 7 Bankruptcy

Once all your schedules and your Statement of Financial Affairs are complete, your attorney will file them with the bankruptcy court and your bankruptcy will be assigned a case number. After that happens, you will get some immediate relief from your creditors through the *automatic stay.*

Stopping Creditor Harassment with the Automatic Stay

The automatic stay requires your creditors to immediately stop trying to collect what you owe them. They will be prohibited from calling or writing to you about your debts, or suing you to collect them, and from taking any of your assets away from you.

As already noted, because it may take time for the bankruptcy court to notify all your creditors about the automatic stay—at least a month in some jurisdictions—your attorney should do that immediately, especially any creditors that may be giving you a hard time about your debts, or that you believe are about to take action against you—foreclose on your home or repossess your car, for example. Your attorney should notify all your secured creditors right away, either by letter or by phone (preferably both). Notifying your creditors about the automatic stay is one of the most important services your attorney will provide, for you will gain some immediate peace of mind knowing that your creditors will leave you alone now that you are in bankruptcy.

If for some reason, however, your attorney does not contact your creditors right away, you can notify them about the automatic stay yourself. For example, if one of your creditors sends you a notice that your debt is going to be sent to collections, write on the notice that you have filed for bankruptcy, provide the creditor with your bankruptcy case number as well as the name, address, and phone number of your attorney, and return the notice to the creditor via certified mail with a return receipt requested.

Some Creditor Collection Actions the Automatic Stay Can't Stop

As powerful as the automatic stay is, it will not stop all creditor collection actions. For example, it won't stop a taxing authority from forcing you to go through a tax audit, notifying you of a tax deficiency, demanding that you file tax returns, or assessing an uncontested tax liability.

Other things the automatic stay won't stop include:

- Any legal actions necessary to establish that you are the father of a child for child support purposes.

- Legal actions to establish or modify your alimony, maintenance, or support (child or spousal) obligations.
- Legal actions to collect any past-due alimony, maintenance, or support you may owe from assets that are not included in your bankruptcy estate. Those assets would be your exempt assets.

Another exception to the automatic stay allows property tax authorities to create and perfect a statutory lien for any taxes that may come due after you file for bankruptcy. In other words, a taxing authority can put a lien on one of your assets after your bankruptcy begins to guarantee payment of your tax debt and if you want to sell that asset while you are in bankruptcy, you must pay the back taxes you owe to get the lien released.

Violating the Automatic Stay

Tell your lawyer if one of your creditors continues to try to collect a debt from you after the automatic stay has been invoked by the court. It is possible that the creditor's actions are the result of a misunderstanding, and the attorney may simply need to notify the creditor once again that you filed for bankruptcy. However, the creditor may be fully aware of the automatic stay and may be trying to collect from you anyway. If that is the case and it appears that the creditor intends to continue trying to collect, your attorney should ask the court to hold the creditor in civil contempt. If your attorney can prove to the court that the creditor intentionally violated the automatic stay, the court may order the creditor to pay you damages, pay your attorney's fee, and give you any other relief that the court thinks is fair. Bottom line, your attorney should not allow any of your creditors to bother you about your debts once your bankruptcy has begun.

H O T   T I P

If a government agency—the IRS, for example—violates the automatic stay, you can try to make the agency pay for any financial damages you may suffer as a result.

FIGURE 4.1
Examples of Priority, Secured, and Unsecured Debts

In bankruptcy, your debts are divided into three categories: priority, secured, and unsecured debts.

Priority debts are debts that you must pay before all other debts in a bankruptcy assuming there are sufficient funds from the sale of your nonexempt property to pay them. These types of debts can include taxes and bankruptcy-related administrative expenses. In reality, however, in most Chapter 7 bankruptcies it is rare that there is any money to pay creditors—even priority creditors. In addition, some kinds of priority debts cannot be wiped out by a Chapter 7 discharge. This means that after your Chapter 7 bankruptcy is over, you will be obligated to pay these debts and if you don't, the creditors you owe the money to can try to collect from you. Examples of this type of priority debt include student loans and payroll taxes that your business withheld but never paid to the IRS.

Secured debt is debt that you have collateralized with an asset. These kinds of debts include a mortgage, home equity loan, car loan, or loans to purchase furniture or equipment.

Unsecured debt is debt that you did not collateralize. This includes credit card debt, some small bank loans, and loans from friends or family.

5

The Automatic Stay

How the Automatic Stay Protects You

No matter what type of bankruptcy you choose, once your bankruptcy petition has been filed, the court will invoke the automatic stay to stop your creditors from taking collection actions against you. The automatic stay is the most dramatic and immediate relief available to consumers who file for bankruptcy. It will protect you as long as you are in an active bankruptcy. The protection of the automatic stay will end if your case is closed or dismissed, or if you receive a discharge of your debts.

Most consumers file for bankruptcy because one of their creditors becomes particularly aggressive about trying to collect the money it is owed. For example, you are threatened with the repossession of your car or with a foreclosure on your home. The automatic stay gives you immediate relief from such threats. Because the automatic stay is so important, let's take a closer look at how it works.

Although the automatic stay goes into effect the moment you file your petition with the court, for you to realize maximum benefit from it, your creditors must be notified of the stay immediately. As already indicated, because the court probably won't notify them right away, your attorney should. If your attorney does not, you can notify your creditors yourself.

> # WARNING
>
> Make sure that you and your attorney agree about which of your creditors will be notified about the automatic stay, when they will be notified, and who will notify them.

The automatic stay applies to most areas of collection. With some exceptions, once it has been invoked:

- Any lawsuits that have been filed against you must be stopped.
- Your creditors cannot enforce any judgments they may already have against you.
- Your creditors cannot repossess your car or furniture and/or foreclose on any real estate you own, including your home.
- Your creditors cannot place a lien on any of your property. The only exception to this prohibition relates to property-taxing authorities.
- Taxing authorities cannot continue trying to collect from you. For example, the Internal Revenue Service cannot garnish your wages or even continue a proceeding in the Tax Court related to any taxes that it says you owe.

The law states that creditors cannot "act to collect, or assess, or recover a claim against the debtor that arose before the commencement of the case." [11 U.S.C. Sec. 362 (a) (6)]

What the Automatic Stay Can and Cannot Do

The automatic stay will not stop any criminal action against you. This exception most commonly applies to people who have written bad checks. Because writing a "hot" check is a criminal offense, the automatic stay will not prevent the creditor to whom you gave the bad check from filing charges against you. Depending on the district where your bankruptcy has been filed, if you bring the criminal charge before the bankruptcy court, the bankruptcy judge may look at the creditor's motive for filing the hot check charge. If the judge decides that the sole motive of that creditor was to collect your debt, the judge may rule that the creditor cannot pursue the hot check charge. However, the judge cannot stop a district attorney from filing criminal charges against you for writing a hot check. Therefore, to be safe, don't write hot checks, even if it means you cannot pay a debt that you owe. If you have written one, however, pay it off as soon as you can.

Automatic Stay and Your Ex-Spouse

The automatic stay cannot stop your ex-spouse from trying to collect past-due alimony, maintenance, and support payments from any assets you own that are not a part of your bankruptcy estate. (In a Chapter 13, all of your property is considered part of your bankruptcy estate, but in a Chapter 7, only your nonexempt property is included in that estate.) The automatic stay, however, can stop the efforts of your former spouse to enforce your obligations under your property agreement. This is the agreement that spells out how you and your ex-spouse will divide up the assets you own together; it is part of your divorce agreement. In Chapter 13, your wages are included in your bankruptcy estate. Therefore, the automatic stay protects them from any efforts your former spouse may make to collect any past-due alimony, maintenance, and support payments you may owe. Because those obligations became due before you filed for Chapter 13, you must pay them through your Chapter 13 reorganization plan. However, any alimony, maintenance, or support payments that you are obligated to pay subsequent to the date that you filed for Chapter 13 must be paid as they come due. If you fall behind on those payments, your ex-spouse can try to collect what he or she is entitled to from any assets that are not in your bankruptcy estate; those assets would be your exempt assets.

W A R N I N G

Your ex-spouse can have a state court judge set or modify your support obligation while you are in a Chapter 13.

WARNING

If you are the former spouse of someone who is in bankruptcy and if your ex is not staying current on his or her alimony, maintenance, or support obligations, consult with a bankruptcy attorney before trying to collect from the assets that are not part of his or her bankruptcy estate. That way, you can be sure that you will not violate the automatic stay in your ex's bankruptcy.

The Automatic Stay and Governmental Agencies

The automatic stay will not protect you if a governmental agency tries to enforce a regulation that you have violated or tries to enforce a judgment against you that is not a money judgment. For example, if your local government told you to move an abandoned car from your property, you would have to do it unless you wanted to suffer the consequences.

Automatic Stay and the IRS

The automatic stay will not stop an IRS audit. Although the IRS cannot try to collect any past-due taxes it may determine that you owe as a result of the audit, it can send you a notice about your tax deficiency. Other taxing authorities, such as your local property tax author-

WARNING

After an automatic stay is in effect, local taxing authorities can put a lien on your property to collect unpaid taxes that become due after your bankruptcy began.

ity, can also assess the amount that you owe in back taxes and then send you a notice about your tax debt. However, no taxing authority, not even the IRS, can try to collect your tax debt while the automatic stay is in effect.

The Automatic Stay and Commodity Futures

Another exception to the automatic stay relates to commodity futures. Because this exception is not an issue for most people, it will not be discussed here. If you deal in commodity futures, consult your bankruptcy attorney.

Relief from the Automatic Stay

Your creditors have the right to ask the court for relief from the automatic stay. If one of your creditors does ask for relief and the court grants its request, the automatic stay won't apply to that creditor and the creditor can sell the collateral it had on the debt. Creditors do not ask for relief very often, however, because it will create more expenses for them related to your debt and because if you have filed for Chapter 13, they know that the bankruptcy court probably would not grant them relief because you might not be able to reorganize if they took any of your assets from you to satisfy your debts. However, if you are in a Chapter 13 and you promised to make payments to a secured creditor directly—your mortgage lender or the creditor that financed your car, for example—and you do not do what you promised, the creditor will file a motion to lift the stay to take back its collateral.

If one of your creditors asks the court for relief, preliminary and final hearings will be scheduled. The court may give the creditor relief if:

- the creditor has a lien on one of your assets;
- the creditor can claim that it will be some time before you can begin paying the money you owe to it and that meanwhile, the asset you used to secure your loan is losing value and its lien is not adequately protected. For instance, if you owe money on your car loan, the court would give the lender the right to demand that you begin paying on that loan immediately.

When a creditor is concerned that its lien is not adequately protected, it may ask the court for permission to take its collateral if you have filed Chapter 13. To do that, however, the creditor must prove

H O T   T I P

If the final hearing on a motion to lift the stay is not concluded within 30 days of the preliminary hearing, the creditor will automatically be granted the relief it asked for unless the judge continues the hearing with the stay remaining in effect.

that you do not have any equity in the asset, that you do not need the asset to help you reorganize your debt, and that you cannot afford to pay for the asset.

W A R N I N G

When creditors petition the court for relief from an automatic stay, they complicate your bankruptcy and increase its cost.

The Automatic Stay and Unexpired Leases

It is important for you to understand how the automatic stay affects:

1. any executory contracts and unexpired leases you have signed, such as the lease for your car or apartment or for the office space or equipment your business is leasing;
2. the past-due debt you owe to your utility company; or
3. the friends or relatives who cosigned your loans.

In Chapters 13 and 7, you have the right to accept or reject an *executory contract* or unexpired lease through the trustee. In other words, if you would like to get out of a contract that you signed and neither you nor the other party to the contract have met all your obligations under the contract, you can end it. For example, you may have signed a contract with a health club that lasts a year or more and that obligates you to make monthly payments to the club. In bankruptcy you can break that contract. That way, you won't have to pay on it anymore, but you will lose your club membership.

Another common problem in bankruptcy involves *unexpired leases.* If you are behind on your rent and maybe even facing eviction, the automatic stay may provide you with a limited amount of help. It may let you stay in the home or apartment you are renting for a certain period of time while you decide whether you want to find a new more affordable place to live or whether you want to stay where you are living now. The automatic stay can also give you time to plan for your move if you decide not to stay where you are currently living.

If you decide that you want to stay where you are, you will have to cure your default, which means that you will have to pay your past-due rental payments. You will have only a limited amount of time to come up with that money. How much time depends on where you live, but it could be several months or as little as a few weeks. The automatic stay could help you in a similar way if you were leasing a car and were behind on your lease payments.

Automatic Stay and Utility Bills

If you owe a substantial amount of money to your utility company, you can use bankruptcy to wipe out that debt on a one-time basis and the utility company cannot "alter, refuse, or discontinue" service to you. In other words, the automatic stay prevents the utility company from disconnecting your service, provided it is notified that you filed bankruptcy. However, to avoid a loss of service, the utility company is legally entitled to demand that you pay it a "reasonable deposit" if you have not already paid one. The court generally defines a "reasonable deposit" to be equal to the average cost of two months of utility service. You will have to come up with the deposit money within 20 days of filing your bankruptcy petition. In other words, when it comes to past-due utility bills, the automatic stay may provide you with very short-lived relief.

Automatic Stay and Codebtors

When you applied for credit, the creditor may have required that you have someone cosign for the credit. This person is legally responsible for paying the debt if you don't. Therefore, you and your cosigner become codebtors. *If you file for Chapter 13, your codebtor will receive special protection from your creditor,* assuming the codebtor cosigned on a consumer-oriented debt, not on a business debt. However, *your codebtor is* not *protected if you file a Chapter 7 bankruptcy.*

Therefore, if you borrowed money with a cosigner to buy a car or some furniture for your personal use and your Chapter 13 reorganization plan does not show that you intend to repay the full amount of that debt, the creditor can ask the court for relief from the automatic stay to collect the amount that you do not intend to pay from your codebtor. The creditor can also ask for relief if your codebtor received some benefit for cosigning. For example, your brother agrees to cosign your car loan and in exchange for his doing you that favor, you pay him some money.

6

The Chapter 7 Process

When you file for Chapter 7, be prepared to have your trustee spend a lot of time reviewing and verifying all the information on your Schedules of Debts and Assets, your Statement of Financial Affairs, and any other financial information the trustee asks for. Although trustees have always reviewed this information, now, as a result of the Bankruptcy Civil Enforcement Initiative, they will scrutinize it more carefully than ever and will probably ask you to provide a lot of additional information. The trustee wants to be certain that you are being 100 percent honest about your finances and wants to determine if there is any way possible that you can file a Chapter 13 bankruptcy rather than a Chapter 7. If the trustee decides that there is, you will be required to file a Chapter 13 rather than move forward with your Chapter 7 bankruptcy. It is a good idea, therefore, to meet with a bankruptcy attorney before you are certain that you will file for bankruptcy to find out what kind of information the trustee in your district is likely to require from you. That way, you can begin to pull that information together and if you do decide to file, your bankruptcy's progress will not be slowed by your having to locate records that the trustee wants. For example, in some districts if the trustee wants you to document the bills you pay each month and if you pay your bills online and do not download the statements that your creditors e-mail to you, you will have to contact those creditors and ask them to send you their information again; or if the trustee wants you to provide canceled checks for the past several months and your bank does not return your canceled checks, you will have to order them, and that will take time.

How Your Creditors May Respond to the Automatic Stay in Your Chapter 7 Bankruptcy

Once your creditors learn that you have filed for Chapter 7, they will respond to your bankruptcy in one of three ways:

1. Accept what you have done.
2. File a *motion to lift the stay.*
3. File a *complaint to disallow a debt from discharge.*

They will have from the date that they are notified of your bankruptcy until 60 days after the date of your first creditors' meeting to decide whether to file the complaint to disallow a debt from discharge. This section of the chapter explains the factors your creditors will probably take into account when they are deciding how to respond. It also explains how each of the three options works.

Accept What You Have Done

Most of your unsecured creditors and many of your secured creditors will simply accept the fact that you have filed for bankruptcy because they do not want to spend any more money or time trying to collect the money that you owe to them. Therefore, these creditors will probably file a proof of claim with the court so that they will be in line to get paid should there be enough money in your bankruptcy to pay them.

File a Motion to Lift the Stay

Some of your secured creditors, especially if you owe any of them a large amount of money, may file a motion to lift the automatic stay. If the court grants their motion, they can try to take back their collateral from you as payment for what you owe them. To do that, however, they will have to show proof to the court that you are behind on your payments, that you cannot afford to catch up on them, and that you have no equity in the assets they want to take from you. You may be won-

dering why any of your secured creditors would go to the trouble of filing these motions. The answer is that if these creditors believe that
they are going to have trouble getting you to pay what you owe them,
they would prefer to take your collateral and sell it so that they can get
at least some of the money you owe them. To help them decide if they
should file a motion to lift the stay, your secured creditors will compare
the cost of filing the motion with the likelihood of recovering their collateral quickly. Alternatively, if you are not paying your secured creditors, they may decide to wait until your Chapter 7 is over and then try
to repossess or foreclose on their collateral. In typical consumer bankruptcy cases, however, secured creditors are encouraged to file motions to lift the stay. As a result, many of these motions are filed.

What Will Happen before the Creditors' Meeting

Soon after your Chapter 7 bankruptcy petition has been filed with
the court and your creditors have been notified of your bankruptcy,
your attorney will begin contacting your secured creditors to let them
know what you intend to do about their collateral—the assets you used
to secure your debts.

If you do not pay one of your secured debts, the creditor can repossess or foreclose on the asset you used as collateral after your bankruptcy is over or while you are still in bankruptcy, assuming the creditor
gets permission from the judge.

When you file for Chapter 7 bankruptcy, you will have to decide
whether you want to keep your secured assets and continue paying the
creditors that are associated with them, or give up the assets. If a secured asset is worth more than what you owe on it, the bankruptcy
trustee will confirm that you have exempted the asset. If you did, the
trustee won't care what you do with it. However, if you did not exempt
the asset and it has some value above what you owe on it, the trustee
will take it and sell it. After the trustee uses the sale proceeds to pay
off the lien on that asset, the trustee will use whatever money may be
left to pay your creditors.

If you want to buy back any of your nonexempt assets from the
trustee, your attorney will contact him or her to make an offer. If your
offer is reasonable and the trustee cannot sell the property for more
than what you have offered, you will be able to buy it, assuming you
can come up with the cash.

Reaffirming Your Debts

If you want to return an exempt asset to one of your secured creditors, your attorney will contact that creditor and make arrangements for you to give it back. If you want to keep that asset, however, your attorney will advise you to continue paying on it according to the terms of your contract with the creditor, and if you are behind on your payments, the attorney will contact the creditor to try to work out a way for you to get caught up on your past-due payments. Although most creditors will let you get caught up, they don't have to. Also, as a condition for letting you keep an exempt asset, they can require that you get caught up on all your missed payments immediately.

When you want to keep an asset and continue paying on it, the creditor will probably require that you enter into a reaffirmation agreement. In this agreement you will agree that the debt you owe to the creditor will survive your bankruptcy and not be discharged. The agreement must be approved by the bankruptcy judge.

Once you enter into a reaffirmation agreement with a creditor, you will have 60 days after the agreement is approved to change your mind. If you do, you must notify the creditor in writing of your decision. If you proceed with the agreement and then later, after your bankruptcy is over, you cannot afford the payments you agreed to make, the creditor can repossess the property, sell it, and make you pay the difference between what the property sold for and what you still owe on the debt. This difference is called a *deficiency*.

Formal Reaffirmations Are Not Recommended

Your attorney should advise you that it is preferable to get the creditor to accept your payments and let you keep the asset without entering into a formal reaffirmation agreement. That way, if you cannot pay the debt after your bankruptcy is over, the worst that can happen is that the creditor will take back the property and sell it, and if the asset does not sell for as much as what you owe on it, you will not have to pay the creditor the deficiency.

Redeeming Property

When you file for Chapter 7, another way to hold on to an exempt asset that you used as collateral is to redeem the property. To redeem it, however, the asset must be worth less than what you owe on it and you must be able to afford to pay the secured creditor the asset's full value. For example, if you owe $1,000 on a furniture loan, but the furniture is worth only $300, you can keep the furniture assuming you can afford to pay the creditor the $300. If you want to redeem an asset, your attorney will contact the secured creditor that has a lien on it and you and the creditor will try to come to an agreement regarding the value of the asset. If you can't, your attorney will file a *motion to redeem the asset.* Then there will be a hearing on the motion so that the bankruptcy judge can decide how much you will have to pay the creditor to redeem the asset.

Most consumers who file Chapter 7 don't redeem assets because they don't have any money to spare and because they will have to pay their bankruptcy attorney an additional fee to redeem if there is a hearing on the matter. They may decide that the asset they want to redeem is not worth the additional expense.

Furthermore, most consumers who have money to spare will file a Chapter 13 rather than a Chapter 7 to pay off their debts over time. This is especially true now that the Bankruptcy Civil Enforcement Initiative is in effect.

Additional Help from Your Attorney

Prior to your creditors' meeting, your attorney will respond to any of your creditors who are angry that you filed for Chapter 7 or who are confused by the process. Part of what you pay your attorney to do is to deal with upset creditors. Hopefully, your attorney will be able to calm them down and help those who are confused understand how your Chapter 7 bankruptcy will proceed. By dealing with these creditors ahead of time, your attorney is trying to avoid any unnecessary litigation related to your bankruptcy so that it won't take longer and cost more.

The Creditors' Meeting

Forty to 60 days after your bankruptcy has begun, your first creditors' meeting will take place. At this meeting, the Chapter 7 trustee and your creditors can question you about your financial affairs.

Preparing for the Hearing

Your attorney will prepare you for this meeting by going over the questions you may be asked. If there is anything unusual or especially sensitive about your case, your attorney will probably review the questions with you prior to the day of the hearing. If your attorney does not expect any tough questions at the meeting, however, he or she may not go over the questions until just before the creditors' meeting while you are at the courthouse.

HOT TIP

Besides knowing ahead of time the questions you will be asked, it is helpful to know the motives behind the trustee's questions.

HOT TIP

If you are nervous about the creditors' meeting, call your attorney to talk over your fears. The attorney should give you the information you need to feel more confident.

The Bankruptcy Code requires that the trustee question you to make sure you are aware of:

(1) the potential consequences of seeking a discharge in bankruptcy, including the effects on your credit history; (2) the debtor's ability to file a petition under a different chapter of this title; (3) the effect of receiving a discharge of debts under this title; (4) the effect of reaffirming a debt, including the debtor's knowledge of the provisions of section 524 (d) of this title. [11 U.S.C. 341]

Don't worry, you need not study or memorize anything to answer the questions you may be asked at the creditors' meeting. There are no wrong answers. The trustee's questions will help him or her make sure that you understand that although filing a Chapter 7 bankruptcy wipes out debts you cannot afford to pay, it will damage your credit history. In other words, there are positive and negative aspects to bankruptcy. The questions will also help the trustee make certain that you cannot afford to pay off your debts through a Chapter 13 bankruptcy rather than a Chapter 7. In fact, under the Bankruptcy Civil Enforcement Initiative, the trustee will try to find a way to push you into a Chapter 13. Also, if you intend to reaffirm any of your debts, the trustee will make sure that you understand that you will have 60 days to change your mind and that if you don't, you will be responsible for paying them.

What Happens at the Creditors' Meeting

After you arrive at the courthouse and find the room where creditors' meetings are held, locate your attorney. Sometimes these meetings are held in private rooms, and you may have to wait your turn outside rather than inside the room. If you are allowed to wait your turn in the meeting room itself, do so. That way, you can listen to the types of questions the trustee asks other debtors who are there for their creditors' meetings for some trustees tend to ask the same questions of each debtor. Pay close attention to how the other debtors answer the trustee's questions and notice how the trustee reacts to their responses. If you are not sure how you would answer a particular question, talk to your attorney before your creditors' meeting begins.

When it is your turn, the trustee will call your name and you will be sworn in. You will probably sit at a table with your attorney, with the trustee sitting either at the head of the table or at the front of the room. The trustee will conduct the meeting.

What Questions Will the Trustee Ask You?

The trustee's questions have two purposes. One purpose is to identify assets that can be liquidated so that the sale proceeds can be applied to your debts. The trustee has a financial incentive to find these assets because the trustee is paid a percentage of any money he or she administers in your bankruptcy. Although the percentage is small, the more assets the trustee can include in your bankruptcy estate, the more money the trustee gets.

The other purpose for the trustee's questions is to determine how honest you were when you provided your attorney with the financial information he or she used to complete the bankruptcy forms that were filed with the court. If the trustee believes that you tried to defraud your creditors by providing inaccurate or incomplete information or by hiding some of your assets, two things will probably happen. You will be reported to the U.S. Attorney's office for possible criminal prosecution, and the trustee will file a complaint with the bankruptcy court, objecting to the discharge of your debts.

Here are some of the questions you will probably be asked at your creditors' meeting to help the trustee make sure that you have been totally forthcoming about your finances and that you are not trying to defraud your creditors:

- *Why did you file for bankruptcy?* The trustee asks this question to find out if you filed because of a business failure. If that is the reason, the trustee will want to make sure that you disclosed that information on your schedules. If you did not, the trustee will ask questions to determine what happened to your business assets. In part, the trustee will be fishing to see if you say anything that tells him or her that you illegally transferred those assets to a friend or relative to keep them out of your bankruptcy.

- *Have you listed all your debts and all your assets on your schedules?* The trustee will note for the record whether you responded "Yes" under oath to questions related to your schedules and if the trustee learns later that you were not telling the truth, he or she will have evidence to charge you with a bankruptcy crime. The trustee also asks you about your schedules to make certain that you did not overlook any information that should be on your schedules. If you did, you will be given an opportunity to add it.

- *How did you come up with values for your assets?* The trustee wants to make sure that your values are realistic. If the trustee thinks that some of the values are too low, he or she may want to get some of your assets independently appraised. When you place too high a market value on some of your assets, the assets might become nonexempt, and the trustee may liquidate them.

- *Have you been in any accidents in the past year?* If you are legally entitled to receive any money in compensation for damages you suffered as the result of an accident and you did not list your claim against the party that injured you as an asset on your schedules, the trustee will insist that you do so. If you cannot exempt the claim, the trustee can settle the claim on your behalf—most likely for much less than you think you should receive—and will apply the settlement money to your debts.

- *Are you entitled to an income tax refund that you have not yet received?* If your answer is yes, you must list the refund as an asset. If you cannot exempt it, the trustee will take it.
- *Are you entitled to an inheritance or is there the possibility you will receive an inheritance within six months of the date that you filed your bankruptcy petition?* Bankruptcy law treats an inheritance as an asset. Therefore, you must list it on your schedules and you will have to exempt the inheritance if you want to keep it.

If one of your relatives dies sometime after the start of your bankruptcy but not more than six months later, and the relative leaves you an inheritance, it is part of your bankruptcy estate. Therefore, you are legally obligated to report the inheritance to the trustee, and the court will determine whether or not you can exempt it. If you cannot, the trustee will take your inheritance, liquidate it as necessary, and apply the money to your debts.

Prior to the creditors' meeting, the trustee may ask you to provide him or her with additional documentation related to your finances, including copies of your bank statements, canceled checks, check registers, copies of your income tax returns, stock certificates, insurance policies, title documents, appraisals, and so on. Then at the creditors' meeting, the trustee will ask you questions based on that information. For example:

- If your bank statements show that you had a larger balance in your account on the day you filed bankruptcy than your schedules reflect, you will be asked to explain the discrepancy. If you cannot exempt the additional funds, the trustee will ask for them.
- If your bank statements show that you wrote checks for large amounts of money close to the time that you filed for bankruptcy, you will be asked to explain what the checks were for. If the trustee concludes that you were paying some of your creditors at the expense of others, the trustee will require the preferred creditors—the ones you paid—to return the money to the court so that the funds can be more fairly distributed among your creditors according to the rules of bankruptcy.

- If your income tax returns show that you are depreciating assets that are not listed on your schedules, you will be asked to explain what became of the property.
- If you bought season football tickets, season tickets to the theater, and so on, and they are not listed as exempt assets on your schedules, the trustee will want to know why.

These are just a few of the questions a trustee might ask you. There could be others, depending on exactly what additional information the trustee asks for and the details of your finances.

Questions That the Trustee Must Ask You

At your creditors' meeting, the trustee is legally required to ask you a series of questions regarding your understanding of the Chapter 7 bankruptcy process and how it may affect you. Among other things, the trustee will talk with you about the potential consequences of filing for Chapter 7, including the fact that it will be in your credit record for ten years and that it will be difficult for you to get new credit at reasonable terms during that time. The trustee will also make sure you understand that you can file a Chapter 13 and that you understand what it means to reaffirm a debt and what will happen when your debts are discharged.

Questions Your Creditors May Ask

Some of your creditors may attend the creditors' meeting and they may ask you questions, too. For example:

- *If there are assets to be liquidated in your bankruptcy, your unsecured creditors may attend to find out how much money they may get.* In practice, however, they usually call the trustee ahead of time to get this information, so few if any of them will actually show up for the meeting. The truth is, in most Chapter 7s, it is rare for unsecured creditors to receive any money. If that is the case in your bankruptcy, your unsecured creditors will be notified before the date of your creditors' meeting that your bankruptcy is a "No Asset Case."
- *Your secured creditors may attend the creditors' meeting to find out if you want to reaffirm the debts that you owe to them.* If your attorney has not already talked with them about a reaf-

firmation, and assuming you want to reaffirm some of your secured debts, then you may do that at the creditors' meeting.

- *Some of the secured creditors may ask you questions to find out if you lied when you provided your attorney with information for your schedules.* For example, they may question you about the financial information you provided to them when you applied for credit and may ask you to explain any discrepancies between the values that you placed on the assets listed on your schedules and the values that you gave to those same assets when you applied for credit. You may also be asked to explain why assets that appeared on your credit application are not listed on your bankruptcy schedules.

If any of your creditors can prove that you lied, they can file complaints against you with the court and ask that the court not discharge the debts you owe to them. If the court sides with them, you will have to pay the debts you owe to those creditors after your bankruptcy is over.

After the creditors' meeting, your attorney will discuss any problems related to your bankruptcy that became apparent at the meeting. Your attorney will also discuss the consequences of those problems and the best way to deal with them.

The 60-Day Period after the Creditors' Meeting

Your creditors will have 60 days after the date of the creditors' meeting to object to the discharge of any of your debts. Once that period is up and assuming there are no objections, your debts will be discharged. During this 60-day period, you should:

- Make sure that all of the creditors are listed on your schedules of debts. Now is the time to add any creditors that you may have overlooked because once your bankruptcy is over, any debts that are not on those schedules may not get discharged and you will have to pay them.
- Make sure that your attorney listed correctly all of your creditors' names and addresses. It is your responsibility to bring any errors and omissions to the attention of your attorney so that he or she can correct your schedules before the discharge date in your bankruptcy.

- If you are reaffirming any of your secured debts so that you can keep your collateral, finalize those arrangements. Once the 60 days have passed and you have obtained a discharge of your debts, you will no longer be protected by the automatic stay and it will be difficult if not impossible to work out a way to keep your secured assets.

The Discharge Hearing

The day of your discharge hearing is the date that your Chapter 7 bankruptcy is over and the court wipes out, or discharges, your debts. It marks the beginning of the fresh start that bankruptcy promises.

Your attorney will explain how your district handles discharge hearings. Depending on the district, you may have to attend a hearing or, instead, the court may just mail you an order of discharge signed by the judge. If you have to attend the hearing, you will sit in a courtroom with a lot of other people who are there for their own bankruptcy discharge. The judge will enter the courtroom, make some brief comments, sign your order officially discharging you of your debts, and wish you well. Later you will receive the order of discharge in the mail.

When you receive your order of discharge, make several copies and store them in a safe place. On occasion, a creditor will ignore your bankruptcy and then one day after it is over, send you a letter or call you demanding that you pay your debt. If this happens, send a copy of your discharge order to the creditor along with a letter noting that the debt the creditor contacted you about has been discharged and can no longer be collected.

You should also send a copy of your discharge order and a copy of your schedules listing your debts to the three national credit-reporting agencies—Equifax, Experian, and TransUnion. Attach this information to a letter asking each credit-reporting agency to add it to your credit record so that your record will reflect the fact that all the debts listed on the order have been discharged. Here are the addresses to write to:

Equifax
Disclosure Department
P.O. Box 740241
Atlanta, GA 30374

Experian
National Consumer Assistance Center
P.O. Box 2104
Allen, TX 75013-2104

TransUnion
Consumer Disclosure Center
P.O. Box 1000
Chester, PA 19002

> ## WARNING
>
> If you do not receive your discharge order within four weeks
> from the date of your bankruptcy discharge, ask your attorney
> to follow up.

Reaffirming a Debt

If you want to reaffirm a debt and you are represented by an attorney, there will probably not be a reaffirmation hearing to decide whether or not the reaffirmation will be approved by the court. Instead, your attorney will file an affidavit saying that you have been told about the consequences of reaffirming a debt and that reaffirmation is not required by the Bankruptcy Code. Getting your reaffirmation approved will depend on whether the judge believes that you are entering into the reaffirmation agreement of your own free will, that you can afford to continue paying on the debt that you want to reaffirm, and that you understand that you can rescind your reaffirmation agreement within 60 days.

7

Preparing Your Chapter 13 Schedules and Debt Reorganization Plan

You have two goals when you file a Chapter 13 bankruptcy: to reduce the amount that you must pay to your creditors by as much as possible and to protect your assets from your creditors while you pay off your debts. Your attorney will help you accomplish these goals in several different ways. For example, your attorney will:

- Fill out your assets and debts schedules using the financial information you provide. The assets schedules will describe the property you own and assign a current value to each asset. The debts schedules will indicate the nature of each of your debts—secured or unsecured, for example—and their amounts.
- Make sure that you claim the maximum amount of property exemptions you are entitled to. Maximizing your exemptions is important because you want to keep as many of your assets as possible and because the value of your exemptions will determine the minimum amount of money you will have to pay your unsecured creditors.
- Scrutinize your budget and statement of income. Your attorney will look at this information to make sure that your budget is realistic and that your reorganization plan is affordable. This is important because if you propose payments to your creditors that are too high, it will be difficult if not impossible for you to

complete your Chapter 13 bankruptcy and you may have to convert it to a Chapter 7. Your attorney will review the expenses in your budget in light of what the court in your district considers reasonable and may ask you to modify certain expenses if he or she believes they are too high or too low based on the court's standards.

Figure 7.1 illustrates the expense categories listed on the budget form you will have to complete when you file for Chapter 13.

- Prepare your debt reorganization plan using the financial information you provide. Although your attorney will be concerned about making your plan affordable, the court will expect you to pay as much as possible on your debts.

Your Chapter 13 Reorganization Plan

In preparing your reorganization plan, your attorney will divide your debts into three categories—*priority, secured,* and *unsecured* claims. Then, following the requirements of the Bankruptcy Code, the attorney will treat each category of debt in a specific way. For example, because priority debts are nondischargeable in bankruptcy, you must pay the full amount of those debts during the term of your plan, which will be in effect for between three and five years.

Taxes, including past-due property taxes and income taxes, are the most common type of priority debt. For example, if you owe $3,000 in past-due property taxes, your plan may show that you intend to pay $50 a month over 60 months (5 years) to pay that debt in full; or if your plan will last for just three years, then your plan would indicate that you will pay a little more than $83 a month to pay off your property tax debt.

Other debts that you must treat as priority claims include past-due alimony, maintenance, and support payments, and criminal fines. For instance, if you were ordered to pay child support and you got behind on your payments, your reorganization plan must show how you intend to get caught up. At the same time, you must make each of your current child support payments throughout the term of the plan.

Your bankruptcy attorney will divide your secured debts into two categories—the money you owe on your homestead (the home you live in) and the money you owe on your other assets, such as your car, furniture, other real estate, etc. When a debt is secured, you have collat-

FIGURE 7.1
Monthly Expenses

Rent or Mortgage Payment		$_____
Utilities:		
Electricity	$_____	
Water	$_____	
Heat	$_____	
Telephone	$_____	
Cable	$_____	
Internet	$_____	
Other	$_____	
Total Utilities:		$_____
Food		$_____
Clothing		$_____
Laundry and Cleaning		$_____
Newspapers, Periodicals and Books (including school books)		$_____
Doctor and Other Medical Expenses		$_____
Transportation (not including auto payments under your reorganization plan)		$_____
Recreation, Clubs, and Entertainment		$_____
Insurance (Not deducted from your wages):		
Auto	$_____	
Life	$_____	
Other	$_____	
Total Insurance:		$_____
Taxes (Not deducted from your wages or included in your mortgage payments)		$_____
Alimony or Support Payments		$_____
Payment for Support of Additional Dependents Not Living at Your Home		$_____
Other (explain):		_____

_____

_____

_____

eralized it with an asset. Therefore, the creditor is legally entitled to take the asset if you default on the debt after it gets the court's permission.

How You Must Pay Your Home Mortgage in Chapter 13

You cannot use bankruptcy to modify the rights of a creditor with a lien on your home. In other words, while your reorganization plan is in effect, you must continue to make your mortgage payments according to the terms of your mortgage loan agreement. The same is true for a home equity loan. However, if any of your payments are past due, you can use Chapter 13 to get caught up on those payments so that you won't lose your home. Therefore, it's a good idea to file for bankruptcy when you think your mortgage lender is about to foreclose on your home. Presently, there is a trend nationally for trustees to require that you pay not only your past-due payments in your plan but the current payment as well. Ask an attorney in your area if that is the practice in your district. If you pay the trustee as you should, the trustee is responsible for making payments to the mortgage company. This could be helpful if you have had trouble in the past with the mortgage company accepting your payments or giving you the proper credit for the payments.

WARNING

Some trustees will require you to pay not only your past-due mortgage payments through your plan but your current payments as well. Ask your attorney if that is the practice in your district.

If your past-due mortgage loan was made after October 22, 1994, you will not have to pay interest on the amount that is in arrears, although there are some exceptions. Those exceptions are:

- Your mortgage agreement specifically obligates you to pay the interest.
- A nonbankruptcy law in your state requires that you pay it.

If you obtained your mortgage loan before October 22, 1994, you will probably have to pay interest on the amount of the loan that may be past due. Usually, however, you can pay the arrearage amount plus the interest through your reorganization plan over a 36-month to a 60-month period.

Some mortgage loan agreements obligate consumers to make balloon payments at the end of their loans. If this applies to you and the date for your balloon payment will occur within five years of the start of your bankruptcy, if you cannot afford to make it, you can provide in your reorganization plan that you will pay the balloon payment over a three- to five-year period.

Paying Other Secured Debts

You can modify the way you pay your car loan, furniture loan, and other secured debts by paying the value of the collateral (the asset that secures the debt) over the term of your reorganization plan rather than paying the balance due on those loans. This usually means that you will end up paying less money to your secured creditors than you agreed to pay when you got the loans. For example, if you owe $10,000 on your car and you are making monthly payments of $350 but the car is only worth $6,000, then you can pay off your car loan during the term of your reorganization plan by paying $6,000 rather than the balance you still owe on the $10,000 loan. As a result, your payments to the car loan lender will be smaller, which means that you will have a better chance of being able to keep your car. The $4,000 balance (the difference between the total amount of your car loan and the value of your car) will be treated as an unsecured debt, which means that you won't have to pay it if you don't have enough money. The next section of this chapter discusses unsecured debts.

You May Not Have to Pay 100 Percent of Your Unsecured Debts

When your attorney deals with your unsecured debts in your reorganization plan, he or she will determine the maximum that you can afford to pay on those debts by looking at the value of your nonexempt property. This is the property that you would have to give up if you had filed a Chapter 7 liquidation bankruptcy rather than a Chapter 13. The rule in bankruptcy is that over the term of your reorganization plan, your unsecured creditors must receive as much as they would have if you had filed for Chapter 7. For example, if you have $1,000 worth of nonexempt property, and your reorganization plan will last for five years, then you must pay at least $16.60 a month to your unsecured creditors over that 60-month period. However, if you can afford to pay more each month after you have paid your living expenses, priority claims, and secured claims, the court will expect you to do so.

Once your attorney has completed your schedules of assets and debts and your reorganization plan, you will be asked to read these documents and sign them. However, do not sign them unless you understand exactly what you are agreeing to pay and feel certain that you can afford the terms of the plan you are proposing to the court. If you have any concerns about the plan, discuss them with your attorney.

Paying on Your Plan

Thirty days after your attorney has filed your schedules and reorganization plan with the court, you must begin making payments to your creditors according to your plan. You will make your payments to the trustee who has been assigned to your case by the bankruptcy court. Your attorney will give you the name and address of the trustee.

Depending on your district, you will either be able to mail your payments directly to the trustee or your employer will be required to deduct the amount of your payments from your paycheck and send the money to the trustee. If your employer will be deducting the payments from your paychecks, tell your attorney ahead of time if you are concerned that the deductions will cause a hardship for you. Your attorney may be able to file a motion with the court asking that you be given permission to mail your payments directly to the trustee instead. Although the court will evaluate your request on its merits, normally it prefers that debtors make their payments through payroll deductions.

HOT TIP

It is illegal for your employer to discriminate against you because you have filed for Chapter 13 bankruptcy.

After Your Plan Has Been Filed

After your schedules and reorganization plan have been filed with the court and the automatic stay has been invoked, your attorney should make sure that all your creditors are notified that you have filed for bankruptcy so that they will stop trying to collect from you.

Ordinarily, your attorney will send each of them a letter informing them of your bankruptcy, but it is also possible that your attorney will notify them by telephone on the day that your petition is filed. Notification by phone is necessary if there is a possibility that any of your secured creditors are about to repossess some of your assets. Make sure that you know which creditors have been notified and whether they were notified by mail or phone.

After your secured creditors have been notified, your attorney will contact them as well as your priority creditors to try to resolve any problems they may have with your bankruptcy. In addition, your attorney will contact the trustee to make sure that he or she has all the necessary documents related to your bankruptcy. It's likely that the trustee will ask for additional information from you now that the Bankruptcy Civil Enforcement Initiative is in place. For example, you may have to provide additional information to prove your living expenses.

The Trustee's Role in Chapter 13

When you file a Chapter 13 reorganization, the court will appoint a trustee to your case. The trustee will administer your reorganization plan, which means that he or she will receive the money you pay on your debts, disburse that money to your creditors, and monitor the progress of your bankruptcy.

In some districts, trustees get involved with Chapter 13 bankruptcies as soon as they begin and in still others they help debtors formulate their reorganization plans. In most districts, however, trustees just review debtors' financial information and their reorganization plans and request additional information.

Meeting with the Trustee for the First Time

In most districts, you will not meet the trustee who is assigned to your case until your first creditors' meeting. By that time, the trustee will have already reviewed your reorganization plan to make sure that your budget is reasonable and that you are paying enough each month on your debts. If the trustee feels that you are paying enough and that your budget is reasonable, he or she will recommend to the judge that your plan be approved; but if the trustee feels that you can pay more or that you have not budgeted enough for some of your living expenses, the trustee will not recommend approval.

Other Major Duties of the Trustee

The trustee will preside over your first creditors' meeting and will also ask you questions during the meeting. The types of questions you will be asked were explained in the previous chapter. In addition, the trustee will be responsible for examining the claims that your creditors submit to the court to get paid during your bankruptcy. Depending on how your district works, the trustee will object to any claims he or she believes are improper or it will be up to you and your attorney to file those objections.

The trustee will be also responsible for recommending to the court whether or not your plan should be approved. The trustee will oppose confirmation of your plan if he or she believes that it is impractical, that you cannot afford to comply with the plan or that you can afford to pay more on your debts, or because the trustee feels that you did not prepare your plan in "good faith."

Although the bankruptcy judge will be the ultimate arbiter of whether or not your plan should be approved, in most districts, the trustee's recommendation carries a lot of weight. Therefore, you must work with your attorney to prepare a realistic budget and plan and you must build and maintain a positive relationship with the trustee. You need a good relationship with the trustee not just because you want him or her to recommend that your plan be approved but because once it is, you will have to work with the trustee while your plan is in effect.

According to the statutory provisions of Chapter 13 bankruptcy, the trustee must advise you about any nonlegal matters related to your reorganization plan and assist you in living up to your plan. It is unclear, however, exactly how the trustee must do these things because there is a difference of opinion about what the words *advise* and *assist* really mean.

Records from the districts that have handled Chapter 13 cases for many years show that those districts with the greatest percentage of successful Chapter 13s are ones in which trustees do more than just disburse the money they receive from debtors to their creditors. In these districts, trustees advise debtors about their finances, give them information about where to acquire new job skills so they can boost their incomes, refer them to programs designed to teach them how to manage their money better, and do everything possible to ensure that the debtors they work with will not develop more financial problems in the future. Also, some districts have mandatory debtor schools that teach financial management skills, while in others, trustees are available at regular hours to meet one-on-one with debtors to answer their financial questions.

If you are in a district where trustees take an active role in advising and assisting debtors, you will find their help very beneficial. Your bankruptcy attorney can tell you how much help you can expect from your trustee.

How Trustees Are Paid

Trustees are paid for their services by receiving a percentage of what you pay on your debts according to your approved reorganization plan. Bankruptcy law says that up to 10 percent of what you pay will go toward the administrative costs associated with your bankruptcy and the trustee's salary. The exact percentage varies by district. For example, if your district allows trustees to take the full 10 percent and your plan shows that you will pay your creditors $100 a month, $90 of that payment will go to your creditors and the other $10 will go to the trustee.

If you cannot pay your creditors 100 percent of what you owe them, you will have to pay only what you can afford to, no matter how much the trustee takes.

The Creditors' Meeting

Usually, your first contact with the court during your Chapter 13 reorganization bankruptcy will be at your creditors' meeting. This meeting is important to getting your plan confirmed by the judge. At the meeting, the trustee will determine whether or not you are acting in good faith by filing a Chapter 13 and whether you deserve the benefits of that type of bankruptcy. Therefore, it is critical that you convey sincerity and honesty at this meeting.

The court will set the date for the creditors' meeting and you will be notified of that date far enough in advance that you should be able to arrange your work schedule around the meeting.

The trustee will preside over the meeting and any creditors who want to can attend to discuss how you have dealt with their claims in your reorganization plan. Usually, the meeting is relatively informal, although it is possible that one of your creditors' attorneys will question you aggressively. The attorney may try to determine if you can pay the creditor more than your plan indicates, if you can really live up to your plan, if you have adequate insurance on the creditors' collateral, etc.

Preparing for the Meeting

Before the meeting begins, your attorney will talk with as many of your secured creditors as possible to try to resolve any outstanding issues they may have with your bankruptcy that could stand in the way of getting your plan confirmed. Those issues might include: exactly how much you owe to each of your creditors, the value of your collateral, how much you are behind on large debts, such as your mortgage, and so on.

While your attorney is busy dealing with your creditors, you will wait for your case to be called by the trustee. If creditors' meetings in your district are held in an open courtroom, you can observe what is happening at the meetings that precede yours while you are waiting, which is good, because knowing what to expect when it's time for your meeting can help calm your nerves.

When your case is called, you, your attorney, and any attorneys who are in the courtroom to represent your creditors will come forward to sit at a table with the trustee. The trustee will swear you in and then will ask you questions about your bankruptcy petition. Among other things, you will be asked to confirm that you are the person who filed the petition, that you still earn the same amount of money as you indicated in your petition, and that all of the information on your debts and assets schedules is true, accurate, and complete.

Notify Your Attorney Before You Make Any Changes

Prior to your creditors' meeting, be sure to let your bankruptcy attorney know if your financial situation has changed in any way since your bankruptcy petition and schedules of assets and debts were filed with the court. That way your attorney will have time to decide what to do about the change(s) and to assess how the change(s) will affect your reorganization plan. Don't do anything that will take your attorney by surprise at the meeting because he or she has worked hard to develop a reorganization plan for you that has a good chance of getting approved by the court. For example, at the creditors' meeting, don't catch your attorney off guard by telling the trustee that you earn less than what your petition shows and what your reorganization plan assumes because earning less means that you will pay your creditors less and that change will decrease the likelihood that the judge will approve your plan. If you are earning less, tell your attorney before the meeting so he or she can prepare another plan.

Here is an example of one way a last-minute change can work against you. Let's assume that your attorney has figured out the minimum amount you need to pay your auto lender so you can keep your car, and the minimum amounts you must pay your other creditors. Then at the meeting you mention that your income has dropped recently. Based on that information, therefore, you may not make enough money to pay your debts according to your plan and may not be able to keep your car.

You must begin paying on your reorganization plan 30 days after you file your petition, which will be before your creditors' meeting and before your plan has been confirmed. If for some reason, however, you have not begun paying on your plan prior to the meeting, you should be ready to make your first payment at the meeting. Doing so will make a good impression on the trustee and will demonstrate that you are operating in good faith. Once you give your payment to the trustee, however, he or she cannot disburse the funds to your creditors until your plan has been confirmed, so if your plan is not, the trustee must return the payment to you. In some districts the payments are disbursed after the creditors' meeting, but before the confirmation hearing. Ask your attorney if that is the case in your district.

Your creditors' meeting will end after all your creditors' issues related to your bankruptcy have been dealt with, after you have answered all the trustee's questions to his or her satisfaction, and after the trustee has issued instructions to you, if any. Most likely, when you leave the meeting, you will know whether or not the trustee is going to recommend that your plan be approved, whether any of your creditors intend to formally object to its confirmation, and the date of your confirmation hearing.

8

Handling Objections to Confirmation: Creditors' Rights and Duties

During your Chapter 13 creditors' meeting, you may learn that one or more of your creditors are objecting to the confirmation of your reorganization plan. They may object because they do not agree with how you have classified their claims in your reorganization plan or because they want you to pay them more during the term of the plan.

Proof of Claims

If your creditors want the opportunity to get paid during your bankruptcy, they must file a *proof of claim* with the court no later than 90 days after the date of your first creditors' meeting. If they don't, they may lose their right to receive any money in your bankruptcy.

If any of your secured creditors don't file their proofs of claim by the deadline, you are entitled to treat them as unsecured creditors in your reorganization plan, which means that they will receive less money than if they had filed their claims on time. Each of those secured creditors, however, will still retain a security interest in the assets you used to secure your debts with them. Therefore, although you may get some immediate relief from the court for those debts, when your Chapter 13 bankruptcy is over or if you decide to sell your collateral, you will have to pay those creditors what you owe them to get clear title to the assets. Without clear title you will not be able to complete the sales.

If any of your unsecured creditors don't file their proofs of claim by the deadline, they will lose all rights to receive any money from you under your Chapter 13 plan. The money they would have received will help pay off the debts you owe to your other creditors.

HOT TIP

If enough of your creditors fail to file proofs of claim by the 90-day deadline, it's possible that you could complete your reorganization plan in less than three years.

How Claims Are Treated

If a creditor files its proof of claim on time, you will have to treat its claim in a certain way in your reorganization plan depending on the nature of the debt. For example, bankruptcy law requires you to pay your priority claims in full. Past-due taxes are the most common type of priority claim, including past-due federal income taxes. You can pay off these kinds of debts during the term of your reorganization plan through monthly installments or in some other way—by selling one of your assets, for example, and using the money to pay the debt.

You must also pay any criminal fines you may owe during the term of your Chapter 13 bankruptcy according to the way that the criminal court judge ordered you to pay them. You cannot use Chapter 13 to discharge criminal fines.

Other debts that you must pay in full during the term of your Chapter 13 bankruptcy are:

- Claims for unpaid alimony, maintenance, and support
- Past-due student loans
- Any money that you owe because you were driving under the influence of illegal drugs or alcohol and you caused an accident and killed or injured someone as a result

How you deal with your secured debts will depend on the exact nature of each debt. Your options are:

- Return your collateral to your secured creditor. The creditor will sell the asset and apply the sale proceeds to your debt. If the asset does not sell for enough to pay the full amount of your debt, you must pay the remaining balance, which is called a *deficiency*. However, that balance becomes an unsecured debt rather than a secured debt and you can treat it just as you would any of your other unsecured debts.

- Modify the rights of a secured creditor so that you can pay the market value of your collateral in monthly installments, with some interest added, during the term of your plan rather than paying the actual amount that you owe to that creditor. In other words, one of the special benefits of filing for Chapter 13 is that you can satisfy most but not all secured debts and keep the assets that collateralize those debts by paying less than what you owe on them. For example, you may want to modify the rights of your auto lender so that you can keep your car. Let's assume that you owe $8,000 on your vehicle and its current value, which is usually determined by the National Automobile Dealers Association Guidebook (the "Blue Book"), is $6,000. If you modify your car loan, you can pay the $6,000 in monthly installments over the length of your reorganization plan, with some interest, rather than the loan's $8,000 outstanding balance. Once you complete your reorganization plan, the car will be 100 percent yours, even though you paid $2,000 less for it. Not only will this arrangement reduce your monthly car payments, but it will also save you a lot of money overall. You can use this same option to keep any furniture, recreational vehicles, or other personal property you have financed. However, you cannot modify your mortgage loan or any other loan that you secured with your home—a home equity loan, for example.

HOT TIP

When you modify a debt, you will end up paying less in interest.

- Pay the secured creditor whatever you still owe on your original purchase. This is a particularly good option if your collateral is worth more than the amount that you owe on it. For example, let's assume that you own a second car that is worth $15,000 and that you still owe $13,000 on it. Assuming you can afford to, you may want to pay the lender that financed your car the balance due on your car loan, the $13,000, to maintain a good relationship with that creditor. For instance, the lender is the credit union where you work and you worry that if you modify the credit union's rights through your Chapter 13 bankruptcy, your job could be affected negatively even though the law says that you cannot be fired simply because you've filed for bankruptcy. Remember, to take advantage of this option, the asset that secures your debt must be worth *more* than what you owe on it.

Although the three options I have just outlined apply to most secured creditors, there are some exceptions. They include:

- You cannot modify your home loan, although you can pay the amount of the loan that may be in default in installments during the term of your reorganization plan. However, while you are paying off the past-due amount, you must stay current on all future mortgage payments. Also, if your entire home loan becomes due according to the terms of your mortgage loan and you cannot afford to pay what you owe, you can use Chapter 13 to be able to pay that amount in installments through your reorganization plan.
- In some states when you file for bankruptcy you can void certain kinds of liens and treat the debts that you owe to the secured creditors with those liens as unsecured debts. You can do this with a nonpurchase-money, nonpossessory secured lien. This kind of lien exists when you borrow money and collateralize it with your furniture or some other asset. Since you are not using the borrowed money to buy the asset, it is referred to as *nonpurchase money,* and since you, not the lender, has possession of the asset, it is referred to as *nonpossessory.*

As for your unsecured debts—debts that are not collateralized, including credit card debts, unpaid medical bills, and so on—you can use Chapter 13 to substantially reduce what you must pay on them each month. Furthermore, because unsecured creditors are usually not entitled to receive interest in bankruptcy, you won't have to pay the 18 percent to 24 percent that you may now be paying on your unsecured debts, which will be a big money saver.

W A R N I N G

As a result of the Bankruptcy Civil Enforcement Initiative, the trustee will check your budget very carefully. The trustee may ask you to verify certain expenses or change your budget so that you can afford to pay more to your unsecured creditors. The trustee will want them to receive as much as possible.

As long as you treat all of your unsecured creditors the same way in your reorganization plan, you may not have to pay them 100 percent of what you owe to them. However, the court will expect you to pay those creditors every single penny that you can. Even so, don't agree to pay more than you can afford.

How to Handle Objections to Your Plan

As was indicated at the start of this chapter, some of your creditors may object to the confirmation of your Chapter 13 debt reorganization plan. The most common reason for objecting is that they do not like the way they have been treated in your plan. In other words, they want more money.

To object to the confirmation of your plan your creditors must file a formal *Objection to Confirmation of the Debtor's Plan* with the court, spelling out exactly what they don't like. Once that happens, your attorney will contact the creditors to discuss their objections and to determine if their objections are valid. If they are, your attorney will try to negotiate compromises with each of the creditors so that they will drop their objections. However, if your attorney is not successful at doing so, there will be a hearing on the objections. This hearing will probably take place at the same time as your confirmation hearing. At the hearing related to your creditors' objections, the creditors' attorneys will explain why the objections were filed and your attorney will present your side. It's possible that witnesses will be called and that you may have to testify as well. At the end of the hearing, the judge will decide what to do about each creditor objection. If the judge decides in your favor, your plan will be confirmed as proposed. However, if the judge decides in favor of your creditors, you will have to modify your reorganization plan accordingly.

WARNING

If you are not current on the payments you are supposed to be making to the trustee under your proposed plan at the time that your confirmation hearing is held, the court may refuse to confirm your plan or it may dismiss your case, which means that your creditors will be legally entitled to try to collect what you owe them. In either case, your only option will be to file a Chapter 7 liquidation.

HOT TIP

These days, falling behind on your payments to the trustee under the terms of your reorganization plan is much less likely than it used to be because a growing number of districts now require that you make your payments through automatic wage deductions. Therefore, the money for your payments will come out of your paychecks and go directly from your employer to the trustee. You will never see it.

9

The Confirmation Hearing

After your creditors' meeting has taken place, the court will set a date and time for your bankruptcy confirmation hearing. At this hearing, your reorganization plan will be formally presented to the bankruptcy judge, who will decide whether to approve or deny it. As explained in the previous chapter, prior to this hearing your creditors and the trustee will have an opportunity to object to your plan's confirmation and their objections will probably be heard at the hearing.

The exact process for the confirmation hearing will depend on your particular district. For example, depending on your district, you may or may not have to attend the hearing, although your attorney must be there. Your attorney will explain how things work in your particular district.

If you must attend the hearing, dress conservatively and do not wear a lot of jewelry. As a rule, bankruptcy judges are conservative and they want to grant the rights and privileges of Chapter 13 to deserving people. If you dress like you have a considerable amount of money—expensive jewelry, a fur coat, a designer purse, etc.—you may not appear deserving and the judge may not confirm your reorganization plan. The same is true if you are rude or have a bad attitude.

At the hearing, the trustee will present your plan to the judge and will either recommend that it be confirmed or denied. The judge may ask you some questions before making his or her decision.

Requirements for Confirmation

Although the confirmation process varies somewhat from district to district, no matter what the process is in your district, the bankruptcy judge will make certain that your Chapter 13 reorganization plan meets certain requirements. If it does not, the judge will not confirm it. These requirements are:

Requirement one. *The proposed reorganization plan must comply with all the rules and provisions of Chapter 13.*

This requirement deals with the technical aspects of Chapter 13. In other words, the bankruptcy judge wants to be sure that all your bankruptcy forms are complete and that they were filed on time. If there are any problems related to your forms, they probably won't prevent the judge from confirming your plan, but you will have to correct the problems first. The problems may irritate the judge, however, because they will delay confirmation of your plan and cause extra work for the court. Of course, if you hired an experienced and capable bankruptcy attorney who understands bankruptcy procedures, knows what the court requires, and is familiar with the rules in your particular district, there should be no problems.

Requirement two. *You have paid your filing fee.*

The fee for filing a Chapter 13 is $194. Most consumers are able to pay this fee; if you cannot afford to, you can ask the court for permission to pay it in installments.

Requirement three. *Your plan shows that you will pay your unsecured creditors at least as much as they would have received if you had filed a Chapter 7 liquidation bankruptcy.*

If you had filed for Chapter 7, the court would have looked at all your assets and allowed you to keep whichever ones you claimed as exempt. Then the trustee would have taken all your nonexempt property, sold it, used the sale proceeds to pay your priority claims, and then, if there was any money left, the trustee would have disbursed the remaining funds to your unsecured creditors. Therefore, assuming that you would have paid your unsecured creditors 20 percent of what you would have owed them if you had filed for Chapter 7, in your Chapter 13 reorganization plan you must pay them at least 20 percent of what they are owed out of your future income during the term of the plan.

Furthermore, your unsecured creditors are not entitled to receive any interest on the debts that you owe them, so paying 20 percent over 36 months is a lot better for you than paying 20 percent from the sale of your assets. Of course, 20 percent is the bare minimum that you must pay them to qualify for a Chapter 13 bankruptcy; the court will expect you to pay more if at all possible. However, many consumers have so much debt and their incomes are so low that they can only afford to pay the minimum. One potential way to pay more to your creditors is to pay them over five years rather than over three years. Five years is the maximum amount of time that your reorganization plan can last.

Requirement four. *You must either let your secured creditors take their collateral back or you must pay them the value of their collateral over the term of your reorganization plan.*

During this time, your secured creditors will continue to have liens on the assets that *collateralize* the debts you owe them. If you want to keep your secured assets, the court will make certain that you can truly afford to.

Requirement five. *You proposed your plan in good faith.*

This requirement more than any other tends to be problematic. This is because bankruptcy law does not define in "good faith" nor does it set out the criteria a judge should use to evaluate this issue. Therefore, bankruptcy judges have a lot of discretion to determine whether a plan has not been proposed in good faith and, therefore, should not be confirmed.

The issue of good faith is most apt to arise if you propose in your plan to pay your unsecured creditors nothing at all or just a small percentage of the total amount that you owe them. Some judges won't confirm such plans because they believe that they were not proposed in good faith. Also, if a judge believes that you do not deserve the benefit of bankruptcy protection, the judge will use your lack of good faith as the hook on which to hang his or her refusal to confirm.

If you are using Chapter 13 because you want to pay as much as possible on your debts, you should not worry about whether the judge will question your good faith. If you can honestly answer the question "Why have I filed for Chapter 13?" with a response such as "Because I am looking for a more affordable way to meet my financial obligations," then you are using bankruptcy as it was intended and the good faith requirement should not be a stumbling block.

Can You Afford a Chapter 13 Plan?

As requirement four indicates, if you want to keep a secured asset, you must pay your creditor the value of that asset. However, you and the creditor must agree on its value and also on the interest rate you must pay during the term of your plan. Until those issues are resolved, the judge will not confirm your plan. If you are working with an inexperienced bankruptcy attorney or if you are handling your own bankruptcy, you will be at a serious disadvantage when you are negotiating these issues with your secured creditors. As a result, you may end up paying more to keep your secured assets than your creditors are really entitled to.

If you and one of your secured creditors cannot agree on the value of an asset, a valuation hearing will be held during which the creditor's attorney and your attorney will present evidence to support what they believe the asset is worth. Then the judge will decide on its market value. You will probably have to testify at the hearing.

Once your reorganization plan has been approved, your secured creditors will retain liens on the assets you are keeping. In fact, in your proposed plan, you must state that those creditors are retaining their liens on the assets you hold on to because once your plan is confirmed all the assets that were under the court's jurisdiction as the result of your Chapter 13 will either be vested back to you or will remain in your bankruptcy estate. In some districts, consumer bankruptcy attorneys normally include in their clients' reorganization plans that these assets will remain the property of their clients' bankruptcy estates because then the automatic stay will continue to apply to the assets. Unless there is a provision in your plan for a secured creditor to retain a lien on your property, vesting the property to you will result in the cred-

WARNING

In a growing number of districts, consumers who file for Chapter 13 must send their house payments to their trustee. Then, the trustee pays their current house payment as well as part of the amount that is past due.

itor losing his or her lien. However, you cannot deal with your home in this way. In other words, you cannot use Chapter 13 to modify the rights of your mortgage lender, although you can use it to catch up on any past-due mortgage payments. Therefore, once the judge approves your reorganization plan, you must continue making the same monthly mortgage payments that you agreed to when you signed your mortgage loan paperwork.

Ordinarily, the judge will not look too closely at what you propose to give your secured creditors in your reorganization plan, because he or she will assume that those creditors have looked out for their own interests and are getting everything they are legally entitled to.

Requirement six. *You can afford to make the debt payments you propose in your reorganization plan.*

Some of your creditors may object to the confirmation of your plan because they do not believe that you will be able to afford to pay your debts according to the terms of your reorganization plan. The bankruptcy judge will also decide whether he or she thinks your plan is realistic. The judge wants your plan to succeed so if he or she concludes that it won't work, the judge will not approve it.

Your income will be the first thing the judge will look at to evaluate whether or not your plan is realistic. You will have to provide proof of your income. Another thing the judge will review is your budget. The judge wants to feel confident you will be able to make your debt payments if your plan is confirmed. Your attorney will have filed the budget when your bankruptcy petition was filed.

Do You Earn Enough to Qualify for Chapter 13?

When you are preparing your reorganization plan, one of your major challenges will be to figure out if you can come up with the money you need to pay your secured creditors so that you can hold on to the secured assets that you do not want to lose. When money is tight, that can be a challenge. For example, if you earn $1,500 a month and your living expenses are $1,400 a month and you must pay your creditors at least $200 a month to hold on to the assets you used as loan collateral, you're in big trouble because you don't have enough money. However, there are a couple of options for resolving this problem so that you can get your plan confirmed. You will have to decide which option to pursue before the date of your confirmation hearing.

One option is to reduce your living expenses. Another is to increase your household income. Neither of these options is realistic if your budget is already bare bones, you are already making as much as you possibly can, and you don't have any assets that you can give back to your secured creditors. If that's the case, filing for Chapter 13 is not a realistic way for you to deal with your financial problems and you will never be able to get your reorganization plan confirmed. That is why it is critical that you work with an experienced bankruptcy attorney as soon as you begin to consider filing for bankruptcy. The attorney will help you determine which type of bankruptcy is best for you based on your finances, which means that you won't waste time pursuing a Chapter 13 when there is no chance that a judge will confirm your plan.

Once Your Plan Is Confirmed

Assuming that your plan meets all the requirements spelled out in this chapter and once all objections to the plan have been resolved, the judge will confirm it. After its confirmation, you will have to continue paying on your debts according to the terms of the plan. (Actually, no later than 30 days after you filed for Chapter 13—before your plan was confirmed—you should have begun paying on those debts.) You either will send your payments directly to the trustee or the payments will be automatically deducted from your paychecks. In some districts, you can decide which option you prefer, but in other districts automatic debits are mandatory. The advantage of automatic debits is that you won't have to remember to make your payments.

10

Modifications to a Chapter 13 Plan, Conversions, and the Hardship Discharge

Confirmation of your reorganization plan signals your new financial start. Now your debt payments are manageable and you are protected by the court from creditor harassment. If you are like most people who file for Chapter 13, your financial situation will improve and your life will begin to return to normal. After your plan has been confirmed, however, it is also possible that new problems will make it difficult for you to live up to your financial obligations under the plan.

W A R N I N G

If you are having problems meeting the terms of your reorganization plan, consult your bankruptcy attorney right away. If you wait too long and you begin falling behind on your debt payments, the trustee or one of your creditors will file a motion to dismiss your case, which means that you will no longer be protected from your creditors' collection actions.

Depending on your situation, you may decide to ask for a moratorium, a modification, a conversion, or a hardship discharge. This chapter explains how each of these options works.

H O T   T I P

If you ask the court for a modification, conversion, or a hardship discharge and one of your creditors objects to your request, the judge is more apt to side with you because obviously you care enough about your plan to have addressed the fact you are having problems living up to it.

Moratoriums

If you are unable to make a payment to a creditor according to the terms of your reorganization plan because of a temporary financial setback—you miss a paycheck because of an illness or accident or because you are between jobs—the trustee will probably let you catch up on any payments you miss. If you miss just one payment and the trustee gives you time to pay it, the creditor that you did not pay may complain but probably won't file a motion to take back its collateral or to have your case dismissed.

Modifications

After your reorganization plan has been approved, something may happen in your life that will make it impossible for you to continue paying your creditors according to the terms of your plan—for example, you lose your job, get a divorce, experience a long illness, etc. If this is the case, try to get your plan modified, which involves asking the court to lower the payments you are obligated to make to your creditors. The court may offer you several ways to modify your plan. It may let you:

1. *Extend the length of time you have to make your plan payments so that the payments will be smaller.* If the term of your plan is 36 months, for example, the court may agree to extend it to 48 months or 60 months (five years), the maximum amount of time you can have in Chapter 13 to pay your debts.

2. *Pay your unsecured creditors less than what your plan says you will pay them as long as they will receive at least as much as they would have if you had filed a Chapter 7 liquidation bankruptcy.* If your plan currently requires you to pay your creditors 80 percent of the value of their claims, you might want to propose paying them only 20 percent. However, the court will expect you to pay as much as you possibly can.

3. *Give up an asset that you are paying for to make your plan more affordable and to retain the rest of your assets.* For instance, right now you may be trying to pay for two vehicles. You might tell the court that you want to give up one of them to lower the total cost of your plan.

How Modifications Work

If you want to modify your reorganization plan, your lawyer will file a modification request with the court and notify all your creditors that you have filed the request so they can formally object to it if they want. If one of your creditors does object, the judge will schedule a hearing. At the hearing, the judge will hear why the creditor is objecting and will listen to your attorney's explanation of why a modification is necessary. Then the judge will decide whether to allow you to modify your plan and whether or not you will have to change the way you intend to treat the creditor who objected to the modification.

If none of your creditors object to your modification request and if your revised plan continues to meet all the basic requirements of the plan that was confirmed initially, the court will allow the modification. However, you will be expected to continue putting all your disposable income toward your debts.

Converting a Chapter 13 to a Chapter 7

Another option when you are having trouble keeping up with your Chapter 13 reorganization plan payments is to convert your bankruptcy to a Chapter 7. This step would be appropriate if you considered a modification and tried every way imaginable to reduce your debt payments so that you could keep making them and they still are not low enough.

When you convert from a Chapter 13 to a Chapter 7 bankruptcy, you will be allowed to keep all your exempt property, but all your non-exempt property will be sold to satisfy your debts. Any unsecured debts that remain unpaid will be formally discharged by the court at the end of your Chapter 7. If you are making payments on any exempt secured assets, such as your car, you must continue making the payments after you convert. Otherwise, you will lose those assets. If you did not pay everything you owed on those debts while you were in Chapter 13, you may have to come up with all your missed payments to hold on to the exempt assets that secure the debts, or you may be able to keep the assets by redeeming them. Talk to your attorney about your options before converting.

How a Conversion Works

The procedure for converting a Chapter 13 bankruptcy to a Chapter 7 liquidation bankruptcy is simple. Your attorney will file a request for conversion with the court, along with any additional information the court requires.

WARNING

If you convert to a Chapter 7, be prepared for your finances to be more closely scrutinized. The trustee will want to make certain that you pay everything possible to your creditors.

If your case gets converted to a Chapter 7 liquidation bankruptcy, a new trustee will be appointed because Chapter 13 trustees don't get involved in Chapter 7 bankruptcies. Also, you will have to attend another creditors' meeting and a discharge hearing will be held to wipe out any debts that remain unpaid.

If you are considering a conversion, you must understand that the only property that will be included in your Chapter 7 bankruptcy estate is the property that you owned at the time you filed your original Chapter 13 bankruptcy petition and that you still owned at the time of the conversion. However, if the court decides that you converted in bad faith—you lied to the court, did not cooperate with the trustee, or did something to defraud one of your creditors—your bankruptcy estate will also include all the assets you owned when you converted.

The Hardship Discharge

A final option when you cannot afford to continue paying on your reorganization plan is to ask the court to grant you a hardship discharge. This kind of discharge is very rare.

The requirements for a hardship discharge are different than the requirements for a modification or conversion. For example, you may qualify for a hardship discharge if:

1. *Your failure to comply with the terms of your Chapter 13 reorganization plan is due to circumstances that are not your fault or that are beyond your control.* For example, you cannot work anymore because of an illness or disability and, therefore, you can't afford to continue paying on your plan. The loss of your job, however, is not enough to merit a hardship discharge because the court expects you to get a new job.
2. *Your unsecured creditors have received as much as they would have received under a straight liquidation bankruptcy, and a modification is impractical.*

To apply for a hardship discharge, your attorney will file a request for the discharge with the court and a hearing will be held to determine if you qualify for one. If you do, most but not all of your unsecured debts will be discharged. Those that will remain as your financial obligation include past-due alimony and child support; priority claims, such as taxes; and some consumer debts that you incurred after you filed for Chapter 13. You also will have to continue paying on your secured debts—your mortgage and your car loan, for instance.

The Discharge Hearing

Once you have made the last payment on your Chapter 13 plan, it will be time for the discharge. The discharge will formally end your responsibility under the plan and your financial fresh start will begin.

Comprehensive Chapter 13 Discharge

A discharge of debts under a Chapter 13 is more comprehensive than a discharge in a Chapter 7 bankruptcy. The only debts that will remain after a Chapter 13 discharge will be child support, spousal maintenance, and support; long-term debts that were specified in the plan such as your home mortgage; and death claims that are the result of your driving while intoxicated or under the influence of drugs. Also, the discharge will not apply to any criminal fines you may owe, although debts arising out of fraudulent conduct, illegal conversion of property, or embezzlement will be discharged if you committed these acts before you filed for Chapter 13.

Usually, there will not be a discharge hearing. Instead, once the court has discharged your debts, it will mail you a discharge notice. If there is a hearing, the judge will notify you by mail of when and where it is to take place. You may not have to attend the hearing, but if you do, there will probably be other debtors in the courtroom. You will not have to speak to the judge. After the hearing, a discharge document signed by the judge will be mailed to you. It will list each of the debts that were discharged. In some districts you will receive your discharge notice at the end of the hearing.

WARNING

If one of your creditors believes that you committed fraud to get your debts discharged, it has one year after the date of your discharge to formally ask the court to revoke the discharge.

Enough about the technical aspects of your discharge. The important thing is that through hard work and self-discipline, you have met the responsibilities of your reorganization plan and lived up to your obligations to your creditors in a Chapter 13 bankruptcy. As a result, you have achieved a worthwhile goal—a financial fresh start. Congratulations!

11

Understanding Taxes and Bankruptcy

Wallace Stevens, an American poet who died in 1955, once wrote that money was a kind of poetry. That may be so. If you don't have any and you owe the tax man, however, your lack of money is a very sad poem indeed. When you owe money to the IRS and have no means of paying it, filing for bankruptcy can offer the best relief. Only in bankruptcy court can you stop an IRS tax collector who is in hot pursuit of you or wipe out some of the taxes you owe.

Tax-Related Problems That Commonly Lead to Bankruptcy

Here are some examples of the kinds of tax problems that commonly lead to bankruptcy:

- Your small business is struggling to stay open and has not been meeting its IRS payroll tax obligations. The amount that your business owes in past-due payroll taxes is more than it can afford to pay so the IRS is threatening to take some of its assets.
- Your income drops or your property taxes increase faster than your income so you cannot afford to pay them. As a result, the taxing authority may be threatening to sue you so that it can take your home, sell it, and apply the proceeds to your property tax debt.

- You are struggling to stay in business and need a little time to turn your business around and to pay its back taxes.
- You and your husband get divorced and as part of your divorce agreement, your husband agrees to pay the income taxes you both owe to the IRS. However, he does not pay them so the IRS comes after you for the money. Because you cannot afford to pay them, you are worried that the IRS will take some of your assets or garnish your wages to collect the taxes. You know that the IRS doesn't care what your divorce agreement says and that it will try to collect from either you or your former spouse.

Obviously, many different types of tax-related problems can force you into bankruptcy. However, all tax-related problems have one thing in common when bankruptcy is your best solution—your finances have reached a crisis point, usually because the taxing authority (federal, state, or local) is unwilling to work with you anymore and is threatening either to take some of your property or to levy against your paycheck or bank account.

WARNING

If the IRS levied against your bank account before you filed for bankruptcy, it can take from that account the money that you owe to it. While you are in bankruptcy, however, the IRS can't try to collect any new monies related to old tax debts.

Stopping the IRS

You can stop the collection efforts of the IRS by filing for bankruptcy because the automatic stay applies even to the IRS. Once the automatic stay is in effect, the IRS will be prohibited from levying your bank account, garnishing your wages, taking your assets, and closing down your business.

Once the automatic stay is in effect, the IRS is prohibited from taking a number of different actions, including:

- *Using future tax refunds to offset your tax liabilities.* In other words, the IRS cannot apply future tax refunds to your existing tax debts.

- *Putting a tax lien on your property.* This is especially important in a Chapter 13 reorganization bankruptcy for it may mean you will pay less interest to the IRS. If the IRS takes a lien against your property before you file for bankruptcy, it will be a secured creditor in your bankruptcy and you will have to pay interest on its claim. However, if the IRS does not have a lien on your property before you file, then you will not owe interest on its claim.

- *Continuing to prosecute you in tax court.*

Beware of What the IRS Can Do

Although the automatic stay prevents the IRS from taking many actions to collect your past-due taxes, there are some things the automatic stay cannot stop. They include:

- *Tax audits.* If you are scheduled for an audit or are already being audited, filing bankruptcy will not stop the audit. While you are in bankruptcy, however, the IRS cannot ask you for any money that the audit may indicate that you owe. If you file for Chapter 7 and the taxes that you owe to the IRS are not dischargeable, the agency can try to collect from you once you are out of bankruptcy. If you file for Chapter 13 and your previous tax returns are being audited, you can modify your Chapter 13 reorganization plan to include any taxes the IRS may decide that you owe as a result of the audit. That way you can pay the taxes through your plan.

- *Tax assessments.* While you are in bankruptcy, the IRS can assess a tax debt against you without getting the bankruptcy court's permission first, assuming you do not object to the assessment. Therefore, interest and penalties can begin to accrue while you are in bankruptcy. However, the IRS cannot attempt to collect what you owe until your bankruptcy is over.

- *Demand that you file tax returns.* While you are in bankruptcy, the IRS can demand that you file any tax returns you have not filed.

Some Past-Due Taxes Can Be Discharged in Bankruptcy

You can wipe out some kinds of taxes through bankruptcy. For example, you can wipe out an income tax debt that became due more than three years before your bankruptcy began as long as you meet certain requirements. These requirements include:

1. You filed the tax return related to the past-due taxes on time. If you did not, the return must have been filed more than two years before the start of your bankruptcy.
2. The taxes you owe must have been assessed more than 240 days before you filed for bankruptcy.
3. The tax return you filed cannot be fraudulent and you cannot have willfully attempted to evade paying taxes.
4. The IRS cannot have a lien on any of your property.

If you do not meet all four of these stringent requirements, you cannot use bankruptcy to discharge an income tax debt.

You should also know that if you borrowed money to pay your income taxes and you do not qualify to have your tax debt wiped out through bankruptcy, then the money you borrowed can't be discharged either. For example, if you got a cash advance on your credit card to pay your taxes and later you filed for bankruptcy, if the credit card company can prove that you borrowed the money to pay your taxes, then it can ask the bankruptcy court to declare that the money not be discharged. Then, once you have completed your Chapter 7 bankruptcy, the credit card company can try to collect from you.

How You Can Benefit from the IRS's Loss of Sovereign Immunity

Previously, if the IRS violated the rules of bankruptcy, you had no legal recourse against the agency and the bankruptcy court could do very little to punish the IRS for its transgression. However, the 1994 changes to the Bankruptcy Code took away the government's right of sovereign immunity in bankruptcy court matters.

As a result, if the IRS violates the automatic stay, the bankruptcy judge can order it to pay any damages that may result from the violation. In other words, you can get a money judgment against the IRS. Therefore, the IRS does not break the rules of bankruptcy and violate the automatic stay as much as it used to, and when it does, the agency is usually willing to correct its mistakes.

However, some restrictions apply to this important change. They are:

1. Although a bankruptcy judge can issue a legal or equitable order against the IRS and can award you actual damages, it cannot order the IRS to pay you punitive damages. Punitive damages are used to discourage a lawbreaker from repeating its illegal behavior.

2. Awards by the court are limited by the hourly rate specified in the United States Code. This means, for example, that if the actual damages you are awarded include paying your attorney's fee, the amount you receive for that expense will be limited by the government rate for attorneys as established in the code. Currently, that rate is $75 an hour, which will almost certainly be less than the hourly rate your attorney charged you. However, something is better than nothing.

3. An order issued by a bankruptcy judge cannot be enforced through the seizure of government property. So if you get a money judgment against the IRS, you can't drive your truck to an IRS office and haul off all its computers to satisfy that judgment.

How Taxes Are Classified in Bankruptcy

When you file a Chapter 7 or Chapter 13 bankruptcy, any taxes you may owe are assigned to one of three different classifications, which are important because they will determine how each of your tax debts will be treated in bankruptcy. Like many debtors, you may owe all three types of taxes. The three classifications are:

1. *Secured.* If the IRS has placed a lien on your property to secure the taxes you owe, those taxes are secured taxes and you cannot discharge them through bankruptcy. Instead, you will have three options to deal with the debt:
   - If you have the cash or can borrow the cash, you can pay the IRS the value of its lien to get the lien released.
   - You can sell the property with the lien on it and use the sale proceeds to pay off the IRS.
   - You can file for Chapter 13 bankruptcy so that you can have three to five years to pay your past-due taxes.

2. *Priority.* This class of taxes is not secured by a property lien and you cannot use bankruptcy to get it discharged. Therefore, the debt will survive a Chapter 7 bankruptcy. As a result, you

must either pay the full amount that you owe to the IRS or file for Chapter 13 so that you can have three to five years to pay the debt.

3. *General Unsecured.* You can discharge this type of tax debt through bankruptcy.

Which Bankruptcy Option Is Best When You Owe Taxes

If all your tax debts can be discharged and you own very little property, your decision is an easy one when you have a tax debt. You should file a Chapter 7 bankruptcy to wipe out the debt. Unfortunately, most bankruptcy cases are not this simple. For instance, what should you do if the IRS has a lien on one of your assets for past-due taxes that would otherwise be dischargeable? It depends. If the value of the property the IRS has a lien against is not much, you may still want to file for Chapter 7 and then pay the IRS the value of its lien to get the lien removed. Or what happens if the value of the asset that the IRS has a lien on is significant and you can't come up with the money necessary to get the lien removed? You could file a Chapter 13 bankruptcy and pay the value of the property to the creditor to get the lien removed. For example, if you owe the IRS $20,000 in dischargeable taxes and it has a lien on one of your assets that is worth $10,000, you must pay $10,000 plus interest to have the lien taken off that property. The balance of your debt to the IRS will become unsecured. You would treat the portion of your tax debt that is dischargeable like any other unsecured debt, and because in a Chapter 13 you are not obligated to pay your unsecured creditors 100 percent of what you owe them (although you must pay as much as possible), you could pay the IRS as much as you can afford to and then whatever is left of your tax debt would be wiped out. If you file Chapter 13 to pay your past-due secured taxes, you will be required to pay interest on those taxes over the length of your plan. The interest rate will be set by the bankruptcy court. Usually, it will be much lower than the interest rate that the IRS charges.

It is possible that you may have so much nondischargeable debt, including past-due taxes, that you won't be able to qualify for Chapter 13. Therefore, you can file a Chapter 7 bankruptcy to wipe out as much debt as possible and then immediately file Chapter 13 to get time to pay the debts that you were not able to get rid of through the Chapter 7. Some attorneys call this a "Chapter 20."

Dealing with Past-Due Trust Fund Taxes

If you own a business and you collected taxes from third parties for the IRS, such as payroll taxes, those taxes are called *trust fund taxes* and they cannot be discharged through bankruptcy. If you are a small business owner (you own your business as a sole proprietorship) and you owe trust fund taxes, and if you are being pressed by the IRS to pay them, you can file a Chapter 13. When you do, the IRS must stop trying to collect the taxes from you and you will get three to five years to pay them. Filing for Chapter 13 is also appropriate if you have already shut down your business and you fell behind on your trust fund taxes while your business was operating. It will protect you from the collection actions of the IRS and at the same time will give you a chance to pay your tax debt.

If you are the owner of a corporation, you are not necessarily safe from the collection actions of the IRS if your corporation owes trust fund taxes. Most likely, the IRS will assess you and any other owners of your business for the full amount of the taxes that your business owes. When individual business owners are assessed for the taxes their business owes, the IRS refers to the tax debt as a penalty. You will not be able to get the penalty discharged through bankruptcy.

How to Handle Your Past-Due Property Taxes

If you do not pay the property taxes you owe on a house or on the land you own, the taxing authority can usually take the house or land and sell it to get the money it's owed. However, you can file for Chapter 13 when you owe past-due property taxes. That way, you will be able to keep your property and you'll get five years to pay your tax debt.

W A R N I N G

A taxing authority can place a lien on your property for taxes that come due *after* you file for bankruptcy. It will not be a violation of the automatic stay.

If You Disagree with the IRS about the Taxes It Says You Owe

If the IRS says that you owe back taxes and you disagree with it about the amount that you owe or if you don't think you owe the money at all, your attorney can litigate that issue in bankruptcy court when you file a Chapter 7 or Chapter 13 bankruptcy. For this to happen, however, you must file a motion objecting to the IRS's claim. After you do, the bankruptcy judge will rule on whether or not you owe the taxes or how much you owe. If the court rules that you owe taxes, it will also determine whether the debt is a secured, priority, or general unsecured debt.

12

Divorce and Bankruptcy

Divorce and bankruptcy often go hand in hand. It is not uncommon for divorced individuals, especially women, to be forced into bankruptcy after a divorce because their change in marital status causes their financial situation to deteriorate. In addition, many men as well as an increasing number of women file for bankruptcy after a divorce because they can't afford to meet the terms of their divorce agreement. Some also deliberately use bankruptcy as a way to get out of obligations they assumed when they signed their divorce agreements.

In an effort to address the relationship between divorce and bankruptcy and to correct some of the social problems the relationship has helped create, the Bankruptcy Reform Act of 1994 made a number of changes related to divorce. (Many of the changes relate to legal separations as well, but this chapter will focus just on divorce. Therefore, if you are separated or about to separate from your spouse, schedule an appointment with a certified bankruptcy attorney to find out how the bankruptcy law could affect you.) The main goals of the 1994 changes were to:

- Provide greater protection to a divorced individual when his or her ex-spouse uses bankruptcy to wipe out their divorce obligations and any other debt-related obligations they agreed to at the time of their divorce.

- Provide greater protection to spouses, ex-spouses, and the children who are due support money.

This chapter examines the most important divorce-related changes to the Bankruptcy Code as a result of the 1994 amendments and discusses their implications. The most important changes were:

- A new category of nondischargeable debt was added to the Bankruptcy Code.
- Some divorce-related debts were made nondischargeable under certain circumstances and conditions.
- Debts related to alimony, maintenance, or support became priority debts.
- Exceptions were added to the automatic stay.
- The status of alimony, maintenance, and support payments was changed in regard to preferential transfers.
- Debtors may no longer use section 522(f)(I) of the Bankruptcy Code to avoid a judicial lien created to secure obligations resulting from a couple's division of property.
- Child support creditors and other representatives can now appear at Bankruptcy Court proceedings.

Exceptions to the Nondischargeability of Alimony, Maintenance, and Support Obligations

Alimony, maintenance, and support obligations are treated as nondischargeable debts in both a Chapter 7 and a Chapter 13 bankruptcy. This means that if a divorced person files for bankruptcy, he or she cannot use it to wipe out past-due payments for these obligations. The former spouse who is owed these past-due payments, however, should not expect to begin receiving them as soon as the debtor has filed for bankruptcy.

If the bankrupt ex-spouse files Chapter 7, the former spouse can try to collect the past-due payments from assets that are not part of the debtor's bankruptcy estate. The ex-spouse can also wait to collect until the debtor's bankruptcy has been discharged and the automatic stay has been lifted.

If the bankrupt ex-spouse files Chapter 13, the debtor must pay all the past-due alimony, maintenance, or support payments owed to his or her ex-spouse during the life of the reorganization plan. It is important to note, however, that filing a bankruptcy in no way affects the debtor's obligation to meet all of his or her alimony, maintenance, or child support payments that come due during the bankruptcy. The debtor must continue making those payments to his or her ex-spouse.

There are two exceptions to the nondischargeability of alimony, maintenance, and support obligations:

1. If the person who is owed the alimony, maintenance, or support voluntarily assigns the debt to another person or entity such as a private collection agency, the debt can be discharged through a Chapter 7 or a Chapter 13 bankruptcy.
2. If the court rules at the request of the debtor that although a debt is designated as alimony, maintenance, or support, it really should be classified as another type of debt related to the debtor's change in marital status—a property settlement obligation, for example—the debt will be discharged. This applies to both Chapter 7 and Chapter 13 bankruptcies.

New Exception to Discharge of Debt

Prior to the 1994 changes in the law, "hold harmless" and property settlement obligations could be discharged through bankruptcy. This meant that if, as part of a couple's divorce agreement, the nondebtor spouse agreed to let the debtor keep an asset or assets in exchange for a promise to pay him or her a set amount of money in installments, or to pay the third-party debts of the nondebtor spouse, or if the nondebtor spouse agreed to accept smaller alimony payments in exchange for being held harmless for debts incurred by both parties during their marriage, the debtor could use bankruptcy to wipe out the obligations he or she incurred by signing that agreement. As a result, if the debtor spouse did not live up to the terms of the couples' divorce agreement, the nondebtor spouse often ended up with a substantial amount of debt to pay and little or no alimony, maintenance, or support to help pay it. Now, however, "hold harmless" and property settlement obligations are nondischargeable under two conditions:

1. The debt will not be discharged if the court believes that the resources of the debtor are sufficient to allow him or her to meet both the nonalimony, maintenance, and support obligations as well as the debtor's alimony, maintenance, and support obligations. If the debtor can prove that he or she won't be able to meet both, all or a portion of the "hold harmless" and

property settlements obligations will be discharged. Also, if the debtor can prove that not getting his or her alimony, maintenance, and support obligations discharged will mean that the debtor won't have enough resources to operate his or her business, the court can opt for a discharge.

2. The debt will not be discharged if the harm done to the non-debtor spouse should the debtor's "hold harmless" and property obligations be discharged outweighs the benefits the debtor would realize from having them erased.

This exception to discharge contains an important catch for the former spouse of a person in bankruptcy. For the court to consider making an obligation of the debtor nondischargeable, the nondebtor spouse must file an adversary proceeding against the debtor within 60 days of the date of the first creditors' meeting in the debtor's bankruptcy. This proceeding is essentially a minilawsuit. What this means is that unless the nondebtor spouse knows the law or retains an attorney once the debtor ex-spouse files for bankruptcy, the adversary proceeding will not be filed and the debtor's property obligations will be discharged. This stipulation in the law also assumes that the nondebtor has the resources necessary to hire an attorney and knows that the debtor has filed for bankruptcy.

How Alimony, Maintenance, and Support Debts Are Treated in Bankruptcy

The 1994 changes to the law also elevated alimony, maintenance, and support obligations to priority status so they are now as important

---

WARNING

Alimony, maintenance, and support debts assigned to another individual or entity as well as debts arising from a marriage that are not in the nature of alimony, maintenance, and support do not have priority status in a bankruptcy.

as tax debts in bankruptcy. Therefore, they must be paid in full during a Chapter 13, and in a Chapter 7, they will be paid before most other creditors if there is enough money. A few types of debts, however, must be paid first. This change has increased the likelihood that an individual whose ex-spouse files for bankruptcy will receive the alimony, maintenance, and support payments that were stipulated in their divorce agreement.

The Automatic Stay

Some divorce-related exemptions to the protection of the automatic stay in bankruptcy relate to the establishment or modification of a court order for the payment of alimony, maintenance, or support. Another exemption applies to the establishment of the paternity of a child for the purposes of ordering a man to pay child support.

The first exemption allows a former spouse to establish or modify an order for alimony, maintenance, or support without getting the bankruptcy court's permission first. Before the bankruptcy law was amended in 1994, the former spouse who was entitled to receive those payments had to file a motion with the court requesting permission to establish or modify an order after his or her ex-spouse filed for bankruptcy. Getting permission typically involved considerable expense for the often cash-strapped former spouse and costly delays. However, if someone wants to initiate a divorce or continue a divorce that has already started after his or her spouse has filed for bankruptcy and their divorce involves the division of the couple's marital property and debts, the spouse who did not file for bankruptcy must file a motion to lift the automatic stay to get the bankruptcy court's permission to proceed with the divorce and with the division of their assets and debts.

The 1994 amendments also exempted from the automatic stay any actions necessary to establish the paternity of a child after a bankruptcy has been filed. So, if a divorced, separated, or unwed woman asks her state's attorney general to help her get child support and then the alleged father of the child files for bankruptcy, the process for establishing paternity can continue. Furthermore, if the man is identified as the child's father, he will be responsible for making child support payments.

Preferential Transfers

If a debtor treats one creditor better than other creditors by making payments to that creditor and not to the others during the year prior to filing for Chapter 7 bankruptcy, the court is entitled to view those payments as "preferential." If it does, the bankruptcy trustee will go after that money so that the funds can be more equitably distributed among all eligible creditors. Prior to the 1994 amendments, payments to a former spouse made during the year prior to filing for bankruptcy could be treated as preferential, but now they cannot be if the debtor files for Chapter 7.

Judicial Liens

In some divorce cases, under a division of property agreement, one spouse will secure the other spouse's promise to pay a debt related to the division of their property by getting a judicial lien placed on an asset owned by the other spouse. Under the old law, if the ex-spouse with the asset filed for bankruptcy, he or she could wipe out the lien if it was on exempt property. However, the 1994 amendments created an exception to this provision. This exception says that if the lien secures the obligation of one spouse under a division of property agreement, it cannot be wiped out through bankruptcy.

13

Conclusion:
Making a Fresh Start

After you have completed your Chapter 13 reorganization plan or had your debts discharged through a Chapter 7 liquidation bankruptcy, you will want to reestablish your credit. Your credit record, however, will show that you filed for bankruptcy and it will contain other negative information that was reported to the credit-reporting agencies as your financial problems were developing. All this information will make it difficult for you to get new credit at reasonable terms for up to ten years, which is the length of time that the federal Fair Credit Reporting Act says negative information can be reported.

Do You Really Want More Credit?

Before telling you how to rebuild your credit, I want you to know that I believe people's lives would be happier and less complicated if they lived more simply and paid for everything with cash. Living like that would provide people with a certain peace of mind because they would only be able to spend what they earned. They would not have to work to pay a seemingly unending stream of future financial obligations as they would if they used credit a lot. I am a realist, however, so I realize that it is difficult to function in our society without credit. After all, credit makes it easier to buy the things you need, especially big-ticket items. Also, having a positive credit history can help get the insurance you need, qualify for a new job or promotion, obtain a security clearance, and even rent a nice place. Therefore, in this chapter, I describe some methods for rebuilding your credit. Remember, however, that your ability to rebuild your credit is really about regaining the confidence of creditors in your ability to manage your finances responsibly and to pay your bills. Achieving that goal will take time.

HOT TIP

For more information about credit records and credit rebuilding as well as tips for how to raise your credit score, read the latest edition of my book, *The Credit Repair Kit* (Dearborn Trade, 2004).

Rebuilding Your Credit

To begin the credit rebuilding process, your first step should be to open a savings account at a bank and to make regular deposits to the account. Once you have between $500 and $1,000 in the account, talk with a loan officer about getting a small loan, using your savings account as collateral.

When you talk to the loan officer, be honest about your past financial problems and explain that you want to rebuild your credit. The loan officer will probably agree to give you the loan for it will be secured by your savings account. If you don't repay the loan according to the terms of your agreement with the bank, the bank can take the money in your savings account. Also, the bank will make money off of you by charging a high rate of interest on the loan.

Once you have repaid the first loan, contact each of the three national credit-reporting agencies—Equifax, Experian, and TransUnion—to make sure that the credit records each of them is maintaining on you includes your loan payment information and that the information related to the loan is accurate. If the information about the loan does not appear in any of your credit files, ask the loan officer you have been working with to add the information. Remember, the whole point of getting the loan and paying it on time is to build a new, positive credit history for yourself so it is important that your loan payment information be reflected in your credit records.

Next, apply for a second larger loan. If you can qualify, make this second loan unsecured. Pay that loan on time, too.

Gradually, through your on-time payments, you will begin demonstrating to creditors that you are a good credit risk. Also, you will have begun building a good relationship with your bank, which you can take advantage of in the future when you want to finance expensive purchases such as an automobile, a home, a home improvement, etc. Furthermore, you can use the bank as a credit reference when you apply for other credit.

After you have been paying on your second loan for several months, contact the three national credit bureaus again to make sure that the payment information related to that loan is being reported and reported accurately. Again, if it is not being reported, ask the bank to report it, and if the credit record information related to your loan payments is not accurate, correct it using the investigation request form that should have come with your report.

Another step to take once you have paid off your first loan is to apply for a Visa or MasterCard. You may be able to apply for one with the bank that loaned you money. However, be sure to shop around for the best deal on a national bankcard because the better the card's terms of credit, the less it will cost you to use the card. Two good sources of information about good deals on national bankcards are:

- Bankrate.com at http://www.bankrate.com.
- CardTrak. This organization publishes a newsletter with up-to-date information on which banks are offering bankcards with attractive terms of credit. You can order the current issue of Card-Trak's newsletter for $5 by going to http://www.cardtrack.com, calling 301-631-9100, or writing to CardTrak at P.O. Box 1700, Frederick, MD 21702.

If you can't qualify for a regular bankcard, apply for one that is secured. This type of bankcard will look exactly like a regular, unsecured card but it works differently. Secured cards were devised to meet the credit needs of people who have damaged credit histories. To use a secured card, you must collateralize your credit purchases by opening a savings account at the bank that issues you the card or by purchasing a certificate of deposit (CD) from that bank. You will be able to charge up to a certain percentage of the money that is in your bank account or of the value of your CD. Using a secured bankcard responsibly over time is an excellent way to demonstrate that you are ready to own a regular bankcard.

HOT TIP

You may want to apply for a gasoline credit card in addition to a national bankcard. However, don't bother applying for retail store charge cards. They tend to be expensive to use and nearly every retailer these days accepts MasterCard and Visa.

WARNING

It is very important to limit the amount of credit you apply for and the number of credit cards you have. One or two national bankcards and a gasoline card are really all that you need. Applying for a lot of credit and having a lot of open credit accounts, even if the accounts have low or no balances, will undermine your efforts to rebuild your credit.

Although you may end up rebuilding your credit a little differently than the method described in this chapter, there are some important things to keep in mind no matter what path you take. First, your goal in obtaining new credit is to convince creditors that you are a good credit risk. To do that you must demonstrate over time that you pay your bills on time, don't have a lot of debt, and have a stable job. Second, having credit is a privilege that you must earn; it is not a right. Third, rebuilding your credit will take time, so be patient and don't be tempted to try shortcuts. In the end, you and your family will be harmed. Fourth, if you are not careful, once you have new credit you may ruin it again. Therefore, if you need to learn better money management skills to help ensure that you don't have to file for bankruptcy again, take a class, read personal finance books, and explore what the Web has to offer. There is a wealth of good personal finance information available to consumers these days. So, get smart about your money and manage it well, and I hope that after you are finished with this book, you will never need to read it again.

A

Chapter 7
Bankruptcy Forms

The forms that follow represent the basic forms that are filed with the court. In addition to these forms, each bankruptcy district in the United States may require filing local forms. So many different local forms exist that it is not practical to present all of them here. Your attorney should be familiar with the local rules in your area and with the additional forms required.

Forms may be purchased from Julius Blumberg, Inc., New York, NY 10013, or from any of its dealers. Reproduction is prohibited.

Official Form B1, P1, 12-03

BlumbergExcelsior, Inc NYC 10013

United States Bankruptcy Court District of	Voluntary Petition

Name of Debtor (If individual, enter Last, First, Middle):	Name of Joint Debtor (Spouse) (Last, First, Middle):
All Other Names used by the debtor in the last 6 years (include married, maiden and trade names):	All Other Names used by the joint debtor in the last 6 years (include married, maiden and trade names):
Last four digits of Soc. Sec. No./Complete EIN or other Tax I.D. No. (if more than one, state all):	Last four digits of Soc. Sec. No./Complete EIN or other Tax I.D. No. (if more than one, state all):
Street Address of Debtor (No. and street, city, state, zip):	Street Address of Joint Debtor (No. and street, city, state, zip):
County of Residence or Principal Place of Business:	County of Residence or Principal Place of Business:
Mailing Address of Debtor (If different from street address):	Mailing Address of Joint Debtor (If different from street address):
Location of Principal Assets of Business Debtor (If different from addresses listed above)	

Information Regarding Debtor (Check the Applicable Boxes)

Venue (Check any applicable box)
- ☐ Debtor has been domiciled or has had a residence, principal place of business or principal assets in this District for 180 days immediately preceding the date of this petition or for a longer part of such 180 days than in any other District.
- ☐ There is a bankruptcy case concerning debtor's affiliate, general partner or partnership pending in this district

Type of Debtor (Check all boxes that apply)		**Chapter or Section of Bankruptcy Code Under Which the Petition is Filed** (Check one box)		
☐ Individual	☐ Railroad			
☐ Corporation	☐ Stockbroker	☐ Chapter 7	☐ Chapter 11	☐ Chapter 13
☐ Partnership	☐ Commodity Broker	☐ Chapter 9	☐ Chapter 12	
☐ Other	☐ Clearing Bank	☐ § 304-Case ancillary to foreign proceeding.		

Nature of Debt (Check one box)		**Filing Fee** (Check one box)
☐ Consumer/Non-Business	☐ Business	☐ Full Filing Fee attached.
		☐ Filing Fee to be paid in installments (Applicable to individuals only)

Chapter 11 Small Business (Check all boxes that apply)
- ☐ Debtor is a small business as defined in 11 U.S.C. § 101.
- ☐ Debtor is and elects to be considered a small business under 11 U.S.C. § 1121(e) (Optional)

Must attach signed application for the court's consideration certifying that the debtor is unable to pay fee except in installments. Rule 1006(b). See Official Form No. 3

Statistical/Administrative Information (Estimates Only)
- ☐ Debtor estimates that funds will be available for distribution to unsecured creditors.
- ☐ Debtor estimates that, after any exempt property is excluded and administrative expenses paid, there will be no funds available for distribution to unsecured creditors.

THIS SPACE FOR COURT USE ONLY

Estimated Number of Creditors	1-15	16-49	50-99	100-199	200-999	1000-over
	☐	☐	☐	☐	☐	☐

Estimated Assets

$0 to $50,000	$50,001 to $100,000	$100,001 to $500,000	$500,001 to $1 million	$1,000,001 to $10 million	$10,000,001 to $100 million	More than $100 million
☐	☐	☐	☐	☐	☐	☐

Estimated Debts

$0 to $50,000	$50,001 to $100,000	$100,001 to $500,000	$500,001 to $1 million	$1,000,001 to $10 million	$10,000,001 to $100 million	More than $100 million
☐	☐	☐	☐	☐	☐	☐

Official Form B1, P2, 12-03   BlumbergExcelsior, Inc NYC 10013

Voluntary Petition *(This page must be completed and filed in every case)*	Name of Debtor(s):

Prior Bankruptcy Case Filed Within Last 6 Years (If more than one, attach additional sheet)		
Location Where Filed:	Case Number:	Date Filed:

Pendin Bankruptcy Case Filed by any Spouse, Partner, or Affiliate of this Debtor (If more than one, attach additional sheet.)		
Name of Debtor:	Case Number:	Date Filed:
District:	Relationship:	Judge:

Signatures

Signature(s) of Debtor(s) (Individual/Joint)

I declare under penalty of perjury that the information provided in this petition is true and correct.
[If petitioner is an individual whose debts are primarily consumer debts and has chosen to file under chapter 7] I am aware that I may proceed under chapter 7, 11,12,13 of title 11, United States Code, understand the relief available under each such chapter, and choose to proceed under chapter 7.
I request relief in accordance with the chapter of title 11, United States Code, specified in this petition.

X _____
Signature of Debtor

X _____
Signature of Joint Debtor

_____
Telephone (If not represented by attorney)

_____
Date

Signature of Attorney

X _____
Signature of Attorney for Debtor(s)

_____
Printed Name of Attorney for Debtor(s)

_____
Firm Name

_____
Address

_____
Telephone Number

_____
Date

Signature(s) of Debtor(s) (Corporation/Partnership)

I declare under penalty of perjury that the information provided in this petition is true and correct, and that I have been authorized to file this petition on behalf of the debtor.

If debtor is a corporation filing under chapter 11, United States Code, specified in this petition.

X _____
Signature of Authorized Individual

_____
Print or Type Name of Authorized Individual

_____
Title of Authorized Individual by Debtor to File this Petition

_____
Date

EXHIBIT A

(To be completed if debtor is required to file periodic reports (e.g., forms 10K and 10Q) with the Securities and Exchange Commission pursuant to Section 13 or 15(d) of the Securities Exchange Act of 1934 and is requesting relief under chapter 11)

☐ Exhibit A is attached and made part of this petition.

EXHIBIT B

(To be completed if debtor is an individual whose debts are primarily consumer debts)

I, the attorney for the petitioner named in the foregoing petition, declare that I have informed the petitioner that [he or she] may proceed under chapter 7, 11, 12, or 13 of title 11, United States Code, and have explained the relief available under each such chapter.

X _____
Signature of Attorney for Debtor(s)   Date

EXHIBIT C

Does the debtor own or have possession of any property that poses or is alleged to pose a threat of imminent and identifiable harm to public health or safety?

☐ Yes, and Exhibit C is attached and made a part of this petition.
☐ No

Signature of Non-Attorney Petition Preparer

I certify that I am a bankruptcy petition preparer as defined in 11 U.S.C. § 110, that I prepared this document for compensation, and that I have provided the debtor with a copy of this document.

_____
Printed Name of Bankruptcy Petition Preparer

_____
Social Security Number (Required by 11 U.S.C. 110(c).)

_____
Address

Names and Social Security numbers of all other Individuals who prepared or assisted in preparing this document:

If more than one person prepared this document, attach additional sheets conforming to the appropriate official form for each person.

X _____
Signature of Bankruptcy Petition Preparer

_____
Date

A bankruptcy petition preparer's failure to comply with the provisions of title 11 and the Federal Rules of Bankruptcy Procedure may result in fines or imprisonment or both 11 U.S.C. § 110; 18 U.S.C. § 156.

Official Form B1, Exhibit C, 12-03   BlumbergExcelsior, Inc NYC 10013

UNITED STATES BANKRUPTCY COURT   ### DISTRICT OF

In re: Debtor(s)   Case No.   (If Known)

EXHIBIT "C." If, to the best of the debtor's knowledge, the debtor owns or has possession of property that poses or is alleged to pose a threat of imminent and identifiable harm to the public health or safety, attach this Exhibit "C" to the petition.

EXHIBIT "C" to Voluntary Petition

1. Identify and briefly describe all real or personal property owned or in possession of the debtor that, to the best of the debtor's knowledge, poses or is alleged to pose a threat of imminent and identifiable harm to the public health or safety (attach additional sheets if necessary):

2. With respect to each parcel of real property or item of personal property identified in question 1, describe the nature and location of the dangerous condition, whether environmental or otherwise, that poses or is alleged to pose a threat of imminent and identifiable harm to the public health or safety (attach additional sheets if necessary):

Form B21 Official Form 21 (12-03)

BlumbergExcelsior, Inc., Publisher NYC 10013
www.blumberg.com

United States Bankruptcy Court

District Of

In re

Set forth here all names including married,
maiden, and trade names used by debtor within
last 6 years.

Debtor

Case No.

Address

Chapter

Employer's Tax Identification (EIN) No(s). [if any]:

Last four digits of Social Security No(s).:

STATEMENT OF SOCIAL SECURITY NUMBER(S)

1. Name of Debtor (enter Last, First, Middle)
   (Check the appropriate box and, if applicable, provide the required information.)

   ☐ Debtor has a Social Security Number and it is:
           (If more than one, state all.)
   ☐ Debtor does not have a Social Security Number.

2. Name of Joint Debtor (enter Last, First, Middle)
   (Check the appropriate box and, if applicable, provide the required information.)

   ☐ Joint Debtor has a Social Security Number and it is:
           (If more than one, state all.)
   ☐ Joint Debtor does not have a Social Security Number.

I declare under penalty of perjury that the foregoing is true and correct.

X _____

       Signature of Debtor   Date

X _____

       Signature of Debtor   Date

*Joint debtors must provide information for both spouses.
Penalty for making a false statement: Fine of up to $250,000 or up to 5 years imprisonment or both.
18 U.S.C, §§152 and 3571.

Blumbergs Law Products Form B6 (6-90)

Julius Blumberg, Inc. NYC 10013

UNITED STATES BANKRUPTCY COURT   **DISTRICT OF**

In re: Debtor(s)   Case No.   (If Known)

See summary below for the list of schedules. Include Unsworn Declaration under Penalty of Perjury at the end.

GENERAL INSTRUCTIONS: Schedules D, E and F have been designed for the listing of each claim only once. Even when a claim is secured only in part, or entitled to priorityonly in part, it still should be listed only once. A claim which is secured in whole or in part should be listed on Schedule D only, and a claim which is entitled to priority in whole or in part should be listed in Schedule E only. Do not list the same claim twice. If a creditor has more than one claim, such as claims arising from separate transactions, each claim should be scheduled separately.

Review the specific instructions for each schedule before completing the schedule.

SUMMARY OF SCHEDULES

Indicate as to each schedule whether that schedule is attached and state the number of pages in each. Report the totals from Schedules A, B, D, E, F, I and J in the boxes provided. Add the amounts from Schedules A and B to determine the total amount of the debtor's assets. Add the amounts from Schedules D, E, and F to determine the total amount of the debtor's liabilities.

Name of Schedule	Attached (Yes No)	Number of sheets	Assets	Liabilities	Other
A - Real Property					
B - Personal Property					
C - Property Claimed as Exempt					
D - Creditors Holding Secured Claims					
E - Creditors Holding Unsecured Priority Claims					
F - Creditors Holding Unsecured Nonpriority Claims					
G - Executory Contracts and Unexpired Leases					
H - Codebtors					
I - Current Income of Individual Debtor(s)					
J - Current Expenditures of Individual Debtor(s)					
Total Number of Sheets of All Schedules					
Total Assets					
Total Liabilities					

Blumberg's Law Products Form B6 A/B, P1(6-90)   Julius Blumberg, Inc. NYC 10013

In re: Debtor(s)   Case No.   (if known)

SCHEDULE A - REAL PROPERTY

DESCRIPTION AND LOCATION OF PROPERTY	NATURE OF DEBTOR'S INTEREST IN PROPERTY	H W J C	CURRENT MARKET VALUE OF DEBTOR'S INTEREST IN PROPERTY WITHOUT DEDUCTING ANY SECURED CLAIM OR EXEMPTION	AMOUNT OF SECURED CLAIM
		Total ->	$	(Report also on Summary of Schedules.)

SCHEDULE B - PERSONAL PROPERTY

TYPE OF PROPERTY	N O N E	DESCRIPTION AND LOCATION OF PROPERTY	H W J C	CURRENT MARKET VALUE OF DEBTOR'S INTEREST IN PROPERTY WITHOUT DEDUCTING ANY SECURED CLAIM OR EXEMPTION
1. Cash on hand				
2. Checking, savings or other financial accounts, certificates of deposit, or shares in banks, savings and loan, thrift, building and loan, and homestead associations, or credit unions, brokerage houses, or cooperatives.				
3. Security deposits with public utilities, telephone companies, landlords, and others.				
4. Household goods and furnishings including audio, video and computer equipment.				
5. Books; pictures and other art objects; antiques; stamp, coin, record, tape, compact disc, and other collections or collectibles.				
6. Wearing apparel.				
7. Furs and jewelry.				
8. Firearms and sports, photographic, and other hobby equipment.				
9. Interests in insurance policies. Name insurance company of each policy and itemize surrender or refund value of each.				

 Form B6B, P2 (6-90)   Julius Blumberg, Inc. NYC 10013

SCHEDULE B
PERSONAL PROPERTY

In re: _____   Debtor(s)   Case No. _____   (if known)

TYPE OF PROPERTY	N O N E	DESCRIPTION AND LOCATION OF PROPERTY	H W J C	CURRENT MARKET VALUE OF DEBTOR'S INTEREST IN PROPERTY WITHOUT DEDUCTING ANY SECURED CLAIM OR EXEMPTION
10. Annuities. Itemize and name each issuer.				
11. Interests in IRA, ERISA, Keogh, or other pension or profit sharing plans. Itemize				
12. Stock and interests in incorporated and unincorporated businesses. Itemize.				
13. Interest in partnerships or joint ventures. Itemize.				
14. Government and corporate bonds and other negotiable and nonnegotiable instruments.				
15. Accounts receivable.				
16. Alimony, maintenance, support, and property settlements to which the debtor is or may be entitled. Give particulars.				
17. Other liquidated debts owing debtor including tax refunds. Give particulars.				
18. Equitable or future interests, life estates, and rights or powers exercisable for the benefit of the debtor other than those listed in Schedule of Real Property.				
19. Contingent and noncontingent interests in estate of a decedent, death benefit plan, life insurance policy, or trust.				
20. Other contingent and unliquidated claims of every nature, including tax refunds, counterclaims of the debtor, and rights to setoff claims. Give estimated value of each.				
21. Patents, copyrights, and other intellectual property. Give particulars.				
22. Licenses, franchises, and other general intangibles. Give particulars.				
23. Automobiles, trucks, trailers, and other vehicles and accessories.				
24. Boats, motors, and accessories.				
25. Aircraft and accessories.				
26. Office equipment, furnishings, and supplies.				
27. Machinery, fixtures, equipment, and supplies used in business.				
28. Inventory.				
29. Animals.				
30. Crops - growing or harvested. Give particulars.				
31. Farming equipment and implements.				
32. Farm supplies, chemicals, and feed.				
33. Other personal property of any kind not already listed. Itemize.				

(Include amounts from any continuation sheets attached. Report total also on Summary of Schedules)   Total -> $ _____

_____ continuation sheets attached

Form B6 C (6,90)   Julius Blumberg, Inc. NYC 10013

In re: Debtor(s)   Case No.   (if known)

SCHEDULE C - PROPERTY CLAIMED AS EXEMPT

Debtor elects the exemptions to which debtor is entitled under (Check one box)

☐ 11 U.S.C. § 522(b)(1): Exemptions provided in 11 U.S.C. § 522(d). Note: These exemptions are available only in certain states.

☐ 11 U.S.C. § 522(b)(2): Exemptions available under applicable nonbankruptcy federal laws, state or local law.

DESCRIPTION OF PROPERTY	SPECIFY LAW PROVIDING EACH EXEMPTION	VALUE OF CLAIMED EXEMPTION	CURRENT MARKET VALUE OF PROPERTY WITHOUT DEDUCTING EXEMPTION

Blumbergs
Law Products   Form B6 D (12-03)

BlumbergExcelsior, Inc., Publisher NYC 10013
www.blumberg.com

In re: Debtor(s)   Case No.   (if known)

SCHEDULE D - CREDITORS HOLDING SECURED CLAIMS

☐ Check this box if debtor has no creditors holding secured claims to report on this Schedule D.

CREDITOR'S NAME AND MAILING ADDRESS INCLUDING ZIP CODE AND ACCOUNT NUMBER (See instructons.)	CO DEBT	H W J C	DATE CLAIM WAS INCURRED, NATURE OF LIEN, AND DESCRIPTION AND MARKET VALUE OF PROPERTY SUBJECT TO LIEN	C U D *	AMOUNT OF CLAIM WITHOUT DEDUCTING VALUE OF COLLATERAL	UNSECURED PORTION IF ANY
A/C #						
			VALUE $			
A/C #						
			VALUE $			
A/C #						
			VALUE $			
A/C #						
			VALUE $			
A/C #						
			VALUE $			
A/C #						
			VALUE $			
A/C #						
			VALUE $			
A/C #						
			VALUE $			
A/C #						
			VALUE $			

_____ continuation sheets attached

Subtotal -> (Total of this page) $

Total -> (use only on last page) $

*If contingent, enter C; if unliquidated, enter U; if disputed, enter D.

(Report total also on Summary of Schedules)

Form B6 E (12-03)

BlumbergExcelsior. Inc.. Publisher NYC 10013
www.blumberg.com

In re: Debtor(s)   Case No.   (if known)

SCHEDULE E - CREDITORS HOLDING UNSECURED PRIORITY CLAIMS

☐ Check this box if debtor has no creditors holding unsecured priority claims to report on this Schedule E

TYPE OF PRIORITY CLAIMS (Check the appropriate box(es) below if claims in that category are listed on the attached sheets)

☐ **Extensions of credit in an involuntary case**   Claims arising in the ordinary course of the debtor's business or financial affairs after the commencement of the case but before the earlier of the appointment of a trustee or the order for relief. 11 U.S.C. § 507 (a) (2).

☐ **Wages, salaries, and commissions**   Wages, salaries, and commissions, including vacation, severance, and sick leave pay owing to employees, and commissions owing to qualifying independent sales representatives up to $4,650* per person, earned within 90 days immediately preceding the filing of the original petition, or the cessation of business, whichever occurred first, to the extent provided in 11 U.S.C. § 507 (a) (3).

☐ **Contributions to employee benefit plans**   Money owed to employee benefit plans for services rendered within 180 days immediately preceding the filing of the original petition, or the cessation of business, whichever occurred first, to the extent provided in 11 U.S.C. § 507 (a) (4).

☐ **Certain farmers and fishermen**   Claims of certain farmers and fishermen, up to $4,650* per farmer or fisherman, against the debtor, as provided in 11 U.S.C. § 507 (a) (5).

☐ **Deposits by individuals**   Claims of individuals up to $2,100* for deposits for the purchase, lease, or rental of property or services for personal, family, or household use, that were not delivered or provided. 11 U.S.C. § 507 (a) (6).

☐ **Alimony, Maintenance, or Support**   Claims of a spouse, former spouse, or child of the debtor for alimony, maintenance, or support, to the extent provided in 11 U.S.C. § 507 (a) (7).

☐ **Taxes and Certain Other Debts Owed to Governmental Units**   Taxes, customs duties, and penalties owing to federal, state, and local governmental units as set forth in 11 U.S.C. § 507 (a) (8).

☐ **Commitments to Maintain the Capital of an Insured Depository Institution**   Claims based on commitments to the FDIC, RTC, Director of the Office of Thrift Supervision, Comptroller of the Currency, or Board of Governors of the Federal Reserve System, or their predecessors or successors, to maintain the capital of an insured depository institution. 11 U.S.C. § 507 (a) (9).

*Amounts are subject to adjustment on April 1, 2004, and every three years thereafter with respect to cases commenced on or after the date of adjustment.

CREDITOR'S NAME AND MAILING ADDRESS INCLUDING ZIP CODE AND ACCOUNT NUMBER (See instructions.)	CODEBTOR	HWJC	DATE CLAIM WAS INCURRED AND CONSIDERATION FOR CLAIM	CUD*	TOTAL AMOUNT OF CLAIM	AMOUNT ENTITLED TO PRIORITY
A/C#						
A/C#						
A/C#						
A/C#						
A/C#						

_____ Continuation sheets attached.

Subtotal -> (Total of this page) $

Total -> (use only on last page of the completed Schedule E) $

* If contingent, enter C; if unliquidated., enter U; if disputed , enter D.

(Report total also on Summary of Schedules)

Form B6 F (12-03)

BlumbergExcelsior, Inc., Publisher NYC 10013
www.blumberg.com

In re: Debtor(s)   Case No.   (if known)

SCHEDULE F - CREDITORS HOLDING UNSECURED NONPRIORITY CLAIMS

☐ Check this box if debtor has no creditors holding unsecured nonpriority claims to report on this Schedule F

CREDITOR'S NAME AND MAILING ADDRESS INCLUDING ZIP CODE AND ACCOUNT NUMBER (See instructions.)	CODEBTOR	H W J C.	DATE CLAIM WAS INCURRED AND CONSIDERATION FOR CLAIM. IF CLAIM IS SUBJECT TO SETOFF, SO STATE.	C U D **	AMOUNT OF CLAIM
A/C #					
A/C #					
A/C #					
A/C #					
A/C #					
A/C #					
A/C #					
A/C #					
A/C #					

_____ Continuation Sheets attached.

Subtotal -> $
(Total of this page)

Total -> $

* If husband, enter H; if wife, enter W; if joint enter J, if community, enter C.

** If contingent, enter C; if unliquidated, enter U; if disputed, enter D.

(use only on last page of completed Schedule F.)

Form B6 G (6-90)   Julius Blumberg, Inc. NYC 10013

In re: Debtor(s)   Case No.   (if known)

SCHEDULE G - EXECUTORY CONTRACTS AND UNEXPIRED LEASES

☐ Check this box if debtor has no executory contracts or unexpired leases.

NAME AND MAILING ADDRESS, INCLUDING ZIP CODE, OF OTHER PARTIES TO LEASE OR CONTRACT.	DESCRIPTION OF CONTRACT OR LEASE AND NATURE OF DEBTOR'S INTEREST. STATE WHETHER LEASE IS FOR NONRESIDENTIAL REAL PROPERTY. STATE CONTRACT NUMBER OF ANY GOVERNMENT CONTRACT.

Form B6 H, (6-90)   Julius Blumberg, Inc. NYC 10013

In re: Debtor(s)   Case No.   (if known)

SCHEDULE H - CODEBTORS

☐ Check this box if debtor has no codebtors.

NAME AND ADDRESS OF CODEBTOR	NAME AND ADDRESS OF CREDITOR

Form B61 (12-03)

BlumbergExcelsior, Inc., Publisher NYC 10013
www.blumberg.com

In re:

| Debtor(s) | Case No. | (if known) |

SCHEDULE I - CURRENT INCOME OF INDIVIDUAL DEBTOR(S)

The column labeled "Spouse" must be completed in all cases filed by joint debtors and by a married debtor in a chapter 12 or 13 case whether or not a joint petition is filed, unless the spouses are separated and a joint petition is not filed.

Debtor's Marital Status:	DEPENDENTS OF DEBTOR AND SPOUSE	
	RELATIONSHIP	AGE

Employment:	DEBTOR	SPOUSE
Occupation		
Name of Employer		
How long employed		
Address of Employer		

Income: (Estimate of average monthly income)

	DEBTOR	SPOUSE
Current monthly gross wages, salary, and commissions (pro rate if not paid monthly.)	$	$
Estimate monthly overtime		
SUBTOTAL	$	$

LESS PAYROLL DEDUCTIONS

    a. Payroll taxes and social security

    b. Insurance

    c. Union dues

    d. Other (Specify)

	DEBTOR	SPOUSE
SUBTOTAL OF PAYROLL DEDUCTIONS	$	$
TOTAL NET MONTHLY TAKE HOME PAY	$	$

Regular income from operation of business or profession or farm

(attach detailed statement)

Income from real property

Interest and dividends

Alimony, maintenance or support payments payable to the debtor for the debtor's

    use or that of dependents listed above.

Social security or other government assistance (Specify)

Pension or retirement income

Other monthly income (Specify)

	DEBTOR	SPOUSE
TOTAL MONTHLY INCOME	$	$

| TOTAL COMBINED MONTHLY INCOME | $ | (Report also on Summary of Schedules) |

Describe any increase or decrease of more than 10% in any of the above categories anticipated to occur within the year following the filing of this document:

Form B6 J, Cont. (6-90)   Julius Blumberg, Inc. NYC 10013

In re: _____   Debtor(s)   Case No.   (if known)

SCHEDULE J - CURRENT EXPENDITURES OF INDIVIDUAL DEBTOR(S)

Complete this schedule by estimating the average monthly expenses of the debtor and the debtor's family. Pro rate any payments made bi-weekly, quarterly, semi-annually, or annually to show monthly rate.

☐ Check this box if a joint petition is filed and debtor's spouse maintains a separate household. Complete a separate schedule of expenditures labeled "Spouse".

Rent or home mortgage payment (include lot rented for mobile home) .... $ _____

Are real estate taxes included? ☐ Yes ☐ No   Is property insurance included? ☐ Yes ☐ No

Utilities Electricity and heating fuel ....

    Water and sewer ....

    Telephone ....

    Other

Home maintenance (repairs and upkeep) ....

Food ....

Clothing ....

Laundry and dry cleaning ....

Medical and dental expenses ....

Transportation (not including car payments) ....

Recreation, clubs and entertainment, newspapers, magazines, etc. ....

Charitable contributions ....

Insurance (not deducted from wages or included in home mortgage payments)

    Homeowner's or renter's ....

    Life ....

    Health ....

    Auto ....

    Other

Taxes (not deducted from wages or included in home mortgage payments)

(Specify)

Installment payments: (In chapter 12 and 13 cases, do not list payments to be included in the plan)

    Auto ....

    Other

Alimony, maintenance, and support paid to others ....

Payments for support of additional dependents not living at your home ....

Regular expenses from operation of business, profession, or farm (attach detailed statement) ....

Other

TOTAL MONTHLY EXPENSES (Report also on Summary of Schedules) .... $ _____

(FOR CHAPTER 12 AND 13 DEBTORS ONLY)

Provide the information requested below, including whether plan payments are to be made bi-weekly, monthly, annually, or at some other regular interval.

A. Total projected monthly income .... $ _____

B. Total projected monthly expenses ....

C. Excess income (A minus B) .... $ _____

D. Total amount to be paid into plan each .... $ _____

                (interval)

Form B6 Cont. (12-03)

BlumbergExcelsior, Inc., Publisher NYC 10013
www.blumberg.com

In re: Debtor(s)   Case No.

                                                                  (if known)

DECLARATION CONCERNING DEBTOR'S SCHEDULES

DECLARATION UNDER PENALTY OF PERJURY BY INDIVIDUAL DEBTOR

I declare under penalty of perjury that I have read the foregoing summary and schedules, consisting of _____ sheets,
                                                   (Total shown on summary page plus 1.)
and that they are true and correct to the best of my knowledge, information, and belief.

Date   Signature: _____
                                              Debtor

Date   Signature: _____
                                     (Joint Debtor, if any) (If joint case, both spouses must sign.)

CERTIFICATION AND SIGNATURE OF NON-ATTORNEY BANKRUPTCY PETITION PREPARER (SEE 11 U.S.C. § 110)

I certify that I am a bankruptcy petition preparer as defined in 11 U.S.C. § 110, that I prepared this document for compensation, and that I have provided the debtor with a copy of this document.

_____   _____
Printed or Typed Name of Bankruptcy Petition Preparer   Social Security No.
                                                       (Required by U.S.C. §110(c).)

_____
Address

Names and Social Security numbers of all other individuals who prepared or assisted in preparing this document:

If more than one person prepared this document, attach additional signed sheets conforming to the appropriate Official Form for each person.

X _____   _____
   Signature of Bankruptcy Petition Preparer   Date

A bankruptcy petition preparer's failure to comply with the provisions of title 11 and the Federal Rules of Bankruptcy Procedure may result in fines or imprisonment or both. 11 U.S.C. § 110; 18 U.S.C. § 156

DECLARATION UNDER PENALTY OF PERJURY ON BEHALF OF A CORPORATION OR PARTNERSHIP

I, the _____ (the president or other officer or an authorized agent of the corporation or a member or an authorized agent of the partnership) of the _____ (corporation or partnership) named as debtor in this case, declare under penalty of perjury that I have read the foregoing summary and schedules, consisting of _____ sheets, and that they are true and correct to the best of my knowledge, information, and belief.   (Total shown on summary page plus 1.)

Date   Signature: _____
                                     (Print or type name of individual signing on behalf of debtor.)

(An individual signing on behalf of a partnership or corporation must indicate position or relationship to debtor.)

Penalty for making a false statement or concealing property: Fine of up to $500,000 or imprisonment for up to 5 years or both. 18 U.S.C.§152 and 3571

 Form 7 Stmt. of Financial
Affairs (12-03)

BlumbergExcelsior, Inc., Publisher NYC 10013
www.blumberg.com

UNITED STATES BANKRUPTCY COURT   DISTRICT OF

In re: Debtor(s)   *Case No.*

STATEMENT OF FINANCIAL AFFAIRS

This statement is to be completed by every debtor. Spouses filing a joint petition may file a single statement on which the information for both spouses is combined. If the case is filed under chapter 12 or chapter 13, a married debtor must furnish information for both spouses whether or not a joint petition is filed, unless the spouses are separated and a joint petition is not filed. An individual debtor engaged in business as a sole proprietor, partner, family farmer, or self-employed professional, should provide the information requested on this statement concerning all such activities as well as the individual's personal affairs.

Questions 1-18 are to be completed by all debtors. Debtors that are or have been in business, as defined below, also must complete Questions 19-25. **If the answer to any question is "None," or the question is not applicable, mark the box labeled "None."** If additional space is needed for the answer to any question, use and attach a separate sheet properly identified with the case name, case number (if known), and the number of the question.

DEFINITIONS

"In business." A debtor is "in business" for the purpose of this form if the debtor is a corporation or partnership. An individual debtor is "in business" for the purpose of this form if the debtor is or has been. within the six years immediately preceding the filing of this bankruptcy case, any of the following: an officer, director, managing executive, or person in control of a corporation; a partner, other than a limited partner, of a partnership; a sole proprietor or self-employed.

"Insider." The term "insider" includes but is not limited to: relatives of the debtor; general partners of the debtor and their relatives; corporations of which the debtor is an officer, director, or person in control; officers, directors, and any person in control of a corporate debtor and their relatives; affiliates of the debtor and insiders of such affiliates; any managing agent of the debtor. 11 U.S.C. §101.

☐ None   **1. Income from Employment or Operation of Business**

State the gross amount of income the debtor has received from employment, trade, or profession, or from operation of the debtor's business from the beginning of this calendar year to the date this case was commenced. State also the gross amounts received during the **two years** immediately preceding this calendar year. (A debtor that maintains, or has maintained, financial records on the basis of a fiscal rather than a calendar year may report fiscal year income. Identify the beginning and ending dates of the debtor's fiscal year.) If a joint petition is filed, state income for each spouse separately. (Married debtors filing under chapter 12 or chapter 13 must state income of both spouses whether or not a joint petition is filed, unless the spouses are separated and a joint petition is not filed.)
Give AMOUNT and SOURCE (If more than one).

☐ None   **2. Income Other than from Employment or Operation of Business**

State the amount of income received by the debtor other than from employment, trade, profession, or operation of the debtor's business during the **two years** immediately preceding the commencement of this case. Give particulars. If a joint petition is filed, state income for each spouse separately. (Married debtors filing under chapter 12 or chapter 13 must state income for each spouse whether or not a joint petition is filed, unless the spouses are separated and a joint petition is not filed.) Give AMOUNT and SOURCE.

3. Payments to Creditors

☐ None   a. List all payments on loans, installment purchases of goods or services, and other debts, aggregating more than $600 to any creditor, made within **90 days** immediately preceding the commencement of this case. (Married debtors filing under chapter 12 or chapter 13 must include payments by either or both spouses whether or not a joint petition is filed, unless the spouses are separated and a joint petition is not filed.)
Give NAME AND ADDRESS OF CREDITOR. DATES OF PAYMENTS. AMOUNT PAID and AMOUNT STILL OWING.

☐ None   b. List all payments made within **one year** immediately preceding the commencement of this case to or for the benefit of creditors who are or were insiders. (Married debtors filing under chapter 12 or chapter 13 must include payments by either or both spouses whether or not a joint petition is filed. unless the spouses are separated and a joint petition is not filed.)
Give NAME AND ADDRESS OF CREDITOR AND RELATIONSHIP TO DEBTOR. DATE OF PAYMENT. AMOUNT PAID and AMOUNT STILL OWING.

4. Suits and Administrative Proceedings, Executions, Garnishments and Attachments

☐ None   a. List all suits and administrative proceedings to which the debtor is or was a party within **one year** immediately preceding the filing of this bankruptcy case. (Married debtors filing under chapter 12 or chapter 13 must include information concerning either or both spouses whether or not a joint petition is filed, unless the spouses are separated and a joint petition is not filed.)
Give CAPTION OF SUIT AND CASE NUMBER. NATURE OF PROCEEDING. COURT OR AGENCY AND LOCATION and STATUS OR DISPOSITION.

☐ None   b. Describe all property that has been attached, garnished. or seized under any legal or equitable process within **one year**

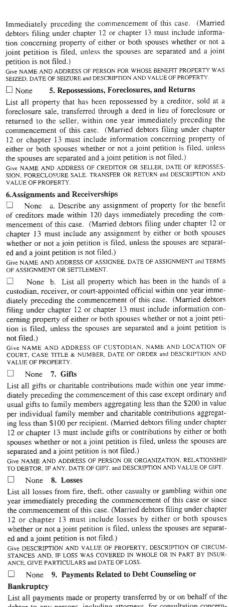

Immediately preceding the commencement of this case. (Married debtors filing under chapter 12 or chapter 13 must include information concerning property of either or both spouses whether or not a joint petition is filed, unless the spouses are separated and a joint petition is not filed.)

Give NAME AND ADDRESS OF PERSON FOR WHOSE BENEFIT PROPERTY WAS SEIZED, DATE OF SEIZURE and DESCRIPTION AND VALUE OF PROPERTY.

☐ None **5. Repossessions, Foreclosures, and Returns**

List all property that has been repossessed by a creditor, sold at a foreclosure sale, transferred through a deed in lieu of foreclosure or returned to the seller, within one year immediately preceding the commencement of this case. (Married debtors filing under chapter 12 or chapter 13 must include information concerning property of either or both spouses whether or not a joint petition is filed, unless the spouses are separated and a joint petition is not filed.)

Give NAME AND ADDRESS OF CREDITOR OR SELLER, DATE OF REPOSSESSION, FORECLOSURE SALE, TRANSFER OR RETURN and DESCRIPTION AND VALUE OF PROPERTY.

6.Assignments and Receiverships

☐ None a. Describe any assignment of property for the benefit of creditors made within 120 days immediately preceding the commencement of this case. (Married debtors filing under chapter 12 or chapter 13 must include any assignment by either or both spouses whether or not a join petition is filed, unless the spouses are separated and a joint petition is not filed.)

Give NAME AND ADDRESS OF ASSIGNEE, DATE OF ASSIGNMENT and TERMS OF ASSIGNMENT OR SETTLEMENT.

☐ None b. List all property which has been in the hands of a custodian, receiver, or court-appointed official within one year immediately preceding the commencement of this case. (Married debtors filing under chapter 12 or chapter 13 must include information concerning property of either or both spouses whether or not a joint petition is filed, unless the spouses are separated and a joint petition is not filed.)

Give NAME AND ADDRESS OF CUSTODIAN, NAME AND LOCATION OF COURT, CASE TITLE & NUMBER, DATE OF ORDER and DESCRIPTION AND VALUE OF PROPERTY.

☐ None **7. Gifts**

List all gifts or charitable contributions made within one year immediately preceding the commencement of this case except ordinary and usual gifts to family members aggregating less than the $200 in value per individual family member and charitable contributions aggregating less than $100 per recipient. (Married debtors filing under chapter 12 or chapter 13 must include gifts or contributions by either or both spouses whether or not a joint petition is filed, unless the spouses are separated and a joint petition is not filed.)

Give NAME AND ADDRESS OF PERSON OR ORGANIZATION, RELATIONSHIP TO DEBTOR, IF ANY, DATE OF GIFT, and DESCRIPTION AND VALUE OF GIFT.

☐ None **8. Losses**

List all losses from fire, theft, other casualty or gambling within one year immediately preceding the commencement of this case or since the commencement of this case. (Married debtors filing under chapter 12 or chapter 13 must include losses by either or both spouses whether or not a joint petition is filed, unless the spouses are separated and a joint petition is not filed.)

Give DESCRIPTION AND VALUE OF PROPERTY, DESCRIPTION OF CIRCUMSTANCES AND, IF LOSS WAS COVERED IN WHOLE OR IN PART BY INSURANCE, GIVE PARTICULARS and DATE OF LOSS.

☐ None **9. Payments Related to Debt Counseling or**

Bankruptcy

List all payments made or property transferred by or on behalf of the debtor to any persons, including attorneys, for consultation concerning debt consolidation, relief under the bankruptcy law or preparation of a petition in bankruptcy within one year immediately preceding the commencement of this case.

Give NAME AND ADDRESS OF PAYEE, DATE OF PAYMENT, NAME OF PAYER IF OTHER THAN DEBTOR and AMOUNT OF MONEY OR DESCRIPTION AND VALUE OF PROPERTY.

☐ None **10. Other Transfers**

List all other property, other than property transferred in the ordinary course of the business or financial affairs of the debtor, transferred either absolutely or as security within one year immediately preceding the commencement of this case. (Married debtors filing under chapter 12 or chapter 13 must include transfers by either or both spouses whether or not a joint petition is file, unless the spouses are separated and a joint petition is not filed.)

Give NAME AND ADDRESS OF TRANSFEREE, RELATIONSHIP TO DEBTOR, DATE, and DESCRIBE PROPERTY TRANSFERRED AND VALUE RECEIVED.

☐   None   **11. Closed Financial Accounts**

List all financial accounts and instruments held in the name of the debtor or for the benefit of the debtor which were closed, sold, or otherwise transferred within one year immediately preceding the commencement of this case. Include checking, savings, or other financial accounts, certificates of deposit, or other instruments; shares and share accounts held in banks, credit unions, pension funds, cooperatives, associations, brokerage houses and other financial institutions. (Married debtors filing under chapter 12 or chapter 13 must include information concerning accounts or instruments held by or for either or both spouses whether or not a joint petition is filed, unless the spouses are separated and a joint petition is not filed.)

Give NAME AND ADDRESS OF INSTITUTION, TYPE OF ACCOUNT, LAST FOUR DIGITS OF ACCOUNT NUMBER AND AMOUNT OF FINAL BALANCE and AMOUNT AND DATE OF SALE OR CLOSING.

☐   None   **12. Safe Deposit Boxes**

List each safe deposit or other box or depository in which the debtor has or had securities, cash, or other valuables within one year immediately preceding the commencement of this case. (Married debtors filing under chapter 12 or chapter 13 must include depositories of either or both spouses whether or not a joint petition is filed, unless the spouses are separated and a joint petition is not filed.)

Give NAME AND ADDRESS OF BANK OR OTHER DEPOSITORY, NAMES AND ADDRESSES OF THOSE WITH ACCESS TO BOX OR DEPOSITORY, DESCRIPTION OF CONTENTS and DATE OF TRANSFER OR SURRENDER, IF ANY.

☐   None   **13. Setoffs**

List all setoffs made by any creditor, including a bank, against a debt or deposit of the debtor within 90 days preceding the commencement of this case. (Married debtors filing under chapter 12 or chapter 13 must include information concerning either or both spouses whether or not a joint petition is filed, unless the spouses are separated and a joint petition is not filed.)

Give NAME AND ADDRESS OR CREDITOR, DATE OF SETOFF and AMOUNT OF SETOFF.

☐   None   **14. Property Held for Another Person**

List all property owned by another person that the debtor holds or controls.

Give NAME AND ADDRESS OF OWNER, DESCRIPTION AND VALUE OF PROPERTY and LOCATION OF PROPERTY.

☐   None   **15. Prior Address of Debtor**

If the debtor has moved within the two years immediately preceding the commencement of this case, list all premises which the debtor occupied during that period and vacated prior to the commencement of this case. If a joint petition is filed, report also any separate address of either spouse.

Give ADDRESS, NAME USED and DATES OF OCCUPANCY.

☐   None   **16. Spouses and Former Spouses**

If the debtor resides or resided in a community property state, commonwealth, or territory (including Alaska, Arizona, California, Idaho, Louisiana, Nevada, New Mexico, Puerto Rico, Texas, Washington, or Wisconsin) within the six-year period immediately preceding the commencement of the case, identify the name of the debtor's spouse and of any former spouse who resides or resided with the debtor in the community property state.

Give NAME.

☐   None   **17. Environmental Information**

For the purpose of this question, the following definitions apply: "Environmental Law" means any federal, state, or local statute or regulation regulating pollution, contamination, releases of hazardous or toxic substances, wastes or material into the air, land, soil, surface water, groundwater, or other medium, including, but not limited to, statutes or regulations regulating the cleanup of these substances, wastes, or material. "Site" means any location, facility, or property as defined under any Environmental Law, whether or not presently or formerly owned or operated by the debtor, including, but not limited to, disposal sites. "Hazardous Material" means anything defined as a hazardous waste, hazardous substance, toxic substance, hazardous material, pollutant, or contaminant or similar term under an Environmental Law.

☐   None   **a**. List the name and address of every site for which the debtor has received notice in writing by a governmental unit that it may be liable or potentially liable under or in violation of an Environmental law. Indicate the governmental unit, the date of the notice, and, if known, the Environmental Law:

Give SITE NAME AND ADDRESS, NAME AND ADDRESS OF GOVERNMENTAL UNIT, DATE OF NOTICE and ENVIRONMENTAL LAW.

☐   None   **b**. List the name and address of every site for which the debtor has provided notice to a governmental unit of a release of Hazardous Material. Indicate the governmental unit to which the notice was sent and the date of the notice.

Give SITE NAME AND ADDRESS, NAME AND ADDRESS OF GOVERNMENTAL UNIT, DATE OF NOTICE and ENVIRONMENTAL LAW.

☐   None   **c**. List all judicial or administrative proceedings, including settlements or orders, under any Environmental Law with respect to which the debtor is or was a party. Indicate the name and address of the governmental unit that is or was a party to the proceeding, and the docket number.

Give NAME AND ADDRESS OF GOVERNMENTAL UNIT, DOCKET NUMBER and STATUS OR DISPOSITION.

18. Nature, Location and Name of Business

☐   None   **a**. If the debtor is an individual, list the names, addresses, taxpayer identification numbers, nature of the businesses and beginning and ending dates of all businesses in which the debtor was an officer, director, partner, or managing executive of a corporation, partnership, sole proprietorship or was a self-employed

(continues on next page)

professional within the **six years** immediately preceding the commencement of this case, or in which the debtor owned 5 percent or more of the voting or equity securities within the **six years** immediately preceding the commencement of this case.

If the debtor is a partnership, list the names and addresses of all businesses in which the debtor was a partner or owned 5 percent or more of the voting securities, within the **six years** immediately preceding the commencement of this case.

If the debtor is a corporation, list the names and addresses of all businesses in which the debtor was a partner or owned 5 percent or more of the voting securities within the **six years** immediately preceding the commencement of this case.

Give NAME, TAXPAYER I.D. NUMBER, ADDRESS, NATURE OF BUSINESS and BEGINNING AND ENDING DATES.

☐ None   b. Identify any business listed in response to subdivision a., above, that is "single asset real estate" as defined in 11 U.S.C. § 101.

Give NAME and ADDRESS.

The following questions are to be completed as shown below.*

19. Books, Records, and Financial Statements

☐ None   a. List all bookkeepers and accountants who within the **two years** immediately preceding the filing of this bankruptcy case kept or supervised the keeping of books of account and records of the debtor.

Give NAME AND ADDRESS and DATES SERVICE RENDERED.

☐ None   b. List all firms or individuals who within the **two years** immediately preceding the filing of this bankruptcy case have audited the books of account and records, or prepared a financial statement of the debtor.

Give NAME, ADDRESS and DATES SERVICES RENDERED.

☐ None   c. List all firms or individuals who at the time of the commencement of this case were in possession of the books of account and records of the debtor. If any of the books of account and records are not available, explain.

Give NAME AND ADDRESS and DATE ISSUED.

☐ None   d. List all financial institutions, creditors and other parties, including mercantile and trade agencies, to whom a financial statement was issued within the **two years** immediately preceding the commencement of this case by the debtor.

Give NAME AND ADDRESS and DATE ISSUED.

20. Inventories

☐ None   a. List the dates of the last two inventories taken of your property, the name of the person who supervised the taking of each inventory, and the dollar amount and basis of each inventory.

Give DATE OF INVENTORY, INVENTORY, SUPERVISOR and DOLLAR AMOUNT OF INVENTORY (specify cost, market or other basis).

☐ None   b. List the name and address of the person having possession of the records of each of the two inventories reported in a., above.

Give DATE OF INVENTORY and NAME AND ADDRESSES OF CUSTODIAN OF INVENTORY RECORDS.

21. Current Partners, Officers, Directors and Shareholders

☐ None   a. If the debtor is a partnership, list the nature and percentage of partnership interest of each member of the partnership.

Give NAME AND ADDRESS, NATURE OR INTEREST and PERCENTAGE OF THE INTEREST.

☐ None   b. If the debtor is a corporation, list all officers and directors of the corporation, and each stockholder who directly or indirectly owns, controls, or holds 5 percent or more of the voting securities of the corporation.

Give NAME AND ADDRESS, TITLE and NATURE AND PERCENTAGE OF STOCK OWNERSHIP.

22. Former Partners, Officers, Directors and Shareholders

☐ None   a. If the debtor is a partnership, list each member who withdrew from the partnership within **one year** immediately preceding the commencement of this case.

Give NAME, ADDRESS and DATE OF WITHDRAWAL.

☐ None   b. If the debtor is a corporation, list all officers or directors whose relationship with the corporation terminated within **one year** immediately preceding the commencement of the case.

Give NAME AND ADDRESS, TITLE and DATE OF TERMINATION.

23. Withdrawals from a Partnership or Distributions by a Corporation

☐ None If the debtor is a partnership or corporation, list all withdrawals or distributions credited or given to an insider, including compensation in any form, bonuses, loans, stock redemption, options exercised and any other perquisite during **one year** immediately preceding the commencement of this case.

Give NAME & ADDRESS OF RECIPIENT, RELATIONSHIP TO DEBTOR, DATE AND PURPOSE OR WITHDRAWAL, and AMOUNT OF MONEY OR DESCRIPTION AND VALUE OF PROPERTY.

24. Tax Consolidation Group.

☐ If the debtor is a corporation, list the name and federal taxpayer identification number of the parent corporation of any consolidated group for tax purposes of which the debtor has been a member at any time within the **six-year period** immediately preceding the commencement of the case.

Give NAME OF PARENT CORPORATION and TAXPAYER IDENTIFICATION NUMBER.

25. Pension Funds.

☐ If the debtor is not an individual, list the name and federal taxpayer identification number of any fund to which the debtor, as an employer, has been responsible for contributing at any time within the **six-year period** immediately preceding the commencement of the case.

Give NAME OF PENSION FUND and TAXPAYER IDENTIFICATION NUMBER.

_____continuation sheets attached

Complete unsworn declaration on page 3076-5

* The following questions are to be completed by every debtor that is a corporation or partnership and by any individual debtor who is or has been, within the **six years** immediately preceding the commencement of this case, any of the following: an officer, director, managing executive, or owner of more than 5 percent of the voting securities or a corporation; a partner, other than a limited partner, of a partnership; a sole proprietor or otherwise self-employed. (An individual or joint debtor should complete this portion of the statement only if the debtor is or has been in business, as defined above, within the six years immediately preceding the commencement of this case. A debtor who has not been in business within those six years should go directly to the signature page.)

[If completed by an individual or individual and spouse]

I declare under penalty of perjury that I have read the answers contained in the foregoing statement of financial affairs and any attachments thereto and that they are true and correct.

Date ——————————   Signature ——————————————————————
                          of Debtor

Date ——————————   Signature ——————————————————————
                          of Joint Debtor
                          (if any)

···

[If completed on behalf of a partnership or corporation]

I, declare under penalty of perjury that I have read the answers contained in the foregoing statement of financial affairs and any attachments thereto and that they are true and correct to the best of my knowledge, information and belief.

Date ——————————   Signature ——————————————————————

                          ——————————————————————
                          Print Name and Title

[An individual signing on behalf of a partnership or corporation must indicate position or relationship to debtor.]

——————— continuation sheets attached.

Penalty for making a false statement: Fine of up to $500,000 or imprisonment for up to 5 years, or both. 18 U.S.C. §§152 and 3571.

···

CERTIFICATION AND SIGNATURE OF NON-ATTORNEY BANKRUPTCY PETITION PREPARER (See 11 U.S.C. § 110)

I certify that I am a bankruptcy petition preparer as defined in 11 U.S.C. § 110, that I prepared this document for compensation, and that I have provided the debtor with a copy of this document.

—————————————————————   —————————————————
Printed or Typed Name of Bankruptcy Petition Preparer   Social Security No.
                                                              (Required by 11 U.S.C. §110(c).)

—————————————————————

—————————————————————
Address

Names and Social Security numbers of all other individuals who prepared or assisted in preparing this document: If more than one person prepared this document, attach additional signed sheets conforming to the appropriate Official Form for each person.

X——————————————————   —————————————————
Signature of Bankruptcy Petition Preparer   Date

A bankruptcy petition preparer's failure to comply with the provisions of title II and the Federal Rules of Bankruptcy Procedure may result in fines or imprisonment or both. 18 U.S.C. § 156.

Form B8 (12-03)

Blumbergs Law Products

BlumbergExcelsior, Inc., Publisher NYC 10013
www.blumberg.com

UNITED STATES BANKRUPTCY COURT

DISTRICT OF

In re:

Debtor(s)   Case No.
                   Chapter

CHAPTER 7 INDIVIDUAL DEBTOR'S STATEMENT OF INTENTION

1. I have filed a schedule of assets and liabilities which includes consumer debts secured by property of the estate.

2. I intend to do the following with respect to the property of the estate which secures those consumer debts: *a. Property to Be Surrendered*

Description of property	Creditor's name

[Check any applicable statement.]

b. Property to Be Retained

Description of property	Creditor's name	Property is claimed as exempt	Property will be redeemed pursuant to 11 U.S.C. § 722	Debt will be reaffirmed pursuant to 11 U.S.C. § 524(c)

Date	Signature of Debtor	Signature of Debtor

CERTIFICATION AND SIGNATURE OF NON-ATTORNEY BANKRUPTCY PETITION PREPARER (SEE 11 U.S.C. § 110)

I certify that I am a bankruptcy petition preparer as defined in 11 U.S.C. § 110, that I prepared this document for compensation, and that I have provided the debtor with a copy of this document.

Printed or Typed Name of Bankruptcy Petition Preparer

Social Security No.
(Required by U.S.C. §110(c).)
Names and Social Security numbers of all other individuals who prepared or assisted in preparing this document:

Address

If more than one person prepared this document, attach additional signed sheets conforming to the appropriate Official Form for each person.

X
Signature of Bankruptcy Petition Preparer   Date

A bankruptcy petition preparer's failure to comply with the provisions of title 11 and the Federal Rules of Bankruptcy Procedure may result in fines or imprisonment or both.
11 U.S.C. § 110; 18 U.S.C. § 156

3085   Statement of compensation: Rule 2016(b). 8-91

UNITED STATES BANKRUPTCY COURT   **DISTRICT OF**

In re   Debtor(s)   Case No.   (If Known)

STATEMENT
Pursuant to Rule 2016(b)

The undersigned, pursuant to Rule 2016(b) Bankruptcy Rules, states that:

(1) The undersigned is the attorney for the debtor(s) in this case.
(2) The compensation paid or agreed to be paid by the debtor(s) to the undersigned is:
   (a) for legal services rendered or to be rendered in contemplation of and in connection
      with this case $ ....
   (b) prior to filing this statement, debtor(s) have paid $ ....
   (c) the unpaid balance due and payable is $ ....
(3) $ of the filing fee in this case has been paid.
(4) The services rendered or to be rendered include the following:
   (a) analysis of the financial situation, and rendering advice and assistance to the debtor(s) in determining whether to file a
      petition under title 11 of the United States Code.
   (b) preparation and filing of the petition, schedules, statement of affairs and other documents required by the court.
   (c) representation of the debtor(s) at the meeting of creditors.

(5) The source of payments made by the debtor(s) to the undersigned was from earnings, wages and compensation for services
   performed, and

(6) The source of payments to be made by the debtor(s) to the undersigned for the unpaid balance remaining, if any, will be from
   earnings, wages and compensation for services performed, and

(7) The undersigned has received no transfer, assignment or pledge of property except the following for the value stated:

(8) The undersigned has not shared or agreed to share with any other entity, other than with members of undersigned's law firm,
   any compensation paid or to be paid except as follows:

Dated: Respectfully submitted, ...*Attorney for Petitioner*

Attorney's name and address...

B

Chapter 13
Bankruptcy Forms

The following forms represent the basic Chapter 13 petition and plan. The plan is used for individuals as well as for small businesses that are sole proprietorships. In addition to these forms, each bankruptcy district in the United States may require filing local forms. So many local forms exist that it is not practical to present all of them here. Your attorney should be familiar with the local rules in your area and with the additional forms required.

The plan provides for the mandatory provisions required by law. However, experienced bankruptcy attorneys will provide a plan that includes additional provisions to give the debtor other rights and safeguards.

Forms may be purchased from Julius Blumberg, Inc., New York, NY 10013, or from any of its dealers. Reproduction is prohibited.

Official Form B1, P1, 12-03   BlumbergExcelsior, Inc NYC 10013

United States Bankruptcy Court **District of**	**Voluntary Petition**
Name of Debtor (If individual, enter Last, First, Middle):	Name of Joint Debtor (Spouse) (Last, First, Middle):
All Other Names used by the debtor in the last 6 years (include married, maiden and trade names):	All Other Names used by the joint debtor in the last 6 years (include married, maiden and trade names):
Last four digits of Soc. Sec. No./Complete EIN or other Tax I.D. No. (if more than one, state all):	Last four digits of Soc. Sec. No./Complete EIN or other Tax I.D. No. (if more than one, state all):
Street Address of Debtor (No. and street, city, state, zip):	Street Address of Joint Debtor (No. and street, city, state, zip):
County of Residence or Principal Place of Business:	County of Residence or Principal Place of Business:
Mailing Address of Debtor (If different from street address):	Mailing Address of Joint Debtor (If different from street address):
Location of Principal Assets of Business Debtor (If different from addresses listed above)	

Information Regarding Debtor (Check the Applicable Boxes)

Venue (Check any applicable box)
☐ Debtor has been domiciled or has had a residence, principal place of business or principal assets in this District for 180 days immediately preceding the date of this petition or for a longer part of such 180 days than in any other District.
☐ There is a bankruptcy case concerning debtor's affiliate, general partner or partnership pending in this district

Type of Debtor (Check all boxes that apply)	**Chapter or Section of Bankruptcy Code Under Which the Petition is Filed** (Check one box)
☐ Individual ☐ Railroad	☐ Chapter 7 ☐ Chapter 11 ☐ Chapter 13
☐ Corporation ☐ Stockbroker	☐ Chapter 9 ☐ Chapter 12
☐ Partnership ☐ Commodity Broker	☐ § 304-Case ancillary to foreign proceeding.
☐ Other ☐ Clearing Bank	

Nature of Debt (Check one box) ☐ Consumer/Non-Business ☐ Business	**Filing Fee** (Check one box) ☐ Full Filing Fee attached. ☐ Filing Fee to be paid in installments (Applicable to individuals only)
Chapter 11 Small Business (Check all boxes that apply) ☐ Debtor is a small business as defined in 11 U.S.C. § 101. ☐ Debtor is and elects to be considered a small business under 11 U.S.C. § 1121(e) (Optional)	Must attach signed application for the court's consideration certifying that the debtor is unable to pay fee except in installments. Rule 1006(b). See Official Form No. 3

Statistical/Administrative Information (Estimates Only)

☐ Debtor estimates that funds will be available for distribution to unsecured creditors.
☐ Debtor estimates that, after any exempt property is excluded and administrative expenses paid, there will be no funds available for distribution to unsecured creditors.

THIS SPACE FOR COURT USE ONLY

Estimated Number of Creditors	1-15	16-49	50-99	100-199	200-999	1000-over
	☐	☐	☐	☐	☐	☐

Estimated Assets	$0 to $50,000	$50,001 to $100,000	$100,001 to $500,000	$500,001 to $1 million	$1,000,001 to $10 million	$10,000,001 to $100 million	More than $100 million
	☐	☐	☐	☐	☐	☐	☐

Estimated Debts	$0 to $50,000	$50,001 to $100,000	$100,001 to $500,000	$500,001 to $1 million	$1,000,001 to $10 million	$10,000,001 to $100 million	More than $100 million
	☐	☐	☐	☐	☐	☐	☐

 Official Form B1, P2, 12-03   **Blumberg**Excelsior, Inc NYC 10013

Voluntary Petition *(This page must be completed and filed in every case)*	Name of Debtor(s):		
Prior Bankruptcy Case Filed Within Last 6 Years (If more than one, attach additional sheet)			
Location Where Filed:	Case Number:		Date Filed:
Pendin Bankruptcy Case Filed by any Spouse, Partner, or Affiliate of this Debtor (If more than one, attach additional sheet.)			
Name of Debtor:	Case Number:		Date Filed:
District:	Relationship:		Judge:

Signatures

Signature(s) of Debtor(s) (Individual/Joint)

I declare under penalty of perjury that the information provided in this petition is true and correct.
[If petitioner is an individual whose debts are primarily consumer debts and has chosen to file under chapter 7] I am aware that I may proceed under chapter 7, 11,12,13 of title 11, United States Code, understand the relief available under each such chapter, and choose to proceed under chapter 7.
I request relief in accordance with the chapter of title 11, United States Code, specified in this petition.

X_____
Signature of Debtor

X_____
Signature of Joint Debtor

_____
Telephone (If not represented by attorney)

_____
Date

Signature of Attorney

X_____
Signature of Attorney for Debtor(s)

_____
Printed Name of Attorney for Debtor(s)

_____
Firm Name

_____
Address

_____

_____
Telephone Number

_____
Date

Signature(s) of Debtor(s) (Corporation/Partnership)

I declare under penalty of perjury that the information provided in this petition is true and correct, and that I have been authorized to file this petition on behalf of the debtor.

If debtor is a corporation filing under chapter 11, United States Code, specified in this petition.

X_____
Signature of Authorized Individual

_____
Print or Type Name of Authorized Individual

_____
Title of Authorized Individual by Debtor to File this Petition

_____
Date

EXHIBIT A

(To be completed if debtor is required to file periodic reports (e.g., forms 10K and 10Q) with the Securities and Exchange Commission pursuant to Section 13 or 15(d) of the Securities Exchange Act of 1934 and is requesting relief under chapter 11)

☐ Exhibit A is attached and made part of this petition.

EXHIBIT B

(To be completed if debtor is an individual whose debts are primarily consumer debts)

I, the attorney for the petitioner named in the foregoing petition, declare that I have informed the petitioner that [he or she] may proceed under chapter 7, 11, 12, or 13 of title 11, United States Code, and have explained the relief available under each such chapter.

X_____
Signature of Attorney for Debtor(s)   Date

EXHIBIT C

Does the debtor own or have possession of any property that poses or is alleged to pose a threat of imminent and identifiable harm to public health or safety?

☐ Yes, and Exhibit C is attached and made a part of this petition.
☐ No

Signature of Non-Attorney Petition Preparer

I certify that I am a bankruptcy petition preparer as defined in 11 U.S.C. § 110, that I prepared this document for compensation, and that I have provided the debtor with a copy of this document.

_____
Printed Name of Bankruptcy Petition Preparer

_____
Social Security Number (Required by 11 U.S.C. 110(c).)

_____
Address

Names and Social Security numbers of all other Individuals who prepared or assisted in preparing this document:

If more than one person prepared this document, attach additional sheets conforming to the appropriate official form for each person.

X_____
Signature of Bankruptcy Petition Preparer

_____
Date

A bankruptcy petition preparer's failure to comply with the provisions of title 11 and the Federal Rules of Bankruptcy Procedure may result in fines or imprisonment or both 11 U.S.C. § 110; 18 U.S.C. § 156.

Official Form B1, Exhibit C, 12-03   BlumbergExcelsior, Inc NYC 10013

UNITED STATES BANKRUPTCY COURT   **DISTRICT OF**

In re: Debtor(s)   Case No.   (If Known)

EXHIBIT "C." If, to the best of the debtor's knowledge, the debtor owns or has possession of property that poses or is alleged to pose a threat of imminent and identifiable harm to the public health or safety, attach this Exhibit "C" to the petition.

EXHIBIT "C" to Voluntary Petition

1. Identify and briefly describe all real or personal property owned or in possession of the debtor that, to the best of the debtor's knowledge, poses or is alleged to pose a threat of imminent and identifiable harm to the public health or safety (attach additional sheets if necessary):

2. With respect to each parcel of real property or item of personal property identified in question 1, describe the nature and location of the dangerous condition, whether environmental or otherwise, that poses or is alleged to pose a threat of imminent and identifiable harm to the public health or safety (attach additional sheets if necessary):

Form B21 Official Form 21 (12-03)   **Blumberg**Excelsior, Inc., Publisher NYC 10013
www.blumberg.com

United States Bankruptcy Court
District Of

In re

    Set forth here all names including married,
maiden, and trade names used by debtor within
last 6 years.

                     Debtor   Case No.

Address

                                   Chapter

Employer's Tax Identification (EIN) No(s). [if any]:

Last four digits of Social Security No(s).:

STATEMENT OF SOCIAL SECURITY NUMBER(S)

1. Name of Debtor (enter Last, First, Middle)
   (Check the appropriate box and, if applicable, provide the required information.)

        ☐ Debtor has a Social Security Number and it is:
                 (If more than one, state all.)
        ☐ Debtor does not have a Social Security Number.

2. Name of Joint Debtor (enter Last, First, Middle)
   (Check the appropriate box and, if applicable, provide the required information.)

        ☐ Joint Debtor has a Social Security Number and it is:
                 (If more than one, state all.)
        ☐ Joint Debtor does not have a Social Security Number.

I declare under penalty of perjury that the foregoing is true and correct.

X _____
           Signature of Debtor   Date

X _____
           Signature of Debtor   Date

---

*Joint debtors must provide information for both spouses.
Penalty for making a false statement: Fine of up to $250,000 or up to 5 years imprisonment or both.
18 U.S.C, §§152 and 3571.

 Form B6 (6-90)

Julius Blumberg, Inc. NYC 10013

UNITED STATES BANKRUPTCY COURT   DISTRICT OF

In re: Debtor(s)   Case No.   (If Known)

See summary below for the list of schedules. Include Unsworn Declaration under Penalty of Perjury at the end.

GENERAL INSTRUCTIONS: Schedules D, E and F have been designed for the listing of each claim only once. Even when a claim is secured only in part, or entitled to priorityonly in part, it still should be listed only once. A claim which is secured in whole or in part should be listed on Schedule D only, and a claim which is entitled to priority in whole or in part should be listed in Schedule E only. Do not list the same claim twice. If a creditor has more than one claim, such as claims arising from separate transactions, each claim should be scheduled separately.

Review the specific instructions for each schedule before completing the schedule.

SUMMARY OF SCHEDULES

Indicate as to each schedule whether that schedule is attached and state the number of pages in each. Report the totals from Schedules A, B, D, E, F, I and J in the boxes provided. Add the amounts from Schedules A and B to determine the total amount of the debtor's assets. Add the amounts from Schedules D, E, and F to determine the total amount of the debtor's liabilities.

Name of Schedule	Attached (Yes No)	Number of sheets	Assets	Liabilities	Other
				Amounts Scheduled	
A - Real Property					
B - Personal Property					
C - Property Claimed as Exempt					
D - Creditors Holding Secured Claims					
E - Creditors Holding Unsecured Priority Claims					
F - Creditors Holding Unsecured Nonpriority Claims					
G - Executory Contracts and Unexpired Leases					
H - Codebtors					
I - Current Income of Individual Debtor(s)					
J - Current Expenditures of Individual Debtor(s)					
Total Number of Sheets of All Schedules					
Total Assets					
Total Liabilities					

Form B6 A/B, P1(6-90)   Julius Blumberg, Inc. NYC 10013

In re: Debtor(s)   Case No.   (if known)

SCHEDULE A - REAL PROPERTY

DESCRIPTION AND LOCATION OF PROPERTY	NATURE OF DEBTOR'S INTEREST IN PROPERTY	H W J C	CURRENT MARKET VALUE OF DEBTOR'S INTEREST IN PROPERTY WITHOUT DEDUCTING ANY SECURED CLAIM OR EXEMPTION	AMOUNT OF SECURED CLAIM
		Total ->	$	(Report also on Summary of Schedules.)

SCHEDULE B - PERSONAL PROPERTY

TYPE OF PROPERTY	N O N E	DESCRIPTION AND LOCATION OF PROPERTY	H W J C	CURRENT MARKET VALUE OF DEBTOR'S INTEREST IN PROPERTY WITHOUT DEDUCTING ANY SECURED CLAIM OR EXEMPTION
1. Cash on hand				
2. Checking, savings or other financial accounts, certificates of deposit, or shares in banks, savings and loan, thrift, building and loan, and homestead associations, or credit unions, brokerage houses, or cooperatives.				
3. Security deposits with public utilities, telephone companies, landlords, and others.				
4. Household goods and furnishings including audio, video and computer equipment.				
5. Books; pictures and other art objects; antiques; stamp, coin, record, tape, compact disc, and other collections or collectibles.				
6. Wearing apparel.				
7. Furs and jewelry.				
8. Firearms and sports, photographic, and other hobby equipment.				
9. Interests in insurance policies. Name insurance company of each policy and itemize surrender or refund value of each.				

 Form B6B, P2 (6-90)   Julius Blumberg, Inc. NYC 10013

SCHEDULE B
PERSONAL PROPERTY

In re: Debtor(s)   Case No.   (if known)

TYPE OF PROPERTY	N O N E	DESCRIPTION AND LOCATION OF PROPERTY	H W J C	CURRENT MARKET VALUE OF DEBTOR'S INTEREST IN PROPERTY WITHOUT DEDUCTING ANY SECURED CLAIM OR EXEMPTION
10. Annuities. Itemize and name each issuer.				
11. Interests in IRA, ERISA, Keogh, or other pension or profit sharing plans. Itemize				
12. Stock and interests in incorporated and unincorporated businesses. Itemize.				
13. Interest in partnerships or joint ventures. Itemize.				
14. Government and corporate bonds and other negotiable and nonegotiable instruments.				
15. Accounts receivable.				
16. Alimony, maintenance, support, and property settlements to which the debtor is or may be entitled. Give particulars.				
17. Other liquidated debts owing debtor including tax refunds. Give particulars.				
18. Equitable or future interests, life estates, and rights or powers exercisable for the benefit of the debtor other than those listed in Schedule of Real Property.				
19. Contingent and noncontingent interests in estate of a decedent, death benefit plan, life insurance policy, or trust.				
20. Other contingent and unliquidated claims of every nature, including tax refunds, counterclaims of the debtor, and rights to setoff claims. Give estimated value of each.				
21. Patents, copyrights, and other intellectual property. Give particulars.				
22. Licenses, franchises, and other general intangibles. Give particulars.				
23. Automobiles, trucks, trailers, and other vehicles and accessories.				
24. Boats, motors, and accessories.				
25. Aircraft and accessories.				
26. Office equipment, furnishings, and supplies.				
27. Machinery, fixtures, equipment, and supplies used in business.				
28. Inventory.				
29. Animals.				
30. Crops - growing or harvested. Give particulars.				
31. Farming equipment and implements.				
32. Farm supplies, chemicals, and feed.				
33. Other personal property of any kind not already listed. Itemize.				

(Include amounts from any continuation sheets attached. Report total also on Summary of Schedules)   Total -> | $

_____ continuation sheets attached

Form B6 C (6,90)   Julius Blumberg, Inc. NYC 10013

In re: _____
                                              Debtor(s)   Case No. _____   (if known)

SCHEDULE C - PROPERTY CLAIMED AS EXEMPT

Debtor elects the exemptions to which debtor is entitled under (Check one box)

☐ 11 U.S.C. § 522(b)(1): Exemptions provided in 11 U.S.C. § 522(d). Note: These exemptions are available only in certain states.

☐ 11 U.S.C. § 522(b)(2): Exemptions available under applicable nonbankruptcy federal laws, state or local law.

DESCRIPTION OF PROPERTY	SPECIFY LAW PROVIDING EACH EXEMPTION	VALUE OF CLAIMED EXEMPTION	CURRENT MARKET VALUE OF PROPERTY WITHOUT DEDUCTING EXEMPTION

Form B6 D (12-03)

BlumbergExcelsior, Inc., Publisher NYC 10013
www.blumberg.com

In re: Debtor(s)   Case No.   (if known)

SCHEDULE D - CREDITORS HOLDING SECURED CLAIMS

☐ Check this box if debtor has no creditors holding secured claims to report on this Schedule D.

CREDITOR'S NAME AND MAILING ADDRESS INCLUDING ZIP CODE AND ACCOUNT NUMBER (See instructons.)	CO DEBT	HWJC	DATE CLAIM WAS INCURRED, NATURE OF LIEN, AND DESCRIPTION AND MARKET VALUE OF PROPERTY SUBJECT TO LIEN	CUD*	AMOUNT OF CLAIM WITHOUT DEDUCTING VALUE OF COLLATERAL	UNSECURED PORTION IF ANY
A/C #						
			VALUE $			
A/C #						
			VALUE $			
A/C #						
			VALUE $			
A/C #						
			VALUE $			
A/C #						
			VALUE $			
A/C #						
			VALUE $			
A/C #						
			VALUE $			
A/C #						
			VALUE $			
A/C #						
			VALUE $			

_____ continuation sheets attached

Subtotal -> (Total of this page) $ _____

Total -> (use only on last page) $ _____

*If contingent, enter C; if unliquidated, enter U; if disputed, enter D.

(Report total also on Summary of Schedules)

Form B6 E (12-03)

BlumbergExcelsior. Inc., Publisher NYC 10013
www.blumberg.com

In re: Debtor(s)   Case No.   (if known)

SCHEDULE E - CREDITORS HOLDING UNSECURED PRIORITY CLAIMS

☐ Check this box if debtor has no creditors holding unsecured priority claims to report on this Schedule E

TYPE OF PRIORITY CLAIMS (Check the appropriate box(es) below if claims in that category are listed on the attached sheets)

☐ **Extensions of credit in an involuntary case**   Claims arising in the ordinary course of the debtor's business or financial affairs after the commencement of the case but before the earlier of the appointment of a trustee or the order for relief. 11 U.S.C. § 507 (a) (2).

☐ **Wages, salaries, and commissions**   Wages, salaries, and commissions, including vacation, severance, and sick leave pay owing to employees, and commissions owing to qualifying independent sales representatives up to $4,650* per person, earned within 90 days immediately preceding the filing of the original petition, or the cessation of business, whichever occurred first, to the extent provided in 11 U.S.C. § 507 (a) (3).

☐ **Contributions to employee benefit plans**   Money owed to employee benefit plans for services rendered within 180 days immediately preceding the filing of the original petition, or the cessation of business, whichever occurred first, to the extent provided in 11 U.S.C. § 507 (a) (4).

☐ **Certain farmers and fishermen**   Claims of certain farmers and fishermen, up to $4,650* per farmer or fisherman, against the debtor, as provided in 11 U.S.C. § 507 (a) (5).

☐ **Deposits by individuals**   Claims of individuals up to $2,100* for deposits for the purchase, lease, or rental of property or services for personal, family, or household use, that were not delivered or provided. 11 U.S.C. § 507 (a) (6).

☐ **Alimony, Maintenance, or Support**   Claims of a spouse, former spouse, or child of the debtor for alimony, maintenance, or support, to the extent provided in 11 U.S.C. § 507 (a) (7).

☐ **Taxes and Certain Other Debts Owed to Governmental Units**   Taxes, customs duties, and penalties owing to federal, state, and local governmental units as set forth in 11 U.S.C. § 507 (a) (8).

☐ **Commitments to Maintain the Capital of an Insured Depository Institution**   Claims based on commitments to the FDIC, RTC, Director of the Office of Thrift Supervision, Comptroller of the Currency, or Board of Governors of the Federal Reserve System, or their predecessors or successors, to maintain the capital of an insured depository institution. 11 U.S.C. § 507 (a) (9).

*Amounts are subject to adjustment on April 1, 2004, and every three years thereafter with respect to cases commenced on or after the date of adjustment.

CREDITOR'S NAME AND MAILING ADDRESS INCLUDING ZIP CODE AND ACCOUNT NUMBER (See instructions.)	CO D E B T	H W J C	DATE CLAIM WAS INCURRED AND CONSIDERATION FOR CLAIM	C U D *	TOTAL AMOUNT OF CLAIM	AMOUNT ENTITLED TO PRIORITY
A/C#						
A/C#						
A/C#						
A/C#						
A/C#						

_____ Continuation sheets attached.

Subtotal -> (Total of this page) $

Total - > (use only on last page of the completed Schedule E) $

* If contingent, enter C; if unliquidated., enter U; if disputed , enter D.

(Report total also on Summary of Schedules)

Form B6 F (12-03)

BlumbergExcelsior, Inc., Publisher NYC 10013
www.blumberg.com

In re: Debtor(s)   Case No.   (if known)

SCHEDULE F - CREDITORS HOLDING UNSECURED NONPRIORITY CLAIMS

☐ Check this box if debtor has no creditors holding unsecured nonpriority claims to report on this Schedule F

CREDITOR'S NAME AND MAILING ADDRESS INCLUDING ZIP CODE AND ACCOUNT NUMBER (See instructions.)	CODEBTOR	H W J C*	DATE CLAIM WAS INCURRED AND CONSIDERATION FOR CLAIM. IF CLAIM IS SUBJECT TO SETOFF, SO STATE.	C U D**	AMOUNT OF CLAIM
A/C #					$
A/C #					
A/C #					
A/C #					
A/C #					
A/C #					
A/C #					
A/C #					
A/C #					

_____ Continuation Sheets attached.

Subtotal -> $
(Total of this page)

Total -> $

* If husband, enter H; if wife, enter W; if joint enter J, if community, enter C.

** If contingent, enter C; if unliquidated, enter U; if disputed, enter D.

(use only on last page of completed Schedule F.)

Form B6 G (6-90)   Julius Blumberg, Inc. NYC 10013

In re: Debtor(s)   Case No.   (if known)

SCHEDULE G - EXECUTORY CONTRACTS AND UNEXPIRED LEASES

☐ Check this box if debtor has no executory contracts or unexpired leases.

NAME AND MAILING ADDRESS, INCLUDING ZIP CODE, OF OTHER PARTIES TO LEASE OR CONTRACT.	DESCRIPTION OF CONTRACT OR LEASE AND NATURE OF DEBTOR'S INTEREST. STATE WHETHER LEASE IS FOR NONRESIDENTIAL REAL PROPERTY. STATE CONTRACT NUMBER OF ANY GOVERNMENT CONTRACT.

Form B6 H, (6-90)   Julius Blumberg, Inc. NYC 10013

In re: Debtor(s)   Case No.   (if known)

SCHEDULE H - CODEBTORS

☐ Check this box if debtor has no codebtors.

NAME AND ADDRESS OF CODEBTOR	NAME AND ADDRESS OF CREDITOR

Form B61 (12-03)

BlumbergExcelsior, Inc., Publisher NYC 10013
www.blumberg.com

In re: Debtor(s)   Case No.   (if known)

SCHEDULE I - CURRENT INCOME OF INDIVIDUAL DEBTOR(S)

The column labeled 'Spouse' must be completed in all cases filed by joint debtors and by a married debtor in a chapter 12 or 13 case whether or not a joint petition is filed, unless the spouses are separated and a joint petition is not filed.

Debtor's Marital Status:	DEPENDENTS OF DEBTOR AND SPOUSE	
	RELATIONSHIP	AGE

Employment:	DEBTOR	SPOUSE
Occupation		
Name of Employer		
How long employed		
Address of Employer		

Income: (Estimate of average monthly income)		DEBTOR	SPOUSE
Current monthly gross wages, salary,and commissions (pro rate if not paid monthly.)		$	$
Estimate monthly overtime			
SUBTOTAL		$	$
LESS PAYROLL DEDUCTIONS			
a. Payroll taxes and social security			
b. Insurance			
c. Union dues			
d. Other (Specify)			
SUBTOTAL OF PAYROLL DEDUCTIONS		$	$
TOTAL NET MONTHLY TAKE HOME PAY		$	$

Regular income from operation of business or profession or farm
(attach detailed statement)
Income from real property
Interest and dividends
Alimony, maintenance or support payments payable to the debtor for the debtor's
    use or that of dependents listed above.
Social security or other government assistance (Specify)

Pension or retirement income
Other monthly income (Specify)

TOTAL MONTHLY INCOME		$	$

TOTAL COMBINED MONTHLY INCOME $ _____   (Report also on Summary of Schedules)

Describe any increase or decrease of more than 10% in any of the above categories anticipated to occur within the year following the filing of this document:

Form B6 J, Cont. (6-90)   Julius Blumberg, Inc. NYC 10013

In re: _____   Debtor(s)   Case No. _____   (if known)

SCHEDULE J - CURRENT EXPENDITURES OF INDIVIDUAL DEBTOR(S)

Complete this schedule by estimating the average monthly expenses of the debtor and the debtor's family. Pro rate any payments made bi-weekly, quarterly, semi-annually, or annually to show monthly rate.

☐ Check this box if a joint petition is filed and debtor's spouse maintains a separate household. Complete a separate schedule of expenditures labeled "Spouse".

Rent or home mortgage payment (include lot rented for mobile home) .... $ ....

Are real estate taxes included? ☐ Yes ☐ No   Is property insurance included? ☐ Yes ☐ No

Utilities Electricity and heating fuel ....

      Water and sewer ....

      Telephone ....

      Other

Home maintenance (repairs and upkeep) ....

Food ....

Clothing ....

Laundry and dry cleaning ....

Medical and dental expenses ....

Transportation (not including car payments) ....

Recreation, clubs and entertainment, newspapers, magazines, etc. ....

Charitable contributions ....

Insurance (not deducted from wages or included in home mortgage payments)

      Homeowner's or renter's ....

      Life ....

      Health ....

      Auto ....

      Other

Taxes (not deducted from wages or included in home mortgage payments)

(Specify)

Installment payments: (In chapter 12 and 13 cases, do not list payments to be included in the plan)

      Auto ....

      Other

Alimony, maintenance, and support paid to others ....

Payments for support of additional dependents not living at your home ....

Regular expenses from operation of business, profession, or farm (attach detailed statement) ....

Other

TOTAL MONTHLY EXPENSES (Report also on Summary of Schedules) .... $ _____

(FOR CHAPTER 12 AND 13 DEBTORS ONLY)

Provide the information requested below, including whether plan payments are to be made bi-weekly, monthly, annually, or at some other regular interval.

A. Total projected monthly income .... $ _____

B. Total projected monthly expenses ....

C. Excess income (A minus B) .... $ _____

D. Total amount to be paid into plan each .... $ _____

                                   (interval)

Form B6 Cont. (12-03)

BlumbergExcelsior, Inc., Publisher NYC 10013
www.blumberg.com

In re: Debtor(s)   Case No.

           (if known)

DECLARATION CONCERNING DEBTOR'S SCHEDULES

DECLARATION UNDER PENALTY OF PERJURY BY INDIVIDUAL DEBTOR

I declare under penalty of perjury that I have read the foregoing summary and schedules, consisting of _____ sheets,
(Total shown on summary page plus 1.)
and that they are true and correct to the best of my knowledge, information, and belief.

Date   Signature: _____
                                     Debtor

Date   Signature: _____
                   (Joint Debtor, if any) (If joint case, both spouses must sign.)

CERTIFICATION AND SIGNATURE OF NON-ATTORNEY BANKRUPTCY PETITION PREPARER (SEE 11 U.S.C. § 110)

I certify that I am a bankruptcy petition preparer as defined in 11 U.S.C. § 110, that I prepared this document for compensation, and that I have provided the debtor with a copy of this document.

_____   _____
Printed or Typed Name of Bankruptcy Petition Preparer   Social Security No.
                                     (Required by U.S.C. §110(c).)

_____
Address
Names and Social Security numbers of all other individuals who prepared or assisted in preparing this document:

If more than one person prepared this document, attach additional signed sheets conforming to the appropriate Official Form for each person.

X _____   _____
   Signature of Bankruptcy Petition Preparer   Date

A bankruptcy petition preparer's failure to comply with the provisions of title 11 and the Federal Rules of Bankruptcy Procedure may result in fines or imprisonment or both. 11 U.S.C. § 110; 18 U.S.C. § 156

DECLARATION UNDER PENALTY OF PERJURY ON BEHALF OF A CORPORATION OR PARTNERSHIP

I, the _____ (the president or other officer or an authorized agent of the corporation or a member or an authorized agent of the partnership) of the _____ (corporation or partnership) named as debtor in this case, declare under penalty of perjury that I have read the foregoing summary and schedules, consisting of _____ sheets, and that they are true and correct to the best of my knowledge, information, and belief.   (Total shown on summary page plus 1.)

Date   Signature: _____
                   (Print or type name of individual signing on behalf of debtor.)

(An individual signing on behalf of a partnership or corporation must indicate position or relationship to debtor.)

Penalty for making a false statement or concealing property: Fine of up to $500,000 or imprisonment for up to 5 years or both. 18 U.S.C.§152 and 3571

3082   Chapter 13 Plan, 8-91

UNITED STATES BANKRUPTCY COURT   **DISTRICT OF**

In re   Debtor(s)   Case No.   (If Known)

CHAPTER 13 PLAN

(If this form is used by joint debtors wherever the word "debtor" or words referring to debtor are used they shall be read as if in the plural.)

1. The future earnings of the debtor are submitted to the supervision and control of the trustee and the *debtor — debtor's employer* shall pay to the trustee the sum of $ *weekly — bi-weekly — semi-monthly — monthly*   for a period of

2. From the payments so received, the trustee shall make disbursements as follows:
   (*a*) Full payment in deferred cash payments of all claims entitled to priority under 11 U.S.C. §507.

   (*b*) Holders of allowed secured claims shall retain the liens securing such claims and shall be paid as follows:

   (*c*) *Subsequent to — pro rata with* dividends to secured creditors, dividends to unsecured creditors whose claims are duly allowed as follows:

3. The following executory contracts of the debtor are rejected:

        Title to the debtor's property shall revest in the debtor *on confirmation of a plan — upon dismissal of the case after confirmation pursuant to 11 U.S.C. §350.*

Dated: ....

                                   Debtor   *Debtor*

Acceptances may be mailed to..   ....

                                                          Post Office Address

Form 7 Stmt. of Financial
Affairs (12-03)

BlumbergExcelsior, Inc., Publisher NYC 10013
www.blumberg.com

UNITED STATES BANKRUPTCY COURT   DISTRICT OF

In re: Debtor(s)   *Case No.*

STATEMENT OF FINANCIAL AFFAIRS

This statement is to be completed by every debtor. Spouses filing a joint petition may file a single statement on which the information for both spouses is combined. If the case is filed under chapter 12 or chapter 13, a married debtor must furnish information for both spouses whether or not a joint petition is filed, unless the spouses are separated and a joint petition is not filed. An individual debtor engaged in business as a sole proprietor, partner, family farmer, or self-employed professional, should provide the information requested on this statement concerning all such activities as well as the individual's personal affairs.

Questions 1-18 are to be completed by all debtors. Debtors that are or have been in business, as defined below, also must complete Questions 19-25. **If the answer to any question is "None," or the question is not applicable, mark the box labeled "None."** If additional space is needed for the answer to any question, use and attach a separate sheet properly identified with the case name, case number (if known), and the number of the question.

DEFINITIONS

"In business." A debtor is "in business" for the purpose of this form if the debtor is a corporation or partnership. An individual debtor is "in business" for the purpose of this form if the debtor is or has been, within the six years immediately preceding the filing of this bankruptcy case, any of the following: an officer, director, managing executive, or person in control of a corporation; a partner, other than a limited partner, of a partnership; a sole proprietor or self-employed.

"Insider." The term "insider" includes but is not limited to: relatives of the debtor; general partners of the debtor and their relatives; corporations of which the debtor is an officer, director, or person in control; officers, directors, and any person in control of a corporate debtor and their relatives; affiliates of the debtor and insiders of such affiliates; any managing agent of the debtor. 11 U.S.C. §101.

☐ None   **1. Income from Employment or Operation of Business**

State the gross amount of income the debtor has received from employment, trade, or profession, or from operation of the debtor's business from the beginning of this calendar year to the date this case was commenced. State also the gross amounts received during the **two years** immediately preceding this calendar year. (A debtor that maintains, or has maintained, financial records on the basis of a fiscal rather than a calendar year may report fiscal year income. Identify the beginning and ending dates of the debtor's fiscal year.) If a joint petition is filed, state income for each spouse separately. (Married debtors filing under chapter 12 or chapter 13 must state income of both spouses whether or not a joint petition is filed, unless the spouses are separated and a joint petition is not filed.)
Give AMOUNT and SOURCE (If more than one).

☐ None   **2. Income Other than from Employment or Operation of Business**

State the amount of income received by the debtor other than from employment, trade, profession, or operation of the debtor's business during the **two years** immediately preceding the commencement of this case. Give particulars. If a joint petition is filed, state income for each spouse separately. (Married debtors filing under chapter 12 or chapter 13 must state income for each spouse whether or not a joint petition is filed, unless the spouses are separated and a joint petition is not filed.) Give AMOUNT and SOURCE.

3. Payments to Creditors

☐ None   a. List all payments on loans, installment purchases of goods or services, and other debts, aggregating more than $600 to any creditor, made within **90 days** immediately preceding the commencement of this case. (Married debtors filing under chapter 12 or chapter 13 must include payments by either or both spouses whether or not a joint petition is filed, unless the spouses are separated and a joint petition is not filed.)
Give NAME AND ADDRESS OF CREDITOR, DATES OF PAYMENTS, AMOUNT PAID and AMOUNT STILL OWING.

☐ None   b. List all payments made within **one year** immediately preceding the commencement of this case to or for the benefit of creditors who are or were insiders. (Married debtors filing under chapter 12 or chapter 13 must include payments by either or both spouses whether or not a joint petition is filed, unless the spouses are separated and a joint petition is not filed.)
Give NAME AND ADDRESS OF CREDITOR AND RELATIONSHIP TO DEBTOR, DATE OF PAYMENT, AMOUNT PAID and AMOUNT STILL OWING.

4. Suits and Administrative Proceedings, Executions, Garnishments and Attachments

☐ None   a. List all suits and administrative proceedings to which the debtor is or was a party within **one year** immediately preceding the filing of this bankruptcy case. (Married debtors filing under chapter 12 or chapter 13 must include information concerning either or both spouses whether or not a joint petition is filed, unless the spouses are separated and a joint petition is not filed.)
Give CAPTION OF SUIT AND CASE NUMBER, NATURE OF PROCEEDING, COURT OR AGENCY AND LOCATION and STATUS OR DISPOSITION.

☐ None   b. Describe all property that has been attached, garnished, or seized under any legal or equitable process within **one year**

Immediately preceding the commencement of this case. (Married debtors filing under chapter 12 or chapter 13 must include information concerning property of either or both spouses whether or not a joint petition is filed, unless the spouses are separated and a joint petition is not filed.)

Give NAME AND ADDRESS OF PERSON FOR WHOSE BENEFIT PROPERTY WAS SEIZED, DATE OF SEIZURE and DESCRIPTION AND VALUE OF PROPERTY.

☐ None   **5. Repossessions, Foreclosures, and Returns**

List all property that has been repossessed by a creditor, sold at a foreclosure sale, transferred through a deed in lieu of foreclosure or returned to the seller, within one year immediately preceding the commencement of this case. (Married debtors filing under chapter 12 or chapter 13 must include information concerning property of either or both spouses whether or not a joint petition is filed, unless the spouses are separated and a joint petition is not filed.)

Give NAME AND ADDRESS OF CREDITOR OR SELLER, DATE OF REPOSSESSION, FORECLOSURE SALE, TRANSFER OR RETURN and DESCRIPTION AND VALUE OF PROPERTY.

6.Assignments and Receiverships

☐ None   a. Describe any assignment of property for the benefit of creditors made within 120 days immediately preceding the commencement of this case. (Married debtors filing under chapter 12 or chapter 13 must include any assignment by either or both spouses whether or not a join petition is filed, unless the spouses are separated and a joint petition is not filed.)

Give NAME AND ADDRESS OF ASSIGNEE, DATE OF ASSIGNMENT and TERMS OF ASSIGNMENT OR SETTLEMENT.

☐   None   b. List all property which has been in the hands of a custodian, receiver, or court-appointed official within one year immediately preceding the commencement of this case. (Married debtors filing under chapter 12 or chapter 13 must include information concerning property of either or both spouses whether or not a joint petition is filed, unless the spouses are separated and a joint petition is not filed.)

Give NAME AND ADDRESS OF CUSTODIAN, NAME AND LOCATION OF COURT, CASE TITLE & NUMBER, DATE OF ORDER and DESCRIPTION AND VALUE OF PROPERTY.

☐   None   **7. Gifts**

List all gifts or charitable contributions made within one year immediately preceding the commencement of this case except ordinary and usual gifts to family members aggregating less than the $200 in value per individual family member and charitable contributions aggregating less than $100 per recipient. (Married debtors filing under chapter 12 or chapter 13 must include gifts or contributions by either or both spouses whether or not a joint petition is filed, unless the spouses are separated and a joint petition is not filed.)

Give NAME AND ADDRESS OF PERSON OR ORGANIZATION, RELATIONSHIP TO DEBTOR, IF ANY, DATE OF GIFT, and DESCRIPTION AND VALUE OF GIFT.

☐   None   **8. Losses**

List all losses from fire, theft, other casualty or gambling within one year immediately preceding the commencement of this case or since the commencement of this case. (Married debtors filing under chapter 12 or chapter 13 must include losses by either or both spouses whether or not a joint petition is filed, unless the spouses are separated and a joint petition is not filed.)

Give DESCRIPTION AND VALUE OF PROPERTY, DESCRIPTION OF CIRCUMSTANCES AND, IF LOSS WAS COVERED IN WHOLE OR IN PART BY INSURANCE, GIVE PARTICULARS and DATE OF LOSS.

☐   None   **9. Payments Related to Debt Counseling or Bankruptcy**

List all payments made or property transferred by or on behalf of the debtor to any persons, including attorneys, for consultation concerning debt consolidation, relief under the bankruptcy law or preparation of a petition in bankruptcy within one year immediately preceding the commencement of this case.

Give NAME AND ADDRESS OF PAYEE, DATE OF PAYMENT, NAME OF PAYER IF OTHER THAN DEBTOR and AMOUNT OF MONEY OR DESCRIPTION AND VALUE OF PROPERTY.

☐   None   **10. Other Transfers**

List all other property, other than property transferred in the ordinary course of the business or financial affairs of the debtor, transferred either absolutely or as security within one year immediately preceding the commencement of this case. (Married debtors filing under chapter 12 or chapter 13 must include transfers by either or both spouses whether or not a joint petition is file, unless the spouses are separated and a joint petition is not filed.)

Give NAME AND ADDRESS OF TRANSFEREE, RELATIONSHIP TO DEBTOR, DATE, and DESCRIBE PROPERTY TRANSFERRED AND VALUE RECEIVED.

☐ None **11. Closed Financial Accounts**

List all financial accounts and instruments held in the name of the debtor or for the benefit of the debtor which were closed, sold, or otherwise transferred within one year immediately preceding the commencement of this case. Include checking, savings, or other financial accounts, certificates of deposit, or other instruments; shares and share accounts held in banks, credit unions, pension funds, cooperatives, associations, brokerage houses and other financial institutions. (Married debtors filing under chapter 12 or chapter 13 must include information concerning accounts or instruments held by or for either or both spouses whether or not a joint petition is filed, unless the spouses are separated and a joint petition is not filed.)

Give NAME AND ADDRESS OF INSTITUTION, TYPE OF ACCOUNT, LAST FOUR DIGITS OF ACCOUNT NUMBER AND AMOUNT OF FINAL BALANCE and AMOUNT AND DATE OF SALE OR CLOSING.

☐ None **12. Safe Deposit Boxes**

List each safe deposit or other box or depository in which the debtor has or had securities, cash, or other valuables within one year immediately preceding the commencement of this case. (Married debtors filing under chapter 12 or chapter 13 must include depositories of either or both spouses whether or not a joint petition is filed, unless the spouses are separated and a joint petition is not filed.)

Give NAME AND ADDRESS OF BANK OR OTHER DEPOSITORY, NAMES AND ADDRESSES OF THOSE WITH ACCESS TO BOX OR DEPOSITORY, DESCRIPTION OF CONTENTS and DATE OF TRANSFER OR SURRENDER, IF ANY.

☐ None **13. Setoffs**

List all setoffs made by any creditor, including a bank, against a debt or deposit of the debtor within 90 days preceding the commencement of this case. (Married debtors filing under chapter 12 or chapter 13 must include information concerning either or both spouses whether or not a joint petition is filed, unless the spouses are separated and a joint petition is not filed.)

Give NAME AND ADDRESS OR CREDITOR, DATE OF SETOFF and AMOUNT OF SETOFF.

☐ None **14. Property Held for Another Person**

List all property owned by another person that the debtor holds or controls.

Give NAME AND ADDRESS OF OWNER, DESCRIPTION AND VALUE OF PROPERTY and LOCATION OF PROPERTY.

☐ None **15. Prior Address of Debtor**

If the debtor has moved within the two years immediately preceding the commencement of this case, list all premises which the debtor occupied during that period and vacated prior to the commencement of this case. If a joint petition is filed, report also any separate address of either spouse.

Give ADDRESS, NAME USED and DATES OF OCCUPANCY.

☐ None **16. Spouses and Former Spouses**

If the debtor resides or resided in a community property state, commonwealth, or territory (including Alaska, Arizona, California, Idaho, Louisiana, Nevada, New Mexico, Puerto Rico, Texas, Washington, or Wisconsin) within the six-year period immediately preceding the commencement of the case, identify the name of the debtor's spouse and of any former spouse who resides or resided with the debtor in the community property state.

Give NAME.

☐ None **17. Environmental Information**

For the purpose of this question, the following definitions apply: "Environmental Law" means any federal, state, or local statute or regulation regulating pollution, contamination, releases of hazardous or toxic substances, wastes or material into the air, land, soil, surface water, groundwater, or other medium, including, but not limited to, statutes or regulations regulating the cleanup of these substances, wastes, or material. "Site" means any location, facility, or property as defined under any Environmental Law, whether or not presently or formerly owned or operated by the debtor, including, but not limited to, disposal sites. "Hazardous Material" means anything defined as a hazardous waste, hazardous substance, toxic substance, hazardous material, pollutant, or contaminant or similar term under an Environmental Law.

☐ None **a.** List the name and address of every site for which the debtor has received notice in writing by a governmental unit that it may be liable or potentially liable under or in violation of an Environmental law. Indicate the governmental unit, the date of the notice, and, if known, the Environmental Law:

Give SITE NAME AND ADDRESS, NAME AND ADDRESS OF GOVERNMENTAL UNIT, DATE OF NOTICE and ENVIRONMENTAL LAW.

☐ None **b.** List the name and address of every site for which the debtor has provided notice to a governmental unit of a release of Hazardous Material. Indicate the governmental unit to which the notice was sent and the date of the notice.

Give SITE NAME AND ADDRESS, NAME AND ADDRESS OF GOVERNMENTAL UNIT, DATE OF NOTICE and ENVIRONMENTAL LAW.

☐ None **c.** List all judicial or administrative proceedings, including settlements or orders, under any Environmental Law with respect to which the debtor is or was a party. Indicate the name and address of the governmental unit that is or was a party to the proceeding, and the docket number.

Give NAME AND ADDRESS OF GOVERNMENTAL UNIT, DOCKET NUMBER and STATUS OR DISPOSITION.

18. Nature, Location and Name of Business

☐ None **a.** If the debtor is an individual, list the names, addresses, taxpayer identification numbers, nature of the businesses and beginning and ending dates of all businesses in which the debtor was an officer, director, partner, or managing executive of a corporation, partnership, sole proprietorship or was a self-employed

(continues on next page)

professional within the **six years** immediately preceding the commencement of this case, or in which the debtor owned 5 percent or more of the voting or equity securities within the **six years** immediately preceding the commencement of this case.

If the debtor is a partnership, list the names and addresses of all businesses in which the debtor was a partner or owned 5 percent or more of the voting securities, within the **six years** immediately preceding the commencement of this case.

If the debtor is a corporation, list the names and addresses of all businesses in which the debtor was a partner or owned 5 percent or more of the voting securities within the **six years** immediately preceding the commencement of this case.

Give NAME, TAXPAYER I.D. NUMBER, ADDRESS, NATURE OF BUSINESS and BEGINNING AND ENDING DATES.

☐ None   b. Identify any business listed in response to subdivision a., above, that is "single asset real estate" as defined in 11 U.S.C. § 101.

Give NAME and ADDRESS.

The following questions are to be completed as shown below.*

19. Books, Records, and Financial Statements

☐ None   a. List all bookkeepers and accountants who within the **two years** immediately preceding the filing of this bankruptcy case kept or supervised the keeping of books of account and records of the debtor.

Give NAME AND ADDRESS and DATES SERVICE RENDERED.

☐ None   b. List all firms or individuals who within the **two years** immediately preceding the filing of this bankruptcy case have audited the books of account and records, or prepared a financial statement of the debtor.

Give NAME, ADDRESS and DATES SERVICES RENDERED.

☐ None   c. List all firms or individuals who at the time of the commencement of this case were in possession of the books of account and records of the debtor. If any of the books of account and records are not available, explain.

Give NAME AND ADDRESS and DATE ISSUED.

☐ None   d. List all financial institutions, creditors and other parties, including mercantile and trade agencies, to whom a financial statement was issued within the **two years** immediately preceding the commencement of this case by the debtor.

Give NAME AND ADDRESS and DATE ISSUED.

20. Inventories

☐ None   a. List the dates of the last two inventories taken of your property, the name of the person who supervised the taking of each inventory, and the dollar amount and basis of each inventory.

Give DATE OF INVENTORY, INVENTORY, SUPERVISOR and DOLLAR AMOUNT OF INVENTORY (specify cost, market or other basis).

☐ None   b. List the name and address of the person having possession of the records of each of the two inventories reported in a., above.

Give DATE OF INVENTORY and NAME AND ADDRESSES OF CUSTODIAN OF INVENTORY RECORDS.

21. Current Partners, Officers, Directors and Shareholders

☐ None   a. If the debtor is a partnership, list the nature and percentage of partnership interest of each member of the partnership.

Give NAME AND ADDRESS, NATURE OR INTEREST and PERCENTAGE OF THE INTEREST.

☐ None   b. If the debtor is a corporation, list all officers and directors of the corporation, and each stockholder who directly or indirectly owns, controls, or holds 5 percent or more of the voting securities of the corporation.

Give NAME AND ADDRESS, TITLE and NATURE AND PERCENTAGE OF STOCK OWNERSHIP.

22. Former Partners, Officers, Directors and Shareholders

☐ None   a. If the debtor is a partnership, list each member who withdrew from the partnership within **one year** immediately preceding the commencement of this case.

Give NAME, ADDRESS and DATE OF WITHDRAWAL.

☐ None   b. If the debtor is a corporation, list all officers or directors whose relationship with the corporation terminated within **one year** immediately preceding the commencement of the case.

Give NAME AND ADDRESS, TITLE and DATE OF TERMINATION.

23. Withdrawals from a Partnership or Distributions by a Corporation

☐ None If the debtor is a partnership or corporation, list all withdrawals or distributions credited or given to an insider, including compensation in any form, bonuses, loans, stock redemption, options exercised and any other perquisite during **one year** immediately preceding the commencement of this case.

Give NAME & ADDRESS OF RECIPIENT, RELATIONSHIP TO DEBTOR, DATE AND PURPOSE OR WITHDRAWAL, and AMOUNT OF MONEY OR DESCRIPTION AND VALUE OF PROPERTY.

24. Tax Consolidation Group.

☐ If the debtor is a corporation, list the name and federal taxpayer identification number of the parent corporation of any consolidated group for tax purposes of which the debtor has been a member at any time within the **six-year period** immediately preceding the commencement of the case.

Give NAME OF PARENT CORPORATION and TAXPAYER IDENTIFICATION NUMBER.

25. Pension Funds.

☐ If the debtor is not an individual, list the name and federal taxpayer identification number of any fund to which the debtor, as an employer, has been responsible for contributing at any time within the **six-year period** immediately preceding the commencement of the case.

Give NAME OF PENSION FUND and TAXPAYER IDENTIFICATION NUMBER.

_____continuation sheets attached

Complete unsworn declaration on page 3076-5

* The following questions are to be completed by every debtor that is a corporation or partnership and by any individual debtor who is or has been, within the **six years** immediately preceding the commencement of this case, any of the following: an officer, director, managing executive, or owner of more than 5 percent of the voting securities or a corporation; a partner, other than a limited partner, of a partnership; a sole proprietor or otherwise self-employed. (An individual or joint debtor should complete this portion of the statement only if the debtor is or has been in business, as defined above, within the six years immediately preceding the commencement of this case. A debtor who has not been in business within those six years should go directly to the signature page.)

[If completed by an individual or individual and spouse]

I declare under penalty of perjury that I have read the answers contained in the foregoing statement of financial affairs and any attachments thereto and that they are true and correct.

Date —————————————— Signature ————————————————————————
of Debtor

Date —————————————— Signature ————————————————————————
of Joint Debtor
(if any)

....

[If completed on behalf of a partnership or corporation]

I, declare under penalty of perjury that I have read the answers contained in the foregoing statement of financial affairs and any attachments thereto and that they are true and correct to the best of my knowledge, information and belief.

Date —————————— Signature ————————————————————

————————————————————
Print Name and Title

[An individual signing on behalf of a partnership or corporation must indicate position or relationship to debtor.]

———— continuation sheets attached.

Penalty for making a false statement: Fine of up to $500,000 or imprisonment for up to 5 years, or both. 18 U.S.C. §§152 and 3571.

....

CERTIFICATION AND SIGNATURE OF NON-ATTORNEY BANKRUPTCY PETITION PREPARER (See 11 U.S.C. § 110)

I certify that I am a bankruptcy petition preparer as defined in 11 U.S.C. § 110, that I prepared this document for compensation, and that I have provided the debtor with a copy of this document.

—————————————————————————
Printed or Typed Name of Bankruptcy Petition Preparer

—————————————————
Social Security No.
(Required by 11 U.S.C. §110(c).)

—————————————————————
Address

Names and Social Security numbers of all other individuals who prepared or assisted in preparing this document: If more than one person prepared this document, attach additional signed sheets conforming to the appropriate Official Form for each person.

X—————————————————————
Signature of Bankruptcy Petition Preparer

——————————————
Date

A bankruptcy petition preparer's failure to comply with the provisions of title II and the Federal Rules of Bankruptcy Procedure may result in fines or imprisonment or both. 18 U.S.C. § 156.

3085   Statement of compensation: Rule 2016(b). 8-91

UNITED STATES BANKRUPTCY COURT   **DISTRICT OF**

In re   Debtor(s)   Case No.   (If Known)

STATEMENT
Pursuant to Rule 2016(b)

The undersigned, pursuant to Rule 2016(b) Bankruptcy Rules, states that:

(1) The undersigned is the attorney for the debtor(s) in this case.

(2) The compensation paid or agreed to be paid by the debtor(s) to the undersigned is:

    (a) for legal services rendered or to be rendered in contemplation of and in connection with this case $ ....

    (b) prior to filing this statement, debtor(s) have paid $ ....

    (c) the unpaid balance due and payable is $ ....

(3) $ _____ of the filing fee in this case has been paid.

(4) The services rendered or to be rendered include the following:

    (a) analysis of the financial situation, and rendering advice and assistance to the debtor(s) in determining whether to file a petition under title 11 of the United States Code.

    (b) preparation and filing of the petition, schedules, statement of affairs and other documents required by the court.

    (c) representation of the debtor(s) at the meeting of creditors.

(5) The source of payments made by the debtor(s) to the undersigned was from earnings, wages and compensation for services performed, and

(6) The source of payments to be made by the debtor(s) to the undersigned for the unpaid balance remaining, if any, will be from earnings, wages and compensation for services performed, and

(7) The undersigned has received no transfer, assignment or pledge of property execept the following for the value stated:

(8) The undersigned has not shared or agreed to share with any other entity, other than with members of undersigned's law firm, any compensation paid or to be paid except as follows:

Dated: Respectfully submitted, ...*Attorney for Petitioner*

Attorney's name and address ....

C

Federal Bankruptcy Exemptions

Bankruptcy Code Section 522(d)

1. The debtor's aggregate interest, not to exceed $18,450 in value, in real property or personal property that the debtor or a dependent of the debtor uses as a residence, in a cooperative that owns property that the debtor or a dependent of the debtor uses as a residence, or in a burial plot for the debtor or a dependent of the debtor.

2. The debtor's interest, not to exceed $2,950 in value, in one motor vehicle. A couple filing can each have a car with $2,950 equity.

3. The debtor's interest, not to exceed $475 in value in any particular item or $9,850 in aggregate value, in household furnishings, household goods, wearing apparel, appliances, books, animals, crops, or musical instruments, that are held primarily for the personal, family, or household use of the debtor or a dependent of the debtor.

4. The debtor's aggregate interest, not to exceed $1,225 in value, in jewelry held primarily for the personal, family, or household use of the debtor or a dependent of the debtor.

5. The debtor's aggregate interest in any property, not to exceed in value $975 plus up to $9,250 of any unused amount of the exemption provided under paragraph (1) of this subsection.

6. The debtor's aggregate interest, not to exceed $1,850 in value, in any implements, professional books, or tools of the trade of the debtor or the trade of a dependent of the debtor.

7. Any unmatured life insurance contract owned by the debtor, other than a credit life insurance contract.

8. The debtor's aggregate interest, not to exceed in value $9,850 less any amount of property of the estate transferred in the manner specified in section 542(d) of this title, in any accrued dividend or interest under, or loan value of, any unmatured life insurance contract owned by the debtor under which the insured is the debtor or an individual of whom the debtor is a dependent.

9. Professionally prescribed health aids for the debtor or a dependent of the debtor.

10. The debtor's right to receive:
   (A) a Social Security benefit, unemployment compensation, or a local public assistance benefit;
   (B) a veterans' benefit;
   (C) a disability, illness, or unemployment benefit;
   (D) alimony, support, or separate maintenance, to the extent reasonably necessary for the support of the debtor and any dependent of the debtor;
   (E) a payment under a stock bonus, pension, profit sharing, annuity, or similar plan or contract on account of illness, disability, death, age, or length of service, to the extent reasonably necessary for the support of the debtor and any dependent of the debtor, unless
      (i) such plan or contract was established by or under the auspices of an insider that employed the debtor at the time the debtor's rights under such plan or contract arose;
      (ii) such payment is on account of age or length of service; and
      (iii) such plan or contract does not qualify under section 401(a), 403(a), 403(b), 408, or 409 of the Internal Revenue Code of 1954 [26 U.S.C. 401(a), 403(a), 403(b), 408, or 409].

11. The debtor's right to receive, or property that is traceable to:
   (A) an award under a crime victim's reparation law;
   (B) a payment on account of the wrongful death of an individual of whom the debtor was a dependent, to the extent reasonably necessary for the support of the debtor and any dependent of the debtor;
   (C) a payment under a life insurance contract that insured the life of an individual of whom the debtor was a dependent on the date of such individual's death, to the extent reasonably necessary for the support of the debtor and any dependent of the debtor;
   (D) a payment, not to exceed $18,450, on account of personal bodily injury, not including pain and suffering or compensation for actual pecuniary loss, of the debtor or an individual of whom the debtor is a dependent; or
   (E) a payment in compensation of loss of future earnings of the debtor or an individual of whom the debtor is or was a dependent, to the extent reasonably necessary for the support of the debtor and any dependent of the debtor.

D

State Bankruptcy Exemptions

Alabama

The homestead exemption has a $5,000 limitation of value.

Personal property may be exempted to a value of $3,000. Also, all family portraits or pictures and all family books.

(Alabama Code Title 6 Sec. 10-2; Sec. 10-5; Sec. 10-6; Sec. 10-7. Alabama Constitution, Article X Sec. 204)

Alaska

The homestead exemption has a $64,800 limitation of value.

Professional books and tools of trade up to an aggregate value of $3,360; wearing apparel, household goods, books, musical instruments, family heirlooms, and portraits up to an aggregate value of $3,600; jewelry to a value of $1,200; pets to a value of $1,200; one motor vehicle to a value of $3,600 (if its full value does not exceed $24,000); a burial plot; necessary health aids. Exemptions may also include retirement plan benefits, unmatured life insurance, and annuity contracts with a loan value of less than $12,000.

(Alaska Statutes Sec. 9.38.010; Sec. 9.30.020; Sec. 9.30.15; Sec. 9.38.030)

Arizona

The homestead exemption has a $100,000 limitation of value.

Personal property that can be exempted to a value of $4,000 includes: household furniture, furnishing, and appliances; food, fuel, and provisions for debtor's use or use of debtor's family for six months; wearing apparel to a value of $500; musical instruments to a value of $250; pets, horses, cattle, and poultry livestock to a value of $500; motor vehicle to a value of $5,000, or $10,000 if disabled; books and personal documents to a value of $250; one watch to a value of $100; life insurance proceeds to a value of $20,000; $150 deposited in one bank account; farm machinery, feed, grain, seed, and animals up to $2,500; retirement accounts.

(Arizona Revised Statutes Sec. 33-1101; Sec. 33-1123; Sec. 33-1124; Sec. 33-1125; Sec. 33-1126; Sec. 33-1130; Sec. 33-1131)

Arkansas

The homestead exemption is limited to one acre of land with improvements up to a value of $2,500. If the homestead is located outside the city limits, exemption is for no more than 160 acres of land; if inside the city limits, the homestead can be on no more than one acre.

A married debtor may claim as exempt certain personal property worth up to $200, or up to $500 if married. Also exempt, tools of the trade and professional library up to $750; a motor vehicle to a value of $1,200; life and disability insurance up to $1,000, IRA contributions made one year prior to bankruptcy up to $20,000.

(Arkansas Statutes Sec. 30-207; Sec. 36-211. Arkansas Constitution Art. 9 Sec. 3-5; Sec. 1, 2)

California

State has two exemptions systems. Debtors must chose one or the other.

System #1

Real or personal property including homestead is up to a value of $50,000 if single and not disabled; $75,000 for families; $125,000 if age 65 or older or disabled; $100,000 if 55 or older, single and earn under $15,000 or married and earn under $20,000 and creditors are forcing sale of homestead.

Also, appliances, furnishings, clothing, and needed food; bank deposits from Social Security Administration up to $2,425 (spouses up to $3,650); burial plot, health aids, jewelry, heirlooms, and art to $6,075 total; motor vehicles to $2,300; pensions from public service; property of business partnership; disability or health benefits; unmatured life insurance benefits needed for support; public benefits including financial aid to students, unemployment benefits, public assistance payments, workers' compensation; and tools of trade including a motor vehicle up to $6,075.

(California Code of Civil Procedure Sec. 703.080; Sec. 704.010; Sec. 704.020; Sec. 704.030; Sec. 704.040; Sec. 704.050; Sec. 704.060; Sec. 704.070; Sec. 704.080; Sec. 704.090; Sec. 704.113; Sec. 704.140; Sec. 704.150; Sec. 704.200; Sec. 704.730; Sec. 706.050)

System #2

Homestead exemption is up to $17,425 in value.

Personal property exemptions may include: health or disability benefits; alimony, child support for support; ERISA-qualified pension benefits; animals, crops, appliances, furnishings, household goods, books, musical instruments, and clothing to $450/item; burial plot to $17,425; health aids; jewelry to $1,150; motor vehicle to $2,775.

(California Code of Civil Procedure Sec. 703.140)

Colorado

Limit is $45,000 in home equity or sales proceeds if sold within the year prior to filing for bankruptcy.

Personal property exemptions include: wearing apparel of the debtor and each dependent to a value of $1,500; jewelry and watches to a value of $1,000; books and family pictures to a value of $1,500; one burial plot per family member; household goods to a value of $3,000; fuel and provisions to a value of $600; motor vehicle to a value of $3,000 ($6,000 if elderly or disabled); professional library up to $3,000; tools of the trade up to $10,000; any amount in an IRS 401(k) or pension plan and right to receive such benefits as Social Security, unemployment, veterans' benefits, public assistance, and pensions—regardless of the amount.

(Colorado Revised Statutes Sec. 13-54-102; Sec. 13-54-104; Sec. 38-41-201; Sec. 38-41-201.6)

Connecticut

The homestead exemption is $75,000 less any liens on the homestead.

Personal property exemptions include: necessary apparel, food, bedding, household appliances, and furniture; burial plot; motor vehicle to a value of $1,500 less the value of all liens; wedding and engagement rings; residential security and utility deposits; public assistance payments, health and disability insurance payments. Exemptions may also be claimed for books, tools, and farm animals necessary for the debtor's occupation.

(Connecticut General Statutes Annotated Sec. 52-352b; Sec. 83-581)

Delaware

No homestead exemption. However, real property held by a married couple may be exempt against debts owed by one spouse.

All debtors may exempt $5,000 in any personal property, schoolbooks, family bible, pianos, organs, family pictures, family library, church pew, burial place, sewing machines, jewelry, and wearing apparel. Also, business partnership property, and pensions and retirement benefits, various pension systems; insurance. Tools of trade necessary for a debtor's business or trade are exempt; $75 in New Castle and Sussex Counties and $50 in Kent County.

(Delaware Code Annotated Title 10 Sec. 4902; Sec. 4903; Sec. 4913)

District of Columbia

The District of Columbia has no homestead law.

Personal property that may be exempted includes: wearing apparel to a value of $300 per person; household furnishings, beds, bedding, stove, radio, sewing machine, cooking utensils to a value of $425; motor vehicle to a value of $2,575 if used mainly for debtor's business; provisions for three months support; fuel for three months; tools of trade and implements for debtor's trade or business up to $1,625; and family pictures and library to a value of $400; certain insurance, public assistance, and unemployment.

(District of Columbia Code Sec. 15-501; Sec. 15-503)

Florida

In general, debtor may exempt homestead. Limited to 1/2 acre within a municipality or 160 acres elsewhere.

Certain personal property may be exempt, including certain portion of wages earned, life insurance policies and annuities, unemployment compensation benefits, retirement funds, disability benefits, health aids, and a motor vehicle up to $1,000 in value.

(Florida Statutes Annotated Sec. 222.05; Sec. 222-11. Florida Constitution Article 10 Sec. 4)

Georgia

The homestead exemption has a $5,000 limit of value.

Personal property that may be exempted includes: motor vehicles with an aggregate value of $3,500; household goods and furnishings, wearing apparel, appliances, books, musical instruments, animals, and crops to a value of $200 per item (total value $5,000); jewelry to a value of $500; Social Security benefits, unemployment benefits, local public assistance, alimony, support or maintenance, professional books, and tools of the trade up to an aggregate value of $1,500.

(Georgia Code Annotated Sec. 44-13-100)

Hawaii

The homestead exemption has a value limitation of $30,000 for a head of household or debtor age 65 or older, and $20,000 for all others.

Personal property that may be exempted includes: one motor vehicle to a value of $2,575; household furnishings and appliances; wearing apparel and books; jewelry and watches to a value of $1,000; burial plot. Exemptions may be taken for tools of trade, all necessary books, furnishings, clothing, appliances, and household furnishings. Also annuities, insurance, disability benefits, pensions, and retirement benefits.

(Hawaii Revised Statutes Sec. 651-92; Sec. 651-121)

Idaho

The homestead exemption has a value limitation of $50,000.

Personal property exemptions include: furnishings and appliances, burial plot, health aids, wearing apparel, books, musical instruments, pets, one firearm up to $500 in value, family portraits, and certain heirlooms to a value of $500 per item and a total value of $5,000 per household; jewelry to a value of $1,000; a motor vehicle to a value of $3,000; a burial plot; professional books, implements, and tools of trade to a value of $1,000; Social Security benefits, veterans' benefits, unemployment compensation, public assistance.

(Idaho Code Sec. 11-207; Sec. 11-603; Sec. 11-604; Sec. 11-605; Sec. 55-1201)

Illinois

The homestead exemption has a $7,500 limit of value.

Personal property that may be exempted includes: wearing apparel, schoolbooks, bible, and family pictures up to $2,000; motor vehicle to a value of $1,200; professionally prescribed health aids, personal injury awards to a value of $7,500; and Social Security benefits, veterans' benefits, disability payments, retirement plan proceeds, life insurance proceeds, alimony.

(Illinois Code of Civil Procedure Sec. 12-803; Sec. 12-901; Sec. 12-1001)

Indiana

The homestead exemption has a $7,500 limit of value.

Personal property that may be exempted includes: tangible property to a value of $4,000 and intangible property to a value of $100; professionally prescribed health aids; interest in a retirement plan; medical savings account.

(Indiana Statutes Annotated Sec. 24-4.5-5-105; Sec. 34-2-28-1)

Iowa

A homestead is generally exempt from judicial sale.

Personal property exemptions include: wearing apparel to a value of $1,000; library, bibles, portraits, pictures, and paintings to a value of $200 per item, $1,000 total; household furniture and furnishings to a value of $2,000 total; shotgun and rifle; farm implements, livestock, and feed to a value of $10,000; musical instruments, auto, $1,000 in accrued wages, tax refund to a value of $5,000, cash on hand up to $100; disability insurance to a value of $15,000; life insurance proceeds up to $10,000.

(Iowa Code Annotated Sec. 561.2; Sec. 627.6; Sec. 642.21)

Kansas

The homestead exemption applies to up to 160 acres of farming land or one acre within a town or city.

Personal property exemptions include: personal property necessary to sustain the basic needs of the debtor and family; motor vehicle not to exceed $20,000 in value; jewelry up to $1,000; tools of the trade equipment, books, furniture, feed, and stock up to $7,500.

(Kansas Statutes Annotated Sec. 60-2301; Sec. 60-2304)

Kentucky

The homestead exemption has a $5,000 limitation of value.

Personal property exemptions include: household furnishings, clothing, and jewelry to a value of $3,000; motor vehicle to a value of $2,500; other property to a value of $1,000; tools of trade up to $300; tools of trade for certain professionals up to $1,000; farmer's tools, equipment, and livestock to a value of $3,000; certain portion of personal injury recoveries, pension, and retirement benefits.

(Kentucky Revised Statutes Sec. 427.010; Sec. 427.030; Sec. 427.040; Sec. 427.060; Sec. 427.150; Sec. 427.160)

Louisiana

The homestead limitation of value is $25,000. Homestead land cannot exceed 200 acres.

Personal property exemptions include: clothing and certain prescribed household items, musical instruments, domestic stock and household pets; wedding or engagement rings up to a value of $5,000; certain trade or professional tools; pensions; payments under an annuity plan; individual retirement accounts; Keoghs; simplified employee pension plans (SEPS).

(Louisiana Revised Statutes Sec. 13:3881; Sec. 20:1)

Maine

The homestead limitation of value is $70,000 for a married couple and $35,000 for a single debtor. If debtor or spouse is disabled or 60 years or older, aggregate exempt value may be $140,000 for a married couple or $70,000 for a single debtor.

Personal property exemptions include: a motor vehicle to a value of $5,000; various household furnishings and furniture, wearing apparel, books, and musical instruments to a value of $200 per item; jewelry to a value of $750; health aids; tools of the trade to an aggregate value of $5,000; personal injury payments up to $12,500; pensions; disability payments; life insurance dividends or interest up to $4,000.

(Maine Revised Statutes Annotated Title 14 Sec. 4422)

Maryland

The homestead limitation has a value of $2,500.

Personal property exemptions include: wearing apparel, books, tools, instruments, or appliances needed for the practice of any trade or profession up to a value of $2,500; debtor's interest in household furnishings and goods, appliances, wearing apparel, books, pets, and other household items up to $500; cash or equivalent up to $3,000; professionally prescribed health aids; money payable in event of sickness, accident, injury, or death; interest in a qualified retirement plan.

(Maryland Annotated Code of Commercial Law Sec. 15-601.1; Maryland Annotated Code of Cts. and Jud. Proc. Sec. 11-504)

Massachusetts

The homestead limitation is up to $300,000.

Personal property exemptions include: necessary wearing apparel, beds and bedding; one heating unit and up to $75 a month for fuel, heat, water, and light; household furniture to a value of $3,000; sewing machine to a value of $200; schoolbooks, library, and bibles to a value of $200; bank account up to $500; cash, savings, or other deposits in a banking institution up to $125; tools of trade up to $500; public assistance payments; an automobile to a value of $700; materials and stock necessary for carrying out debtor's trade or profession to a value of $500; tackle and nets used for fishing to a value of $500.

(Massachusetts General Laws Annotated Chap. 188 Sec. 1; Chap. 235 Sec. 34; Chap. 246 Sec. 28A)

Michigan

The homestead limitation is up to $3,500.

Personal property exemptions include: all family pictures, wearing apparel of every person or family, and fuel for comfortable subsistence of each householder and his or her family for six months; all household goods, furniture, utensils, books, and appliances to a value of $1,000; a church pew; a burial plot; tools of trade up to $1,000; disability benefits; individual retirement account; qualified pensions, profit sharing stock bonus, or other plan.

(Michigan Compiled Laws Annotated Sec. 600.6023)

Minnesota

The homestead limitation is up to $200,000, but if used for agricultural purposes, the limit is $500,000.

Personal property exemptions include: bible, library, musical instruments, church pew, and burial plot; wearing apparel; one watch; utensils and foodstuffs of debtor and family; household furniture, household appliances, phonographs, radios, and televisions up to $8,100 in value; motor vehicle to a value of $3,600; personal injury recoveries. Also exempt are: farm machines and implements, livestock, farm produce, and standing crops to a value of $13,000; tools of trade, implements, machines, instruments, office furniture, stock in trade, and library necessary for debtor's trade or profession to a value of $9,000; retirement plans up to $54,000; employee benefits up to $54,000; unmatured life insurance up to $7,200.

(Minnesota Statutes Annotated Sec. 550.37)

Mississippi

The homestead exemption limitations are 160 acres in size and $75,000 in value.

Personal property exemptions include: $10,000 in any tangible personal property including household goods, wearing apparel, motor vehicles, trade implements, health aids and/or cash; life insurance up to $50,000; personal injury judgments up to $10,000; homeowners insurance up to $75,000; IRAs and Keoghs; Social Security benefits; public assistance benefits; unemployment benefits.

(Mississippi Code Sec. 85-3-1; Sec. 85-3-4; Sec. 85-3-17; Sec. 85-3-21)

Missouri

The homestead exemption is real property to a value of $15,000.

Personal property exemptions include: wearing apparel, household furnishings and goods, appliances, books, musical instruments, animals, and crops to an aggregate value of $1,000; jewelry to a value of $500; motor vehicle to a value of $1,000; any implements, professional books, or tools of the trade not to exceed $2,000 in aggregate; Social Security payments; veterans' benefits; unemployment benefits.

(Annotated Missouri Statutes Sec. 513.430; Sec. 513.440; Sec. 513.475; Sec. 525.030)

Montana

Homestead exemption limitations are no more than $100,000 for an individual and no more than $200,000 for a married couple.

Personal property exemptions for head of family or person over 60 include: wearing apparel, household furnishings and goods, appliances, books, jewelry, firearms and other sporting goods, animals, feed, crops, and musical instruments up to $600 in any item and not exceeding $4,500 in aggregate; professionally prescribed health aids; tools of the trade, implements, and professional books up to $3,000 in aggregate value; one motor vehicle up to $2,500; Social Security benefits; veterans' benefits; disability payments.

(Montana Code Annotated Sec. 25-13-611; Sec. 25-13-612; Sec. 25-13-613; Sec. 25-13-614; Sec. 25-13-617; Sec. 70-32-104)

Nebraska

The homestead exemption for a head of family is limited to no more than $12,500.

Personal property exemptions include: the immediate personal possessions of the debtor and his or her family; wearing apparel, household furniture, and furnishings to a total fair market value of $1,500; fuel and provisions for six months; books or tools of trade or automobile up to an aggregate value of $2,400; tools of trade up to $2,400; insurance annuity contracts and insurance policy proceeds up to $10,000.

(Revised Statutes of Nebraska Sec. 12-517; Sec. 25-1552; Sec. 25-1556; Sec. 25-1558; Sec. 40-101)

Nevada

The homestead exemption is up to $200,000.

Personal property exemptions include: one vehicle to a value of $15,000 if debtor's equity does not exceed $15,000; library to a value of $1,500; all family pictures, keepsakes, necessary household goods, and yard equipment up to $10,000; private libraries up to $1,500; money not to exceed $500,000 in present value held in qualified retirement plans, employee pension plan, or profit sharing plans; farm stock, farm trucks, farm tools and equipment, supplies, and seeds up to a value of $4,500.

(Nevada Revised Statutes Sec. 21.090; Sec. 115.010)

New Hampshire

The homestead exemption is real property or manufactured housing to a value of $50,000.

Personal property exemptions include: wearing apparel; beds, bedsteads, and bedding; household furniture to a value of $3,500; one cook stove, one heating stove, and one refrigerator and necessary utensils; sewing machine; jewelry to a value of $500; automobile to a value of $4,000; personal library, bibles, and schoolbooks to a value of $800; fuel and provisions to a value of $400; tools of trade to a value of $5,000; insurance proceeds up to $5,000; no more than four tons of hay.

(New Hampshire Revised Statutes Annotated Sec. 480:1; Sec. 511:2; Sec. 512:21)

New Jersey

Personal property exemptions include: wearing apparel; household goods and furnishings up to a value of $1,000; interests in a corporation or shares of stock, goods, and chattels, and any personal property (not including wearing apparel) to a value of $1,000; disability payments; workers' compensation payments; retirement benefits.

(New Jersey Statutes Annotated Sec. 2A:17-19; Sec. 2A:17-56; Sec. 2A:26-4)

New Mexico

The homestead exemption for a debtor who is married, widowed, or supporting another person has a value limitation of $30,000. If the homestead is jointly owned by two persons, each joint owner is entitled to an exemption of $30,000.

Personal property exemptions include: personal items in the amount of $500; jewelry to a value of $2,500; motor vehicle to a value of $4,000; other personal property to a value of $500; clothing, furniture, medical/health equipment for personal use; any interest in or proceeds from a pension or retirement fund; certain life, accident, and health insurance benefits not exceeding $5,000.

(New Mexico Statutes Annotated Sec 42-10-1; Sec. 42-10-2; Sec. 42-10-9; Sec. 42-10-10)

New York

The homestead exemption is real property, a mobile home, or an interest in a condominium or cooperative apartment to a value of $10,000 above liens and encumbrances.

Personal property exemptions include: wearing apparel, household furniture, and various appliances, stoves, and fuel for 60 days; one sewing machine up to $5,000; church pew; motor vehicle not exceeding $2,400; a wedding ring and a watch not exceeding $35 in value, up to $5,000; schoolbooks, family pictures, and bible to a value of $5,000; other books up to $50; wearing apparel, household furniture, one refrigerator, one TV, one radio, utensils, crockery, tableware up to $5,000; necessary tools and implements; family food for 60 days; domestic animals and family food for 60 days; annuity contract benefits up to $5,000; bodily injury payments up to $7,500.

(New York Civil Practice Law and Rules Sec. 5205; Sec. 5206. New York Debtor and Creditor Law Sec. 282-284)

North Carolina

Equity in homestead is up to $10,000. If debtor's spouse also files for Chapter 7, maximum is $20,000.

Motor vehicle up to $1,500; household goods, wearing apparel, appliances, books, animals, crops, or musical instruments up to $3,500 for the debtor plus $750, but not to exceed $3,000 in total for each dependent; tools of the trade not to exceed $750; life insurance proceeds; professionally prescribed health aids; compensation for personal injury or death; qualified individual retirement accounts and retirement annuities.

(General Statutes of North Carolina Sec. 1C-1601)

North Dakota

The homestead exemption is $80,000.

Personal property exemptions include: family pictures; church pew; family bible and all schoolbooks not to exceed $1,000; wearing apparel, provisions for the debtor and family necessary for one year's supply, crops and grain not to exceed 160 acres of land; personal property including money up to $5,000 for a married couple and up to $2,500 for a single debtor; one motor vehicle up to $1,200; qualified pension plan; Social Security benefits, veterans' disability pension benefits.

(North Dakota Century Code Sec. 28-22-02; Sec. 28-22-03.1; Sec. 28-22-04; Sec. 28-22-05; Sec. 32-09.1-.03; Sec. 47-18-01)

Ohio

The homestead exemption limitation of value is $5,000 of real or personal property used as a residence.

Personal property exemptions include: motor vehicle to a value of $1,000; $400 in cash; refrigerator and stove to a value of $300 each; personal injury awards up to $5,000; household goods and furnishings up to $1,500 if claiming homestead, otherwise up to a maximum of $2,000; jewelry up to $1,500 if claiming homestead and up to $2,000 if not; tools of trade up to $750.

(Ohio Revised Code Sec. 2329.66)

Oklahoma

The homestead exemption is real property limited in value to $5,000.

Personal property exemptions include: wearing apparel up to $4,000; all household and kitchen furniture; implements of husbandry necessary to farm the homestead up to a value of $5,000; tools, apparatus, and books used in any trade or profession; all books, portraits, and pictures; professionally prescribed health aids; five milk cows and their calves under six months old, two horses, bridles, and saddles; one motor vehicle not to exceed $3,000; one gun; qualified retirement plans; death or workers' compensation plans.

(Oklahoma Statutes Annotated Title 31 Sec. 1 and 2)

Oregon

The homestead exemption value limitation for real property or a mobile home is $25,000 for a single debtor and $33,000 for a couple.

Personal property exemptions include: books, pictures, and musical instruments up to the value of $600; wearing apparel, jewelry, and other personal items to a value of $1,800; household goods and furniture, radios, a television, and utensils up to a value of $3,000; musical instruments, books, and pictures to a value of $600; vehicle to a value of $1,700; rifle, shotgun, or one pistol up to $1,000; domestic animals and poultry kept for family use for total value of $1,000; spousal support, child support, or separate maintenance; all professionally prescribed health aids for debtor and spouse.

(Oregon Revised Statutes Sec. 23.160; Sec. 23.164; Sec. 23.185; Sec. 23.200; Sec. 23.240)

Pennsylvania

Personal property exemptions include: wearing apparel, sewing machine, bibles, schoolbooks, uniforms, qualified retirement funds and accounts, pension or annuity, insurance proceeds, Social Security payments, workers' compensation payments.

(Pennsylvania Consolidated Statutes Annotated Title 42 Sec. 8123; Sec. 8124; Sec. 8127)

Rhode Island

Homestead exemption is up to a value of $150,000.

Personal property exemptions include: wearing apparel; work tools up to $1,200, and the professional library of someone who is in a professional practice; jewelry up to $1,000; household furniture and goods up to $8,600; motor vehicle not to exceed $10,000; books, including schoolbooks and bible, up to $300; certain qualified retirement or annuity accounts.

(General Laws of Rhode Island Sec. 9-26-4)

South Carolina

The homestead exemption is up to a value of $5,000; may increase to $10,000 for joint owners.

Personal property exemptions include: wearing apparel, household goods and furniture, appliances, musical instruments, books, crops, and animals to a value of $2,500; jewelry to a value of $500; motor vehicle to a value of $1,200; cash and other liquid assets to a value of $1,000 in lieu of the homestead exemption; insurance; business partnership property; tools of trade to a value of $750; Social Security; unemployment compensation; public assistance.

(Code of Laws of South Carolina Sec. 15-41-200)

South Dakota

The homestead exemption is up to $30,000.

Personal property exemptions include: goods, chattels, merchandise, money, or other personal property not exceeding in the aggregate a value of $4,000 for a single person or $6,000 for a head of household; miscellaneous books and musical instruments up to $200; farm equipment up to $1,250; life insurance proceeds up to $10,000.

(South Dakota Codified Laws Sec. 15-20-12; Sec. 43-31-4; Sec. 43-45-2; Sec. 43-45-4)

Tennessee

The homestead exemption value limitation is $5,000.

Personal property exemptions include: money and funds on deposit with banks and other financial institutions up to $4,000; wearing apparel; all family portraits and pictures, the family bible, and schoolbooks; tools of the trade to a value of $1,900; personal injury payments; other personal property including cash and bank accounts to a value of $4,000; qualified retirement funds; Social Security payments; unemployment payments; veterans' benefits; disability payments.

(Tennessee Code Annotated Sec. 26-2-102; Sec. 26-2-103; Sec. 26-2-106; Sec. 26-2-111; Sec. 26-2-301; Sec. 26-2-305)

Texas

The homestead exemption is limited to no more than 10 acres of land and improvements within a town or city, not more than 200 acres and improvements in a rural area for a family, and not more than 100 acres and improvements for a single debtor in a rural area.

Personal property exemptions include: personal property with an aggregate fair market value of up to $60,000 for a family or $30,000 for an individual. This property may include: home furnishings; farming or ranch vehicles and implements; books, tools, and equipment; wearing apparel; jewelry; athletic and sporting equipment; two firearms; a motor vehicle for each person in the household who has a driver's license; alimony, maintenance, support, and separate maintenance; qualified retirement plan, annuity, or account.

(Texas Property Code Annotated Sec. 41.001; Sec. 42.002)

Utah

The homestead exemption for a single person is up to $20,000 and for jointly owned property, $40,000.

Personal property exemptions include: burial plot; essential health aids; disability, illness, or unemployment benefits; veterans' benefits; child support; one clothes washer and dryer; one refrigerator and freezer; one stove; one microwave; one sewing machine; all carpets; 12 months of provisions for individual or family use; all wearing apparel, not including fur and jewelry; all beds and bedding; insurance proceeds; one motor vehicle used for business or professional purposes not exceeding $2,500; books and musical instruments up to $500; sofa, chairs, and related furnishings up to $500 in aggregate value; dining room chairs and table for one family up to a value of $500; qualified retirement plans; insurance plans.

(Utah Code Sec. 78-23-3; Sec. 78-23-5; Sec. 78-23-8)

Vermont

The homestead exemption value limitation is $75,000.

Personal property exemptions include: motor vehicle not to exceed $2,500; professional or trade books or tools up to $5,000; household furnishings, goods or appliances, books, wearing apparel, animals, crops, or musical instruments not to exceed $5,000; appliances needed for heating; one stove, one refrigerator, one freezer; ten cords of firewood; five tons of coal or 500 gallons of heating oil; 500 gallons of bottled gas; Social Security benefits; alimony, support, or separate maintenance; disability or illness benefits; veterans' benefits; professionally prescribed health aids.

(Vermont Statutes Annotated Title 12 Sec. 2740; Title 27 Sec. 101)

Virginia

The homestead exemption value limitation is $5,000 with an additional $500 in value per dependent.

Personal property exemptions for a householder include: motor vehicles up to $2,000; family bible, wedding and engagement rings, family portraits, and heirlooms not to exceed $5,000; wearing apparel up to $1,000; household furniture and furnishings to a value of $5,000.

(Code of Virginia Sec. 34-4; Sec. 34-4.1; Sec. 34-6; Sec. 34-26; Sec. 34-27; Sec. 34-29)

Washington

The homestead limitation of value is $40,000.

Personal property exemptions include: wearing apparel not exceeding a value of $1,000 per person; household goods, furniture and appliances, and yard and home equipment to a value of $2,700; family pictures and keepsakes to a value of $1,500; libraries to a value of $1,500; motor vehicle to a value of $2,500; cash or bank accounts up to $100; professional library, office furniture, and equipment and supplies up to $5,000; tools of trade up to $5,000; certain retirement plan benefits; insurance proceeds; public assistance payments; unemployment benefits.

(Revised Code of Washington Annotated Sec. 6.12.050; Sec. 6.16.020; Sec. 7.33.280)

West Virginia

The homestead exemption has a value limitation of $25,000.

Personal property exemptions include: wearing apparel, household goods and furnishings, appliances, books, musical instruments, animals, and crops to a total value of $8,000 (limit of $400 per item); jewelry to a value of $1,000; professionally prescribed health aids for debtor or dependent of debtor; motor vehicle to a value of $2,400; payments made to a prepaid tuition trust on behalf of beneficiaries; disability payments; alimony, support, or separate maintenance; Social Security payments; unemployment benefits; local public assistance payments; veterans' benefits.

(West Virginia Code Sec. 38-10-4)

Wisconsin

The homestead exemption limit of value is $40,000.

Personal property exemptions include: tools of trade, business and farm property not to exceed $7,500; consumer goods up to $5,000; household furnishings up to $5,000; motor vehicles not to exceed $1,200; retirement benefits; federal disability payments; deposit accounts in aggregate of $1,000.

(Wisconsin Statutes Annotated Sec. 815.18; Sec. 815.20)

Wyoming

The homestead exemption limit is $10,000.

Personal property exemptions include: wearing apparel including wedding rings; household furnishings and provisions to a value of $2,000; bible, schoolbooks, pictures, burial plot, furniture, bedding, provisions, and other household items up to $2,000; motor vehicle up to $2,400 in value; professional library and instruments to a value of $2,000; retirement plans; Social Security payments; veterans' benefits; black lung benefits; workers' compensation payments; unemployment benefits.

(Wyoming Statutes Annotated Sec. 1-17-411; Sec. 1-20-101; Sec. 1-20-105; Sec. 1-20-106)

E

Common Motions, Adversaries, Objections, and Applications

When there is a dispute in the bankruptcy process between a debtor and the trustee or between the debtor and one or more of his or her creditors, and one or more parties to the dispute want the bankruptcy judge to resolve the issue, a motion, adversary, or objection will have to be filed. If the debtor wants the judge to give him or her permission to do something, then the debtor must file a request or application with the court. The debtor's attorney will prepare and file the paperwork.

The following represent the most common motions, adversaries, objections, and applications consumer debtors may encounter during their bankruptcy together with an explanation of the circumstances that apply to each one.

Motion to lift automatic stay. This is the most common motion filed in court during a bankruptcy. It is usually filed by a secured creditor who has not been paid for a long time. When a creditor files this motion, it is asking the bankruptcy judge to decide whether or not it can take back its collateral—for instance, your car—or whether the court will require that you begin making adequate protection payments to the creditor if you keep the asset you used as collateral. The payments are intended to help protect the creditor's interest in that asset.

Motion to dismiss. This motion will be filed either by one of your creditors or by the trustee if one of them thinks that you should not be entitled to stay in bankruptcy. For example, if you file a Chapter 13 adjustment of debt bankruptcy and you miss some of the payments on your reorganization plan, the trustee will file a motion to dismiss your case for failure to pay.

Motion to redeem. If you are in a Chapter 7 bankruptcy, you may file this motion if you and one of your creditors cannot come to an agreement on the value of an asset you want to keep, or redeem. The motion asks the judge to decide on its value. Once that happens, you must pay the asset's value to the creditor and, in return, you will be allowed to keep the asset free of any liens. The balance of the debt you owe on that asset will be wiped out by your bankruptcy.

Objection to discharge. This adversary may be filed against you when you file for Chapter 7 if the trustee or one of your creditors believes that you have broken any bankruptcy rules or have tried to defraud the court. If the adversary is successful, none of your debts will be discharged, which means that you will still owe them at the end of your bankruptcy.

Objection to dischargeability. One of your creditors may file this adversary against you to prevent its debt from being wiped out through bankruptcy. Usually, the creditor will allege that you committed some kind of fraud, such as lying on one of your financial statements, to obtain the loan.

Objection to Chapter 13 plan. This objection may be filed by either the trustee or a creditor if one of them believes that your proposed plan does not fulfill the requirements of confirmation or when one of your creditors believes its claim is not being treated fairly in your bankruptcy.

Objection to exemptions. This adversary may be filed against you when the trustee or one of your creditors believes that an asset you have exempted so that you can keep it should really be treated as a nonexempt asset and, therefore, should be sold to satisfy your debts. This objection must be filed within 30 days of the creditors' meeting in your bankruptcy.

Motion for evaluation. You will file this motion if you want to keep a secured asset by paying its current value rather than what you actually owe on it and you and the creditor to whom you owe the debt that the asset secures cannot agree on the asset's value. By filing the motion you will be asking the court to decide what it is worth.

Motion to determine tax liability. You would use this motion if you want to file for Chapter 13 but are not sure how much you owe to the Internal Revenue Service, since you must know exactly how much you owe to all your creditors, including the IRS, in order to prepare your reorganization plan. You must also know whether any of your IRS tax debt can be treated as a general unsecured claim and be paid off at less than 100 percent. You will get all that information by filing this motion.

Modification of Chapter 13 plan. You would file this motion if you want to change some aspect of your confirmed Chapter 13 reorganization plan because you are having trouble living up to the plan and want to stay in Chapter 13. You would probably make this request because you have experienced a drop in your income or there has been some other negative change in your financial status.

Motion to avoid lien. Depending on your state of residence, you can use this motion to remove a lien that one of your creditors has placed on some of your household goods to secure a loan it made to you. Your goal would be to keep those assets. This type of loan is called a nonpurchase-money, nonpossessory loan. If the judge approves your motion, the amount you owe on the loan will be wiped out through your bankruptcy. This type of motion can also be used to remove judgment liens from exempt property.

Application to reaffirm a debt. Although it is not recommended that you file this kind of motion, you would file it if you want the bankruptcy court to approve an agreement you have made with one of your creditors to pay the debt you owe to it even though you would wipe out the debt through your bankruptcy.

F

Resources

The information in this section provides names and contact information for organizations, Web sites, and publications that can help you deal with your debts, understand the bankruptcy process, and manage your finances responsibly.

Dealing with Debt

The National Foundation for Credit Counseling (NFCC) is a nonprofit organization with a network of more than 1,300 credit-counseling offices around the country. These offices provide low cost/no cost debt counseling and budgeting services to consumers who are in financial trouble. They try to help these consumers avoid bankruptcy by negotiating new, more affordable debt repayment schedules with their creditors. To locate the NFCC office closest to you, go to http://www.nfcc.org or call 800-388-2227.

Debtors Anonymous (DA) is a nonprofit organization that helps people with spending addictions overcome their problems using the proven techniques of Alcoholics Anonymous. To find a DA chapter near you, go to http://www.debtorsanonymous.org or call 781-452-2743.

Life or Debt: A One-Week Plan for a Lifetime of Financial Freedom, Stacy Johnson, Ballantine Books, 2001.

The Complete Cheapskate: How to Get Out of Debt, Stay Out and Break Free from Money Worries Forever, Mary Hart, St. Martin's Press, 2003.

Debt-Free By 30: Practical Advice for the Young, Broke & Upwardly Mobile, Jason Anthony and Karl Cluck, Plume, 2001.

Frugal Living for Dummies, Deborah Taylor-Hough, Wiley, 2003.

The Get Out of Debt Kit, Deborah McNaughton, Dearborn Trade Publishing, 2002.

Good Advice for a Bad Economy, John Ventura and Mary Reed, Berkley Books, 2003.

Surviving Debt: A Guide for Consumers, Jonathan Sheldon and Gary Klein, National Consumer Law Center, 1996.

Bankruptcy

The American Bankruptcy Institute (ABI) provides information about managing debt and filing for bankruptcy in the Consumer Corner section of its Web site, http://www.abiworld.org/consumer. You can also find a board-certified bankruptcy attorney in your area at the site.

Managing Your Money Responsibly and Living on Less

Bankrate.com, http://www.bankrate.com. This Web site offers lots of easy-to-understand-and-practice advice about everyday financial matters, including getting and using credit, dealing with debt, managing money, and so on. You can also sign up for a free Bankrate.com newsletter.

National Consumer Law Center (NCLC) is a national organization that works on behalf of low-income consumers. Among other things, it helps consumers deal with debt-collection problems, foreclosures and repossessions, loss of utility service, and so on. To find an NCLC consumer law attorney in your area, go to http://www.consumerlaw.org or call 617-542-8010.

Debtsmart E-mail Newsletter. This free newsletter provides money-saving techniques, budgeting advice, information about using coupons, and more. See http://www.debtsmart.com.

The Budget Kit, 4th edition, Judy Lawrence, Dearborn Trade, 2004.

Cheap Talk with Frugal Friends: Over 600 Tips, Tricks and Creative Ideas for Saving Money, Angie Zalwski, Deana Ricks, Starburst Publishers, 2001.

The Complete Tightwad Gazette III, Amy Dacyczyn, Villard, 1996.

Frugal Friends: Making the Most of Your Hard-Earned Money, Jonni McCoy, Dimensions, 2003.

How to Save Money Every Day, Ellie Kay, Bethany House, 2001.

Mary Hunt's Debt-Proof Living, Mary Hunt, Broadway & Hollman Publishers, 1999.

50 Simple Things You Can Do to Improve Your Finances: How to Spend Less, Save More and Make the Most of What You Have, Ilyce Glink, Three Rivers Press, 2001.

Rebuilding Credit

After Bankruptcy: Simple Steps to Rebuilding Your Credit and Your Life, Anne Whiteley, Solstice Publishing, 2001.

Bounce Back from Bankruptcy: A Step-by-Step Guide to Getting Back on Your Financial Feet, Paula Langguth Ryan, Pellingham, Casper Communications, 2001.

The Credit Repair Kit, 4th edition, John Ventura, Dearborn Trade, 2004.

The Ultimate Credit Handbook, 3rd edition, Gerri Detweiller, Plume, 2003.

How to Locate Trustees

Should you need to contact the trustee involved in your bankruptcy case, this section provides the names, addresses, and phone numbers of the Chapter 7 and Chapter 13 Panel and Standing Trustees throughout the United States as well as in St. Thomas, the Virgin Islands, and Christiansted, Saint Croix and Virgin Islands. Also included are the names, addresses, and phone numbers of the U.S. Trustees Regional Management officials. They oversee the work of the trustees in each region and monitor individual bankruptcy cases.

Chapter 7 Panel Trustees

ALABAMA

The U.S. Trustee Program does not administer bankruptcy estates in Alabama at this time. Questions about cases in Alabama should be addressed to:

The Administrative Office of the U.S. Courts
Bankruptcy Judges Division
1 Columbus Circle, N.E.,
    Suite 4-250
Washington, DC 20544
Phone: 202-502-1900

ALASKA

Note: The individuals listed are private parties, not government employees.

William M. Barstow III
P.O. Box 240261
Anchorage, AK 99524
E-mail: wbarstow@gci.net
Phone: 907-274-9253

Kenneth Battley
629 L Street, Suite 201
Anchorage, AK 99501
Phone: 907-274-6683

Larry D. Compton
400 D Street, Suite 210
Anchorage, AK 99501
E-mail: akchapter13@gci.net
Phone: 907-276-6660
Fax: 907-258-3348

ARIZONA

Note: The individuals listed are private parties, not government employees.

Robert P. Abele
P.O. Box 5478
Mesa, AZ 85211-5478
E-mail: rabele@azbktrustee.com
Phone: 480-844-1624

Ronald L. Ancell
1721 W. Klamath Drive
Tucson, AZ 85704
E-mail: rancell@epitrustee.com
Phone: 520-888-4210

David A. Birdsell
216 N. Center
Mesa, AZ 85201
E-mail: dabtrustee@hotmail.com
Phone: 480-644-1080

Roger W. Brown
P.O. Box 32967
Phoenix, AZ 85064-2967
E-mail: rrwwbb@hotmail.com
Phone: 602-274-4231

Robert J. Davis
P.O. Box 55120
Phoenix, AZ 85078-5120
E-mail: RDAVI3@AMFAM.com
Phone: 602-993-4245

Daniel R. Dominguez
2210 N. Indian Ruins Road
Tucson, AZ 85715
E-mail: ddominguez@epitrustee
    .com
Phone: 520-296-8838

Constantino Flores
411 N. Central Avenue, Suite 900
Phoenix, AZ 85004
Phone: 602-506-4111

Jill H. Ford
11108 E. Honda Bow Road
Scottsdale, AZ 85262
Phone: 480-488-5175

James D. Fox
P.O. Box 599
Scottsdale, AZ 85252-0599
Phone: 480-946-1412

Maureen Gaughan
P.O. Box 6729
Chandler, AZ 85246
E-mail: maureengaughan@cox.net
Phone: 480-899-2036

Lothar H. Goernitz
P.O. Box 32961
Phoenix, AZ 85064-2961
E-mail: lgoernitz@epitrustee.com
Phone: 602-263-5413

Stanley J. Kartchner
7090 N. Oracle Road, Suite 178-204
Tucson, AZ 85704
E-mail: sjkartchner@epitrustee.com
Phone: 520-742-1210

Beth E. Lang
1955 W. Grant Road, Suite 125
Tucson, AZ 85745
E-mail: bethlang@earthlink.net
Phone: 520-884-1880

Robert A. MacKenzie
301 E. Virginia Avenue, Suite 3500
Phoenix, AZ 85004
E-mail: ram@ramlawltd.com
Phone: 602-229-8575

Sebastian W. Manera
5104 N. 32nd Street,
    Apartment 434
Phoenix, AZ 85018
Phone: 602-468-2856

Diane M. Mann
P.O. Box 12970
Scottsdale, AZ 85261-2970
E-mail: dmm1126@aol.com
Phone: 602-368-7886

Anthony H. Mason
1850 N. Central Avenue, #330
Phoenix, AZ 85004
E-mail: tony2388@earthlink.net
Phone: 602-808-7770

Sharon Maxwell
177 N. Church Avenue, Suite 625
Tucson, AZ 85701
E-mail: smaxwell@epitrustee.com
Phone: 520-623-7401

Gayle E. Mills
P.O. Box 36317
Tucson, AZ 85740
E-mail: mills@theriver.com
Phone: 520-797-8279

Louis A. Movitz
P.O. Box 3137
Carefree, AZ 85377-3137
E-mail: louis.movitz@psinet.com
Phone: 602-488-9629

William E. Pierce
P.O. Box 429
Chino Valley, AZ 86323-0429
E-mail: wept@commspeed.net
Phone: 928-636-6210

Charles L. Riley, Jr.
P.O. Box 6640
Chandler, AZ 85246-6640
E-mail: trust.riley@psinet.com
Phone: 480-839-4224

Theodor C. Albert
P.O. Box 1860
Costa Mesa, CA 92626-1860
E-mail: talbert@awglawyers.com
Phone: 714-445-1021

Karl T. Anderson
700 E. Tahquitz Canyon Way,
   Suite H
Palm Springs, CA 92262
Phone: 760-778-4889

Peter C. Anderson
6055 E. Washington Boulevard,
   Suite 608
Los Angeles, CA 90040-2466
Phone: 323-727-9589

Christopher R. Barclay
600 Anton Boulevard, Suite 1350
Cosa Mesa, CA 92626-7195
Phone: 714-662-0800

Sandra L. Bendon
15411 Redhill Avenue, Suite A
Tustin, CA 92780
Phone: 714-258-7992

James L. Brown
3660 Wilshire Boulevard,
   Suite 1118
Los Angeles, CA 90010
Phone: 213-251-2330

Thomas H. Casey
22342 Avenida Epresa, Suite 260
Rancho Santa Margarita, CA
   92688
Phone: 949-766-8787

Linda J. Chu
515 S. Flower Street, Suite 4400
Los Angeles, CA 90071
Phone: 213-688-1300

Arturo M. Cisneros
3403 Tenth Street, Suite 711
Riverside, CA 92501
Phone: 909-328-3124

Charles W. Daff
2122 N. Broadway, Suite 200
Santa Ana, CA 92706
Phone: 714-541-0511

Richard K. Diamond
2029 Century Park East, 3rd Floor
Los Angeles, CA 90067-3005
Phone: 310-277-0077

Carolyn Anne Dye
1925 Century Park, Suite 1150
Los Angeles, CA 90067-2712
Phone: 310-789-2054

Howard Marc Ehrenberg
333 S. Hope Street, 35th Floor
Los Angeles, CA 90071
Phone: 213-626-2311

David Y. Farmer
1254 Marsh Street
San Luis Obispo, CA 93401
Phone: 805-541-1626

Helen R. Frazer
17871 Park Plaza Drive, Suite 200
Cerritos, CA 90703
Phone: 562-653-3200

David A. Gill
2029 Century Park East, 3rd Floor
Los Angeles, CA 90067-3005
Phone: 310-277-0077

Jeffrey I. Golden
650 Town Center Drive, Suite 950
Costa Mesa, CA 92626
Phone: 714-966-1000

Amy L. Goldman
221 N. Figueroa Street, Suite 1200
Los Angeles, CA 90012
Phone: 213-250-1800

Rosendo Gonzalez
515 S. Figueroa Street, Suite 1970
Los Angeles, CA 90071
Phone: 213-452-0071

Robert L. Goodrich
3600 Lime Street
Building 2, Suite 221
Riverside, CA 92501
Phone: 909-341-9304

David Keith Gottlieb
15233 Ventura Boulevard, 9th Floor
Sherman Oaks, CA 91403-2201
Phone: 818-325-8441

David R. Hagen
6400 Canoga Avenue, Suite 311
Woodland Hills, CA 91367
Phone: 818-992-1940

David L. Hahn
22342 Avenida Empressa, Suite 260
Rancho Margarita, CA 92688
Phone: 949-888-1010

Norman L. Hanover
3880 Lemon Street, 5th Floor
Riverside, CA 92502
Phone: 909-680-1257

James J. Joseph
2029 Century Park East, 3rd Floor
Los Angeles, CA 90067-3005
Phone: 310-277-0077

Nancy Knupfer
2029 Century Park East, 3rd Floor
Los Angeles, CA 90067
Phone: 310-277-0077

Weneta M. A. Kosmala
P.O. Box 16279
Irvine, CA 92623-9998
E-mail: wkosmala@kosmalalaw.com
Phone: 714-708-8190

Brad D. Krasnoff
221 N. Figueroa Street, Suite 1200
Los Angeles, CA 90012
Phone: 213-250-1800

Heide C. Kurtz
2515 S. Western Avenue, Suite 11
San Pedro, CA 90732
Phone: 310-832-3604

Sam S. Leslie
6310 San Vicente Boulevard,
   Suite 320
Los Angeles, CA 90048
Phone: 323-549-6900

Richard A. Marshack
26632 Towne Center Drive,
   Suite 300
Foothill Ranch, CA 92610-2808
Phone: 949-340-3400

Sandra K. McBeth
2450 Professional Parkway,
   Suite 240
Santa Maria, CA 93455
Phone: 805-938-9223

John J. Menchaca
510 W. Sixth Street, Suite 400
Los Angeles, CA 90014
Phone: 213-629-9094

Elissa Diane Miller
333 S. Hope Street, 35th Floor
Los Angeles, CA 90071
Phone: 213-626-2311

Jerry Namba
625 E. Chapel Street
Santa Maria, CA 93454
Phone: 805-922-2575

Karen S. Naylor
P.O. Box 504
Santa Ana, CA 92702-0504
E-mail: knaylor@Burd-Naylor.com
Phone: 949-262-1748

R. Todd Neilson
10100 Santa Monica Boulevard,
   Suite 410
Los Angeles, CA 90067
Phone: 310-282-9911

Dennis W. King
3151 S. Vaughn Way, #510
Aurora, CO 80014
E-mail: KingDJ7@aol.com
Phone: 303-751-3200

Kevin P. Kubie
311 W. 24th Street
Pueblo, CO 81003
Phone: 719-545-1153

Douglas E. Larson
422 White Avenue, #323
Grand Junction, CO 81501
Phone: 970-245-8021

David E. Lewis
1314 Main Street, #102
Louisville, CO 80027
Phone: 303-666-1217

Jennifer M. McCallum
132 Kolar Court
Erie, CO 80516
E-mail: trusteemccallum@
mccallumlaw.net
Phone: 303-774-4052

Paul V. Moss
311 W. 24th Street
Pueblo, CO 81003
Phone: 719-544-2100

Jon S. Nicholls
1725 Gaylord Street, #100
Denver, CO 80206-1208
Phone: 303-329-9700

David A. Palmer
P.O. Box 4244
Grand Junction, CO 81502-4244
E-mail: dpalmer@acsol.net
Phone: 970-241-1925

M. Stephen Peters
3760 Vance Street, #200
Wheatridge, CO 80033
Phone: 303-422-8501

Simon E. Rodriguez
P.O. Box 36324
Denver, CO 80236
E-mail: Lawyercolo@aol.com
Phone: 303-837-9300

Joseph G. Rosania
390 Interlocken Crescent, #490
Broomfield, CO 80021
Phone: 303-661-9292

Charles W. Schlosser, Jr.
1888 Sherman Street, Suite 650
Denver, CO 80203
Phone: 303-831-0733

Harvey Sender
1999 Broadway, #2305
Denver, CO 80202
Phone: 303-296-1999

Cynthia V. Skeen
P.O. Box 218
Georgetown, CO 80444
E-mail: cynthia.skeen@psinet.com
Phone: 303-569-3134

Janice A. Steinle
PMB 505, 9249 S. Broadway, #200
Highlands Ranch, CO 80129
Phone: 303-794-8034

Jeffrey A. Weinman
730 17th Street, Suite 240
Denver, CO 80202
Phone: 303-572-1010

CONNECTICUT

Note: The individuals listed are private parties, not government employees.

Richard L. Belford
9 Trumbull Street
New Haven, CT 06511
Phone: 203-865-0867

Thomas C. Boscarino
628 Hebron Avenue, Building 3
Glastonbury, CT 06033
Phone: 860-659-5657

Ronald I. Chorches
1010 Wethersfield Avenue
Hartford, CT 06114
Phone: 860-296-9972

Richard M. Coan
495 Orange Street
New Haven, CT 06511
Phone: 203-624-4756

Michael John Daly
378 Boston Post Road
P.O. Drawer 966
Orange, CT 06477-0966
Phone: 203-795-1211

Barbara H. Katz
57 Trumbull Street
New Haven, CT 06510-1004
Phone: 203-772-4828

Eric R. Lopez
205 Center Street
West Haven, CT 06516
Phone: 203-934-5688

Bonnie C. Mangan
1050 Sullivan Avenue, Suite A3
South Windsor, CT 06074
Phone: 860-644-4204

Roberta Napolitano
350 Fairfield Avenue
Bridgeport, CT 06604
Phone: 203-333-1177

Anthony S. Novak
1260 Silas Deane Highway
Wethersfield, CT 06109-4331
Phone: 860-257-1980

John J. O'Neil
255 Main Street
Hartford, CT 06106
Phone: 203-527-3171

Neal Ossen
21 Oak Street
Hartford, CT 06106
Phone: 203-728-6635

DELAWARE

Note: The individuals listed are private parties, not government employees.

Jeoffrey L. Burtch
824 Market Street Mall, Suite 1000
Wilmington, DE 19899-1680
P.O. Box 1680
Wilmington, DE 19899-1680
E-mail: jlburtch@ctlaw.org
Phone: 302-652-5379

Montague S. Claybrook
919 N. Market Street, Suite 550
Wilmington, DE 19801
E-mail: mclaybrook@
navigantconsulting.com
Phone: 302-661-7700
Fax: 302-661-1772

Alfred T. Giuliano
750 Route 73 S., Suite 110
Marlton, NJ 08053
E-mail: atgiuliano@
giulianomiller.com
Phone: 856-596-7000
Fax: 856-596-8688

George L. Miller
1628 John F. Kennedy Boulevard
8 Penn Center, Suite 950
Philadelphia, PA 19103
Phone: 215-561-0950

DISTRICT OF COLUMBIA

Note: The individuals listed are private parties, not government employees.

Marc E. Albert
1150 18th Street, N.W., Suite 800
Washington, DC 20036
Phone: 202-785-9100

Kevin R. McCarthy
818-0 Greensboro Drive, Suite 875
McLean, VA 22102
Phone: 703-770-9260

Bryan S. Ross
1800 K Street, N.W., Suite 624
Washington, DC 20006
Phone: 202-659-2214

Wendell W. Webster
1819 H Street, N.W., Suite 300
Washington, DC 20006
Phone: 202-659-8510

William D. White
818-0 Greensboro Drive, Suite 875
McLean, VA 22102
Phone: 703-770-9260

FLORIDA

Note: The individuals listed are private parties, not government employees.

TRUSTEE(S) COVERING THE MIDDLE DISTRICT OF FLORIDA

Doreen R. Abbott
P.O. Box 56257
Jacksonville, FL 32241-6257
E-mail: dabbott@epiqtrustee.com
Phone: 904-886-9459

Robert Altman
P.O. Box 922
Palatka, FL 32178-0922
E-mail: raltman@se.rr.com
Phone: 386-325-4691
Fax: 386-325-9765

Efrain Aponte
450 Crown Oak Centre
Longwood, FL 32750
Phone: 407-260-8268

Gregory L. Atwater
P.O. Box 1815
Orange Park, FL 32073
E-mail: ath20@netmail.att.net
Phone: 904-264-2273

Andrea P. Bauman
P.O. Box 907
Highland City, FL 33846
E-mail: abauman@epitrustee.com
Phone: 863-701-7047

V. John Brook, Jr.
2520 Ninth Street, N.
St. Petersburg, FL 33704
Phone: 727-821-5010

Gene T. Chambers
P.O. Box 533987
Orlando, FL 32853-3987
E-mail: g.chambers@inetmail.att.net
Phone: 407-872-7575

Carolyn A. Chaney
P.O. Box 530248
St. Petersburg, FL 33747-0248
E-mail: carolyn.chaney@psinet.com
Phone: 727-864-9851

Aaron Robert Cohen
P.O. Box 4218
Jacksonville, FL 32201
E-mail: aaroncohen@epitrustee.com
Phone: 904-722-1866

Gregory K. Crews
300 W. Adams Street, Suite 200
Jacksonville, FL 32202
Phone: 904-354-1750

Angela L. W. Esposito
P.O. Box 549
Odessa, FL 33556-0549
E-mail: welch.esposito@verizon.net
Phone: 813-901-9561

Scott R. Fransen
1470 E. Michigan Street
Orlando, FL 32856-0848
Phone: 407-482-5800

Lauren P. Greene
13611 Park Boulevard, Suite G
Seminole, FL 33776
Phone: 727-393-0384

Ralph Jay Harpley
1602 W. Sligh Avenue
Tampa, FL 33604
Phone: 813-931-1700

Thomas S. Heidkamp
P.O. Box 61169
Fort Myers, FL 33906-1169
E-mail: tsh@lhbk.com
Phone: 239-275-7797

Marie E. Henkel
3560 S. Magnolia Avenue
Orlando, FL 32806
Phone: 407-438-6738

Kenneth D. Herron, Jr.
P.O. Box 2327
Orlando, FL 32802
Phone: 407-648-0058

Larry S. Hyman
P.O. Box 18614
Tampa, FL 33679
E-mail: lhyman@epitrustee.com
Phone: 813-251-6534

Shari Streit Jansen
P.O. Box 50667
Sarasota, FL 34232-0305
E-mail: sjansen@epitrustee.com
Phone: 941-378-3330

Diane L. Jensen
P.O. Drawer 1507
Fort Myers, FL 33902
E-mail: dianejensen@paveslaw.com
Phone: 239-334-2195

Gordon P. Jones
P.O. Box 600459
Jacksonville, FL 32260-0459
E-mail: gtrustee@aol.com
Phone: 904-262-7373

Valerie Hall Manuel
P.O. Box 1258
Jacksonville, FL 32201
E-mail: valeriem@psinet.com
Phone: 904-355-9441

Leigh R. Meininger
P.O. Box 1946
Orlando, FL 32802-1946
E-mail: lmeininger@epitrustee.com
Phone: 407-246-1585

Stephen L. Meininger
711 N. Florida Avenue, Suite 260
Tampa, FL 33602
Phone: 813-301-1025

Robert F. Melone
P.O. Box 7107
Wesley Chapel, FL 33543
E-mail: rfmelone@melonelaw.com
Phone: 813-907-3379

Douglas N. Menchise
300 Turner Street
Clearwater, FL 34616
Phone: 727-442-2186

George E. Mills, Jr.
P.O. Box 995
Gotha, FL 34734-0995
E-mail: gem9334@aol.com
Phone: 407-292-5780

Marika Tolz
1804 Sherman Street
Hollywood, FL 33020
E-mail: Tolzoffice@aol.com
Phone: 954-923-6536

Kenneth A. Welt
3790 N. 28th Terrace
Hollywood, FL 33020
Phone: 954-929-8000

GEORGIA

Note: The individuals listed are
private parties, not government
employees.

TRUSTEE(S) COVERING THE
MIDDLE DISTRICT OF GEORGIA

Paul L. Cames
314 Corder Road
P.O. Box 8499
Warner Robins, GA 31088
E-mail: paul.cames@
   camesandburge.com
Phone: 478-922-0922
Fax: 478-929-2568

Michael Patrick Cielinski
900 Second Avenue
P.O. Box 1615
Columbus, GA 31902
E-mail: jwaters44@mindspring.com
Phone: 706-323-4357
Fax: 706-323-1722

William M. Flatau
355 Cotton Avenue
Macon, GA 31201
E-mail: billflatau@hotmail.com
Phone: 478-742-6481
Fax: 478-742-0108

Ernest V. Harris
P.O. Box 1586
1045 S. Milledge
Athens, GA 30603
E-mail: ehlaw@bellsouth.net
Phone: 706-613-1953
Fax: 706-613-0053

Walter W. Kelley
P.O. Box 70879
Albany, GA 31708
E-mail: wkelley@
   kellylovetteandmullis.com
Phone: 229-888-9128
Fax: 229-888-0966

David E. Mullis
1102 Williams Street
P.O. Box 945
Valdosta, GA 31604
E-mail: DMullis@
   kelleyandmullis.com
Phone: 229-219-0014
Fax: 229-219-0074

J. Coleman Tidwell
154 Broadway
P.O. Box 1796
Macon, GA 31202
E-mail: colemantidwell@
   hotmail.com
Phone: 478-743-3890
Fax: 478-742-5688

Joy R. Webster
544 Mulberry Street, Suite 400
P.O. Box 1773
Macon, GA 31201
E-mail: jwebster@epitrustee.com
Phone: 478-742-1889
Fax: 478-742-7101

TRUSTEE(S) COVERING THE
NORTHERN DISTRICT OF
GEORGIA

L. Lou Allen
2971 Flowers Road, S., Suite 181
Atlanta, GA 30347
Phone: 770-455-3660

Paul Henry Anderson, Jr.
600 W. Peachtree Street, N.W.,
   Suite 1460
Atlanta, GA 30308
E-mail: asteele@gwtwlaw.com
Phone: 404-892-4144

Herbert C. Broadfoot II
2400 International Tower
229 Peachtree Street, N.E.
Atlanta, GA 30303-1629
Phone: 404-588-0500

Gary W. Brown
12 Jackson Street
Newnan, GA 30263
Phone: 770-251-1567

Dale R. F. Goodman
1801 Peachtree Street, Suite 210
Atlanta, GA 30309
Phone: 404-237-0800

Neil C. Gordon
1201 W. Peachtree Street, N.E.
2800 One Atlantic Center
Atlanta, GA 30309
Phone: 404-873-8596

S. Gregory Hays
3343 Peachtree Road, Suite 750
Atlanta, GA 30326-1085
Phone: 404-926-0051

Griffin E. Howell III
P.O. Box 551
Griffin, GA 30224
E-mail: newton_howell@
   mindspring.com
Phone: 770-227-0110

William J. Layng, Jr.
P.O. Box 56227
Atlanta, GA 30343
E-mail: blayng@mannbracken.com
Phone: 404-487-5563

Jordan E. Lubin
540 Power Springs Street,
   Suite 17-C
Marietta, GA 30064
Phone: 770-424-8281

Theo Davis Mann
28 Jackson Street
Newnan, GA 30264
Phone: 770-253-2222

James R. Marshall
170 Mitchell Street
Atlanta, GA 30303
E-mail: bktrustee@yahoo.com
Phone: 404-526-8869

Martha A. Miller
229 Peachtree Street, N.E.,
   Suite 2415
Atlanta, GA 30303
Phone: 404-607-9008

Tracey L. Montz
2100 Roswell Road, Suite 200C-406
Marietta, GA 30062
Phone: 404-713-6472

Betty A. Nappier
P.O. Box 1649
Cumming, GA 30028
E-mail: banappier@yahoo.com
Phone: 770-529-9371

Albert F. Nasuti
40 Technology Parkway S.,
   Suite 300
Norcross, GA 30092
Phone: 770-925-0111

Frances F. Gecker
311 S. Wacker Drive, Suite 3000
Chicago, IL 60606
Phone: 312-360-6607

John E. Gierum, Jr.
1030 W. Higgins Road, Suite 220
Park Ridge, IL 60068
Phone: 847-318-9130

Ilene F. Goldstein
425 Huehl Road, Suite 16B
Northbrook, IL 60062
Phone: 847-498-9595

David E. Grochocinski
800 Ravinia Place
Orland Park, IL 60462
Phone: 708-226-2700

Leonard M. Groupe
555 Skokie Boulevard
Northbrook, IL 60062
Phone: 847-480-1020

Megan G. Heeg
215 E. First Street, Suite 100
Dixon, IL 61021
Phone: 815-288-4949

Brenda Porter Helms
3400 W. Lawrence Avenue
Chicago, IL 60625
Phone: 630-267-7300

David R. Herzog
77 W. Washington Street,
    Suite 1717
Chicago, IL 60602
Phone: 312-977-1600

Glenn R. Heyman
135 S. LaSalle Street, #1540
Chicago, IL 60603
Phone: 312-641-6777

Daniel Hoseman
77 W. Washington Street,
    Suite 1220
Chicago, IL 60602
Phone: 312-372-5139

Leroy G. Inskeep
203 N. LaSalle Street, #1800
Chicago, IL 60601
Phone: 312-368-4067

Robert B. Katz
223 W. Jackson Boulevard,
    Suite 1010
Chicago, IL 60606
Phone: 312-705-1400

Alexander S. Knopfler
225 N. Michigan Avenue,
    Suite 1100
Chicago, IL 60601
Phone: 312-819-6363

Gina B. Krol
105 W. Adams Street, Suite 1100
Chicago, IL 60602
Phone: 312-368-0300

David P. Leibowitz
222 W. Washington Street
Waukegan, IL 60085-5618
Phone: 847-249-9100

Thomas J. Lester
100 Park Avenue
Rockford, IL 61101
Phone: 815-963-8488

Phillip D. Levey
2722 N. Racine Avenue
Chicago, IL 60614
Phone: 312-726-4475

Louis W. Levit
150 N. Michigan Avenue,
    Suite 2500
Chicago, IL 60601
Phone: 312-558-1000

Philip V. Martino
203 N. LaSalle Street, Suite 1800
Chicago, IL 60601
Phone: 312-368-2165

Richard J. Mason
150 N. Michigan Avenue,
    Suite 2500
Chicago, IL 60601
Phone: 312-558-1000

Andrew J. Maxwell
105 W. Adams Street, Suite 3200
Chicago, IL 60603
Phone: 312-368-1080

Alex D. Moglia
1325 Remington Road, Suite H
Schaumburg, IL 60173
Phone: 847-884-8282

Charles J. Myler
111 W. Downer Place
Aurora, IL 60506
Phone: 630-897-8475

Bernard J. Natale
308 W. State Street, Suite 470
Rockford, IL 61101
Phone: 815-964-4700

Norman B. Newman
191 N. Wacker Drive, Suite 1800
Chicago, IL 60606
Phone: 312-521-2000

Joseph D. Olsen
1318 E. State Street
Rockford, IL 61104-2228
Phone: 815-965-8635

Gus A. Paloian
55 E. Monroe Street, Suite 4200
Chicago, IL 60603
Phone: 312-346-8000

Ronald R. Peterson
One IBM Plaza, 38th Floor
Chicago, IL 60611
Phone: 312-222-9350

N. Neville Reid
190 S. LaSalle Street, Suite 3900
Chicago, IL 60603
Phone: 312-782-0600

Roy A. Safanda
11 East Side Drive
Geneva, IL 60134
Phone: 630-262-1761

Joel A. Schechter
53 W. Jackson Boulevard,
    Suite 1025
Chicago, IL 60604
Phone: 312-332-0267

Thomas E. Springer
611 S. Addison Road
Addison, IL 60101
Phone: 630-530-9999

Catherine L. Steege
One IBM Plaza, 38th Floor
Chicago, IL 60611
Phone: 312-222-9350

Jay A. Steinberg
One IBM Plaza
330 N. Wabash Avenue, 34th Floor
Chicago, IL 60611
Phone: 312-755-2676

James E. Stevens
One Madison Street
Rockford, IL 61104
Phone: 815-962-6611

Thomas B. Sullivan
800 Ravinia Place
Orland Park, IL 60462
Phone: 708-226-2700

Edward P. Dechert
217 N. Main Street
Kokomo, IN 46903-0665
Phone: 765-459-0764

Dennis J. Dewey
107 State Street
Newburgh, IN 47630
Phone: 812-853-3357

Gregory S. Fehribach
50 S. Meridian Street, #700
Indianapolis, IN 46204
Phone: 317-638-2400

Joanne B. Friedmeyer
135 N. Pennsylvania Street,
    Suite 2000
Indianapolis, IN 46204
Phone: 317-264-5000

Ellen K. Fujawa
P. O. Box 526
Greenwood, IN 46142
E-mail: efujawa@epitrustee.com
Phone: 317-888-4555

Jenice R. Golson-Dunlap
One Virginia Avenue, Suite 850
Indianapolis, IN 46204
Phone: 317-263-3580

Paul D. Gresk
Gateway Plaza, #410
950 N. Meridian Street
Indianapolis, IN 46204
Phone: 317-237-7911

Joseph W. Hammes
One Indiana Square, Suite 2100
Indianapolis, IN 46204
Phone: 317-639-5444

Michael J. Hebenstreit
151 N. Delaware Street, Suite 2000
Indianapolis, IN 46204
Phone: 317-638-5555

Donald G. Henderson
1635 I Street
Bedford, IN 47421-0909
P.O. Box 909
Bedford, IN 47421-0909
Phone: 812-279-9614

Rex M. Joseph, Jr.
South Point Professional Centre
5150 E. Stop 11 Road, Suite 12
Indianapolis, IN 46237
Phone: 317-859-0000

Robert S. Koor
215 W. Main Street
Muncie, IN 47305
Phone: 765-282-5592

Thomas A. Krudy
236 E. 15th Street
Indianapolis, IN 46202
Phone: 317-635-4428

R. Stephen LaPlante
915 Main Street, Suite 100
P.O. Box 3326
Evansville, IN 47732-3326
Phone: 812-421-1911

Elliott D. Levin
500 Marriott Center
342 Massachusetts Avenue
Indianapolis, IN 46204
Phone: 317-634-0300

Richard W. Lorenz
P.O. Box 46
Spencer, IN 47460-0046
E-mail: Fourmdavis@yahoo.com
Phone: 812-829-2221

John J. Petr
111 Monument Circle, Suite 900
700 Guaranty Building
Indianapolis, IN 46204-5175
Phone: 317-692-9000

Gregory K. Silver
342 Massachusetts Avenue, #400
Indianapolis, IN 46204
Phone: 317-263-9417

William J. Tabor
P.O. Box 328
Terre Haute, IN 47808
Phone: 812-877-3750

David J. Theising
P.O. Box 2850
Indianapolis, IN 46206
E-mail: theising@iquest.net
Phone: 317-635-9000

William J. Tucker
111 Monument Circle, #452
Indianapolis, IN 46204
Phone: 317-635-5005

Michael J. Walro
426 E. Main Street
Madison, IN 47250
Phone: 812-265-3617

Anastasia M. Wissel
P.O. Box 68
Decker, IN 47524-0068
E-mail: swissel@sbcglobal.net
Phone: 317-408-2851

Randall Lee Woodruff
115-A E. 9th Street
Anderson, IN 46016
Phone: 765-644-6464

IOWA

Note: The individuals listed are private parties, not government employees.

TRUSTEE(S) COVERING THE NORTHERN DISTRICT OF IOWA

Michael C. Dunbar
P.O. Box 1377
Waterloo, IA 50704
E-mail: mdunbar@cfu.net
Phone: 319-233-6327

Larry S. Eide
800 Brick and Tile Building
Mason City, IA 50401
P.O. Box 1588
Mason City, IA 50401
Phone: 515-423-4264

Paul J. Fitzsimmons
850 White Street
Dubuque, IA 52001
Phone: 319-588-4088

Wil L. Forker
505 Sixth Street, Suite 530
Sioux City, IA 51101
Phone: 712-252-1395

Renee K. Hanrahan
3519 Center Point Road, N.E.,
    Suite 200
Cedar Rapids, IA 52402
Phone: 319-378-0232

Wesley B. Huisinga
115 Third Street, S.E., Suite 500
Cedar Rapids, IA 52401
P.O. Box 2107
Cedar Rapids, IA 52406-2107
Phone: 319-365-9461

Donald H. Molstad
505 Sixth Street, Suite 308
Sioux City, IA 51101
Phone: 712-255-8036

Sheryl L. Schnittjer
310 Franklin Street
P.O. Box 375
Delhi, IA 52223
Phone: 563-922-9702

David A. Sergeant
1728 Central Avenue
P.O. Box 1315
Fort Dodge, IA 50501
Phone: 515-576-0333

Brian A. Goldman
36 S. Charles Street, 24th Floor
1500 Charles Center South
Baltimore, MD 21201
Phone: 410-547-1400

Charles R. Goldstein
2 N. Charles Street, Suite 400
Baltimore, MD 21201
Phone: 410-454-6800
Fax: 410-454-9801

Steven H. Greenfeld
5028 Wisconsin Avenue, N.W.,
    Suite 300
Washington, DC 20016
Phone: 202-537-7050

Zvi Guttman
P.O. Box 32308
Baltimore, MD 21282
E-mail: ZviGuttman@aol.com
Phone: 410-580-0500

Gregory P. Johnson
8455 Colesville Road, Suite 1080
Silver Spring, MD 20910
Phone: 301-608-3700

Richard M. Kremen
6225 Smith Avenue
Baltimore, MD 21209-3600
Phone: 410-580-3000

George W. Liebmann
8 W. Hamilton Street
Baltimore, MD 21201
Phone: 410-752-5887

Wendelin I. Lipp
4800 Hampden Lane, 7th Floor
Bethesda, MD 20814
Phone: 301-656-7603

Sean C. Logan
821 N. Charles Street
Baltimore, MD 21201
Phone: 410-539-8580

Janet M. Nesse
1150 18th Street, Suite 800
Washington, DC 20036
Phone: 202-785-9100

David E. Rice
2 Hopkins Plaza, Suite 1800
Baltimore, MD 21201
Phone: 410-244-7779

Michael G. Rinn
111 Warren Road, Suite 4
Cockeyville, MD 21030-2429
Phone: 410-683-1040

Cheryl E. Rose
50 W. Edmonston Drive, Suite 600
Rockville, MD 20850
Phone: 301-838-2010

Gary A. Rosen
One Church Street, Suite 802
Rockville, MD 20850
Phone: 301-251-0202

Roger Schlossberg
134 W. Washington Street
Hagerstown, MD 21740
Phone: 301-739-8610

Joel I. Sher
36 S. Charles Street, Suite 2000
Baltimore, MD 21201
Phone: 410-385-0202

Lori S. Simpson
2 N. Charles Street, Suite 500
Baltimore, MD 21201
Phone: 410-468-0054

Bud S. Tayman
6303 Ivy Lane, Suite 140
Greenbelt, MD 20770
Phone: 301-474-8831

Michael G. Wolff
11300 Rockville Pike, Suite 408
Rockville, MD 20852
Phone: 301-984-6266

MASSACHUSETTS

Note: The individuals listed are
private parties, not government
employees.

John James Aquino III
260 Franklin Street
Boston, MA 02110
Phone: 617-723-3500

Joseph H. Baldiga
1700 Bank of Boston Tower
100 Front Street
Worcester, MA 01608
Phone: 508-791-8500

William G. Billingham
506 Plain Street
Marshfield, MA 02050
Phone: 617-837-5252

Joseph S. Braunstein
3 Center Plaza
Boston, MA 02108
Phone: 617-523-9000

John Alfred Burdick, Jr.
340 Main Street, Suite 800
Worcester, MA 01608
Phone: 508-752-4633

Joseph G. Butler
50 Staniford Street, Suite 200
Boston, MA 02114-2500
Phone: 617-723-9800

Debora A. Casey
97 Whiting Street
Hingham, MA 02043
Phone: 617-749-8068

Joseph B. Collins
101 State Street
Springfield, MA 01103
Phone: 413-734-6411

Gary W. Cruickshank
21 Custom House Street, Suite 920
Boston, MA 02110
Phone: 617-330-1960

Mark Guy DeGiacomo
99 High Street, 20th Floor
Boston, MA 02110-2320
Phone: 617-451-9300

John O. Desmond
24 Union Avenue, Suite 4
Framingham, MA 01702
Phone: 508-879-9638

Kathleen P. Dwyer
8 Essex Center Drive
Peabody, MA 01960
E-mail: kdwyer@mhdpc.com
Phone: 978-774-7123
Fax: 978-774-7164

Stewart F. Grossman
101 Arch Street
Boston, MA 02110
Phone: 617-951-2800

Jack E. Houghton, Jr.
78 Bartlett Avenue
Pittsfield, MA 01201
Phone: 413-447-7385

Donald R. Lassman
P.O. Box 920385
Needham, MA 02492
Phone: 781-455-8400

David B. Madoff
101 Arch Street
Boston, MA 02110
Phone: 617-951-2505

Harold B. Murphy
One Beacon Street
Boston, MA 02108
Phone: 617-423-0400

David M. Nickless
495 Main Street
Fitchburg, MA 01420
Phone: 978-342-4590

David W. Ostrander
P.O. Box 1237
Northampton, MA 01061-1237
E-mail: David@Ostranderlaw.com
Phone: 413-585-9300

Lynne F. Riley
69 Thorndike Street
Cambridge, MA 02141
Phone: 617-876-3755

Matthew D. Rockman
340 Main Street, Suite 800
Worcester, MA 01608
Phone: 508-797-0525

Stephan M. Rodolakis
446 Main Street, 21st Floor
Worcester, MA 01608
Phone: 508-798-2480

Stephen E. Shamban
P.O. Box 850973
639 Granite Street
Braintree, MA 02185-0973
Phone: 508-849-1136

Tali A. Tomsic
P.O. Box 307
North Andover, MA 01845
E-mail: Nfaigel@aol.com
Phone: 978-687-8711

Gary M. Weiner
95 State Street, Suite 918
Springfield, MA 01103
Phone: 413-732-6840

Steven Weiss
1441 Main Street
Springfield, MA 01103
Phone: 413-737-1131

MICHIGAN

Note: The individuals listed are
private parties, not government
employees.

TRUSTEE(S) COVERING THE
EASTERN DISTRICT OF MICHIGAN

David W. Allard, Jr.
2600 Buhl Building
535 Griswold Street
Detroit, MI 48226
Phone: 313-961-6141

Collene K. Corcoran
803 W. Big Beaver Road,
   Suite 203-B
Troy, MI 48084
Phone: 248-988-1370
Fax: 248-989-1014

George P. Dakmak
600 Ford Building
615 Griswold Street
Detroit, MI 48226
Phone: 313-964-0800

Frederick J. Dery
803 W. Big Beaver, Suite 353
Troy, MI 48084
Phone: 313-362-4655

Douglas S. Ellmann
308 W. Huron
Ann Arbor, MI 48103
Phone: 313-668-4800

Karen E. Evangelista
903 Opdyke, Suite A
Auburn Hills, MI 48326
E-mail: kee1008@aol.com
Phone: 248-276-2533

Randall L. Frank
310 Davidson Building
Bay City, MI 48707
P.O. Box 2220
Bay City, MI 48707
Phone: 517-893-2461

Stuart A. Gold
24901 Northwestern Highway,
   Suite 444
Southfield, MI 48075
Phone: 810-350-8220

G. E. Grogan
3176 Penobscot Building
Detroit, MI 48226
Phone: 313-963-6240

Daniel C. Himmelspach
4371 State Street
Saginaw, MI 48603
Phone: 517-790-0400

Gene R. Kohut
21 Kercheval Avenue, Suite 285
Gross Pointe Farms, MI 48236
Phone: 313-886-9765
Fax: 313-886-9762

Wendy T. Lewis
456 E. Milwaukee
Detroit, MI 48202
Phone: 313-875-5555

Kyung-jin Lim
645 Griswold, Suite 3900
Detroit, MI 48226
Phone: 313-237-0850

Michael A. Mason
516 W. Court Street
Flint, MI 48503
Phone: 810-234-4941

Homer W. McClarty
24400 Northwestern Highway,
   Suite 204
Southfield, MI 48075
Phone: 810-352-7686

Kenneth Andrew Nathan
29100 Northwestern Highway
260 Franklin Center
Southfield, MI 48034
Phone: 810-351-0099

Mark H. Shapiro
24901 Northwestern Highway,
   Suite 611
Bloomfield Hills, MI 48075
Phone: 248-352-4700

Basil T. Simon
422 W. Congress, Suite 350
Detroit, MI 48226
Phone: 313-962-6400

Sheila Solomon
527 N. Main Street
Royal Oak, MI 48067
Phone: 248-414-4035

Michael A. Stevenson
29200 Southfield Road,
   Suite 210
Southfield, MI 48076
Phone: 248-423-8200

Samuel D. Sweet
P.O. Box 757
Ortonville, MI 48462-0757
E-mail: trusteesweet@hotmail.com
Phone: 248-236-0985
Fax: 248-236-0984

Charles Joseph Taunt
700 E. Maple Road, Second Floor
Birmingham, MI 48009-6359
Phone: 248-647-1127

Charles L. Wells III
903 N. Opdyke Road, Suite A1
Auburn Hills, MI 48326
E-mail: charlwel2@aol.com
Phone: 248-276-0285
Fax: 248-276-0675

TRUSTEE(S) COVERING THE
WESTERN DISTRICT OF
MICHIGAN

Rose Ellen Bareham
P.O. Box 207
Frankenmuth, MI 48837
E-mail: RoseBareham@msn.com
Phone: 517-622-8553

James Wesley Boyd
412 S. Union Street
Traverse City, MI 49684
Phone: 231-941-3446

Thomas Allen Bruinsma
6812 Old 28th Street, Suite E
Grand Rapids, MI 49546
Phone: 616-975-2010

Darrell R. Dettmann
148 W. Washington Street
Marquette, MI 49855
Phone: 906-228-7355

Lisa E. Gocha
675 E. 16th Street, #255
Holland, MI 49423
Phone: 616-395-5205
Fax: 616-662-4148

James William Hoerner
One Timber Trail, S.E.
Ada, MI 49301
Phone: 616-676-0365

Stephen L. Langeland
350 E. Michigan Street, Suite 200
Kalamazoo, MI 49007
Phone: 616-382-3703

Marcia R. Meoli
503 Century Lane
Holland, MI 49422-1559
P.O. Box 1559
Holland, MI 49422-1559
Phone: 616-396-1245

Jeffrey A. Moyer
2757 44th Street, S.W., Suite 304BB
Wyoming, MI 49509
P.O. Box 337
Grandville, MI 49468-0337
Phone: 616-724-1892

Colleen M. Olson
Grandview Plaza, Suite 3309
10850 E. Traverse Highway
Traverse City, MI 49684
Phone: 231-946-6878

John A. Porter
6059 Cannon Highlands Drive, N.E.
Belmont, MI 49417
Phone: 616-874-4800

Thomas C. Richardson
136 E. Michigan Avenue, Suite 8000
Kalamazoo, MI 49007
P.O. Box 51067
Kalamazoo, MI 49005-1067
E-mail: thomasrichardson2@
    earthlink.net
Phone: 269-388-7600

Thomas R. Tibble
2813 W. Main Street
Kalamazoo, MI 49007
Phone: 616-342-9482

MINNESOTA

Note: The individuals listed are private parties, not government employees.

Paul W. Bucher
206 S. Broadway, Suite 505
P.O. Box 549
Rochester, MN 55903-0549
Phone: 507-288-9111

Julia A. Christians
120 S. Sixth Street, Suite 2500
Minneapolis, MN 55402
Phone: 612-338-5815

Michael S. Dietz
505 Marquette Bank Building
P.O. Box 549
Rochester, MN 55903
Phone: 507-288-9111

Terri A. Georgen
P.O. Box 16355
St. Paul, MN 55101-2133
E-mail: TGeorgen@GeorgenLaw
    .com
Phone: 651-699-6980

John A. Hedback
2855 Anthony Lane S., Suite 201
St. Anthony, MN 55418
Phone: 612-789-1331

Michael J. Iannacone
444 Cedar Street, Suite 575
St. Paul, MN 55101
Phone: 651-224-3361

Mary Jo A. Jensen-Carter
1339 E. County Road D
Vadnais Heights, MN 55109
Phone: 651-486-7475

Robert R. Kanuit
4814 W. Arrowhead Road, Suite 230
Hermantown, MN 55811
Phone: 218-722-7722

Dorraine A. Larison
1010 W. St. Germain, Suite 600
St. Cloud, MN 56301
Phone: 320-252-4414

Brian F. Leonard
100 S. 5th Street, Suite 1200
Minneapolis, MN 55402
Phone: 612-332-1030

Dwight R.J. Lindquist
527 Marquette Avenue, Suite 1510
Minneapolis, MN 55402
Phone: 612-332-8871

Nauni Jo Manty
3601 W. 76th Street, Suite 250
Minneapolis, MN 55435
Phone: 952-646-0400

Timothy D. Moratzka
1400 AT&T Tower
901 Marquette Avenue
Minneapolis, MN 55402-2859
Phone: 612-305-1400

Charles W. Ries
P.O. Box 7
Mankato, MN 56002-0007
E-mail: CW_Ries@MRR-Law.com
Phone: 507-625-6600

Randall Seaver
12400 Portland Avenue S., Suite 132
Burnsville, MN 55337
Phone: 952-890-0888

John R. Stoebner
2500 One Financial Plaza
120 S. 6th Street
Minneapolis, MN 55402
Phone: 612-338-5815

Patti J. Sullivan
P.O. Box 16406
St. Paul, MN 55116
E-mail: Patti@mm.com
Phone: 651-699-4825

David G. Velde
1118 Broadway
Alexandria, MN 56308
Phone: 320-763-6561

Tamara L. Yon
407 N. Broadway
Crookston, MN 56716
Phone: 218-281-2400

MISSISSIPPI

Note: The individuals listed are private parties, not government employees.

TRUSTEE(S) COVERING THE
NORTHERN DISTRICT OF
MISSISSIPPI

Alexander Brown Gates
P.O. Box 216
Sumner, MS 38957
E-mail: Abgates@network.com
Phone: 662-375-8728

Erlene W. Krigel
4550 Belview
Kansas City, MO 64111
Phone: 816-756-5800

Jere L. Loyd
507 Francis Street, #208-12
St. Joseph, MO 64501
Phone: 816-364-3020

Fred Charles Moon
3275 E. Ridgeview Street, Suite C
Springfield, MO 65803
Phone: 417-862-3704
Fax: 417-862-1936

Dan R. Nelson
1845 S. National
Springfield, MO 65808-4288
P.O. Box 4288
Springfield, MO 65808-4288
Phone: 417-877-5900

Thomas J. O'Neal
901 St. Louis Street, #1200
Springfield, MO 65806
Phone: 417-869-3353

Aunna L. Peoples
4550 Main Street, Suite 217
Kansas City, MO 64111
Phone: 816-531-2700

Robert A. Pummill
6801 W. 107th Street, Suite 1000
Overland Park, MO 66212
Phone: 913-648-8877

John Charles Reed
325 Jefferson Street
Jefferson City, MO 65102
Phone: 573-635-8500

Norman E. Rouse
20th and Prosperity Road
P.O. Box 1846
Joplin, MO 64802-1846
Phone: 417-782-2222

Maureen A. Scully
P.O. Box 30233
Kansas City, MO 64112
E-mail: scullyn@umkc.edu
Phone: 816-235-6139

Janice C. Stanton
104 W. 9th Street, Suite 303
Kansas City, MO 64105
Phone: 816-421-7770

David C. Stover
9800 N.W. Polo Drive, Suite 100
Kansas City, MO 64153
Phone: 816-454-5600

Bruce E. Strauss
1044 Main Street, 7th Floor
Kansas City, MO 64105
Phone: 816-221-8855

MONTANA

Note: The individuals listed are private parties, not government employees.

Darcy M. Crum
P.O. Box 2720
Great Falls, MT 59403-2720
Phone: 406-727-8400

Gary S. Deschenes
104 Fourth Street N., Suite 201
Great Falls, MT 59403
P.O. Box 3466
Great Falls, MT 59403
Phone: 406-761-6112

William M. Kebe, Jr.
129 W. Park
Butte, MT 59703
P.O. Box 509
Butte, MT 59703
Phone: 406-782-5800

Craig D. Martinson
303 N. Broadway, Suite 830
Billings, MT 59101
Phone: 406-248-9346

Ross P. Richardson
116 W. Granite
Butte, MT 59703
P.O. Box 399
Butte, MT 59703
Phone: 406-723-3219

Richard J. Samson
310 W. Spruce
Missoula, MT 59807
P.O. Box 8479
Missoula, MT 59807
Phone: 406-721-7772

Donald W. Torgenrud, Jr.
109 1st Avenue
St. Ignatius, MT 59865
P.O. Box 490
St. Ignatius, MT 59865
Phone: 406-745-2711

Joseph V. Womack
303 N. Broadway, Suite 805
Billings, MT 59102
Phone: 406-252-7200

NEBRASKA

Note: The individuals listed are private parties, not government employees.

Joseph H. Badami
301 S. 13th Street, Suite 500
Lincoln, NE 68508
Phone: 402-437-8521

Philip M. Kelly
105 E. 16th Street
Scottsbluff, NE 69363
Phone: 308-632-7191

Rick D. Lange
1201 Lincoln Mall, Suite 102
Lincoln, NE 68508
Phone: 402-475-5100

Richard D. Myers
11404 W. Dodge Road,
    Suite 500
Omaha, NE 68154
Phone: 402-492-9200

Stacy C. Nossaman-Petitt
115 Railway Street, Suite B-107
Scottsbluff, NE 69363
Phone: 308-632-3089

Thomas D. Stalnaker
8805 Indian Hills Drive, #325
Omaha, NE 68114
Phone: 402-393-5421

James J. Stumpf
11623 Arbor Street, #100
Omaha, NE 68144
Phone: 402-333-1200

John A. Wolf
P.O. Box 460
Grand Island, NE 68802
E-mail: Jwolflaw@cccusa.net
Phone: 308-384-1635

NEVADA

Note: The individuals listed are private parties, not government employees.

Angelique L. M. Clark
P.O. Box 50070
Sparks, NV 89435
Phone: 775-356-8099

Jeri Ann Coppa-Knudson
145 Mt. Rose Street
Reno, NV 89509
Phone: 702-329-1528

Timothy S. Cory
520 S. 4th Street, #220
Las Vegas, NV 89101
Phone: 702-388-1996

Richard A. Davis
2810 W. Charleston Boulevard,
   G-71
Las Vegas, NV 89102
Phone: 702-880-4200

Tom R. Grimmett
2275 Corporate Circle, Suite 120
Henderson, NV 89074
Phone: 702-740-4152

S. Scott Hopping
P.O. Box 38
Elko, NV 89830
E-mail: scotthopping@aol.com
Phone: 775-777-9116
Fax: 775-778-9505

William A. Leonard, Jr.
5030 Paradise Road, #A-201
Las Vegas, NV 89119
Phone: 702-262-9322

James F. Lisowski, Sr.
1771 E. Flamingo Road, Suite 115 B
Las Vegas, NV 89101
Phone: 702-737-6111

Stanley W. Pack
P.O. Box 620834
Las Vegas, NV 89162-0834
E-mail: stanpacktrustee@yahoo.com
Phone: 702-453-5914
Fax: 702-453-4813

Anabelle G. Savage
3336 Spring Creek Circle
Reno, NV 89509
Phone: 775-324-6121

Barry L. Solomon
1000 Bible Way, Suite 40
Reno, NV 89502
Phone: 775-324-0922

Yvette P. Weinstein
6450 Spring Mountain Road, #14-G
Las Vegas, NV 89146
Phone: 702-364-8919

NEW HAMPSHIRE

Note: The individuals listed are
private parties, not government
employees.

Michael S. Askenaizer
60 Main Street, Suite 200
Nashua, NH 03060
Phone: 603-594-0300

Victor W. Dahar
20 Merrimack Street
Manchester, NH 03101
Phone: 603-622-6595

Edmond J. Ford
10 Pleasant Street, Suite 400
Portsmouth, NH 03801
Phone: 603-433-2002

Steven M. Notinger
402 Amherst Street, Suite 204
Nashua, NH 03603
Phone: 603-886-7266

Timothy P. Smith
67 Middle Street
Manchester, NH 03101
Phone: 603-623-0036

NEW JERSEY

Note: The individuals listed are
private parties, not government
employees.

Bunce D. Atkinson
P.O. Box 8415
Red Bank, NJ 07701
E-mail: ADKLaw@aol.com
Phone: 732-530-5300
Fax: 732-530-9877

Karen E. Bezner
567 Park Avenue, Suite 103
Scotch Plains, NJ 07076
Phone: 908-322-8484
Fax: 908-322-0560

Donald V. Biase
22 Oak Drive
Roseland, NJ 07068
Phone: 973-618-1008
Fax: 973-226-2258

John A. Casarow, Jr.
32 N. Pearl Street
Bridgeton, NJ 08302
Phone: 856-455-0566
Fax: 856-455-6593

Nicholas J. Delzotti
11 Franklin Street, 3rd Floor
Newark, NJ 07102
Phone: 973-622-3464
Fax: 973-622-6422

Andrea Dobin
50 W. State Street
Trenton, NJ 08607
Phone: 609-392-2100
Fax: 609-392-7956

Barbara A. Edwards
The Vanguard Building
21-00 Route 208 S.
Fair Lawn, NJ 07410
Phone: 201-796-3100
Fax: 201-791-0350

Charles M. Forman
218 Route 17 N.
Rochelle, NJ 07662
Phone: 201-845-1000
Fax: 201-845-9112

Barry W. Frost
691 Route #33
Trenton, NJ 08619
Phone: 609-890-1500
Fax: 609-890-6961

John W. Hargrave
216 Haddon Avenue, Suite 510
Westmont, NJ 08108
Phone: 856-854-3410
Fax: 856-854-0187

Nancy Isaacson
100 Morris Avenue, 3rd Floor
Springfield, NJ 07081
Phone: 973-258-0500
Fax: 973-258-0707

Gary S. Jacobson
P.O. Box 276
Liberty Corner, NJ 07938-0276
E-mail: gsjtrustee@aol.com
Phone: 908-647-1022
Fax: 908-647-7721

Steven P. Kartzman
101 Gibraltar Drive, Suite 2F
Morris Plains, NJ 07950
Phone: 967-267-0220
Fax: 973-267-2402

Jonathan Kohn
50 Park Place
Newark, NJ 07102
Phone: 973-622-7713
Fax: 973-733-9817

David E. Krell
56 Fayette Street
Bridgeton, NJ 08302
Phone: 856-455-6000
Fax: 856-451-2029

Jeffrey A. Lester
374 Main Street
Hackensack, NJ 07601
Phone: 201-487-5544
Fax: 201-487-4026

Theodore Liscinski, Jr.
265 Davidson Avenue, Suite 200
Somerset, NJ 08873
Phone: 732-469-9008
Fax: 732-469-7655

Jay L. Lubetkin
100 Executive Drive, Suite 100
West Orange, NJ 07052
Phone: 973-243-8600
Fax: 973-243-8677

Carmen J. Maggio
19 Main Avenue
Clifton, NJ 07014
Phone: 973-661-1311
Fax: 973-661-3066

Joseph D. Marchand
117-119 W. Broad St.
Bridgeton, NJ 08302
P.O. Box 298
Bridgeton, NJ 08302
E-mail: JMarchand@epiqtrustee.com
Phone: 856-451-7600
Fax: 856-451-6535

John M. McDonnell III
609 Main Street
Toms River, NJ 08754-0476
P.O. Box 476
Toms River, NJ 08754-0476
E-mail: JohnMcDonnellEsq@
  aol.com
Phone: 732-341-7551
Fax: 732-505-3109

Linda L. McMackin
669 Grove Road
Thorofare, NJ 08086
Phone: 856-848-3600
Fax: 856-848-3818

Stacey L. Meisel
354 Eisenhower Parkway,
  Suite 2800
Livingston, NJ 07039
Phone: 973-422-1100
Fax: 973-422-9122

Steven R. Neuner
Willow Ridge Executive Office Park
750 Route 73 S., Suite 210
Marlton, NJ 08053
Phone: 856-596-2828
Fax: 856-985-6176

Joseph J. Newman
4 Concord Street
Cranford, NJ 07016
Phone: 908-276-9371
Fax: 908-276-2547

Michael I. Okechuku
936 Broad Street, 2nd Floor
Newark, NJ 07102
Phone: 973-848-1400
Fax: 973-848-0466

Thomas J. Orr
321 High Street, 2nd Floor
Burlington, NJ 08016
Phone: 609-386-8700
Fax: 609-386-7765

Eric R. Perkins
3 University Plaza, 5th Floor
Hackensack, NJ 07601
Phone: 201-488-9080
Fax: 201-488-5580

Albert Russo
268 Broad Street
Red Bank, NJ 07701
Phone: 732-741-1212
Fax: 732-741-3888

Barry R. Sharer
1103 Laurel Oaks Road, Suite 105B
Voorhees, NJ 08043
Phone: 856-435-3200
Fax: 856-435-4868

Andrew S. Sklar
701 White Horse Road
Adams Place, Suite 5
Voorhees, NJ 08043
Phone: 856-435-5394
Fax: 856-435-8469

Peggy E. Stalford
100 Main Street
Allenhurst, NJ 07711
Phone: 732-517-8555
Fax: 732-517-8545

Douglas S. Stanger
2900 Fire Road, Suite 102A
East Harbor Twp., NJ 08234
Phone: 609-645-1881
Fax: 609-645-9932

Charles A. Stanziale
22 Crestmont Road
Montclair, NJ 07042
Phone: 973-746-6000
Fax: 973-746-5849

Benjamin A. Stanziale, Jr.
91 Main Street
West Orange, NJ 07052
Phone: 973-731-9393
Fax: 973-731-9401

Daniel E. Straffi
670 Commons Way
Toms River, NJ 08755
Phone: 732-341-3800
Fax: 732-341-3548

Thomas J. Subranni
1624 Pacific Avenue
Atlantic City, NJ 08401
Phone: 609-347-7000
Fax: 609-345-4545

John W. Sywilok
51 Main Street
Hackensack, NJ 07601
Phone: 201-487-9390
Fax: 201-487-9393

Brian S. Thomas
327 Central Avenue, Suite 104
Linwood, NJ 08221
Phone: 609-601-6066
Fax: 609-601-6061

Robert B. Wasserman
225 Millburn Avenue, Suite 207
Millburn, NJ 07041
P.O. Box 1029
Millburn, NJ 07041
E-mail: attys@wjslaw.com
Phone: 973-467-2700
Fax: 973-467-8126

David A. Wolff
One Gateway Center
Newark, NJ 07102-5386
Phone: 973-621-9020
Fax: 973-621-7406

Daniel J. Yablonsky
1600 Route 208 N.
Hawthorne, NJ 07506
Phone: 973-427-2277
Fax: 973-427-0110

Catherine E. Youngman
9-10 Saddle River Road
Fair Lawn, NJ 07410-5793
Phone: 201-791-4400
Fax: 201-791-5659

NEW MEXICO

Note: The individuals listed are private parties, not government employees.

Linda S. Bloom
P.O. Box 218
Albuquerque, NM 87103-0218
Phone: 505-764-9600

Thomas J. Gaffney
80 W. Huron Street
Buffalo, NY 14202
Phone: 716-852-1102

Kenneth W. Gordon
100 Meridian Centre Boulevard,
    Suite 120
Rochester, NY 14618
Phone: 585-244-1070

Warren H. Heilbronner
2400 Chase Square
Rochester, NY 14604
Phone: 585-232-5300

John H. Heyer II
604 Exchange National Bank
    Building
P.O. Box 588
Olean, NY 14760
Phone: 716-372-0395

Morris L. Horwitz
2696 Sheridan Drive
Tonawanda, NY 14150-9414
Phone: 716-838-4300

Edwin R. Ilardo
5899 S. Park Avenue
P.O. Box 887
Hamburg, NY 14075-0887
Phone: 716-646-1190

C. Bruce Lawrence
2400 Chase Square
Rochester, NY 14604
Phone: 585-232-5300

William E. Lawson
500 Convention Tower
Buffalo, NY 14202
Phone: 716-854-3015

Douglas J. Lustig
2 State Street, Suite 1600
Rochester, NY 14614
Phone: 585-261-6461

Lucien A. Morin II
25 E. Main Street, Suite 500
Rochester, NY 14614
Phone: 716-546-2500

John Henry Ring III
360 Dingens Street
Cheektowaga, NY 14206
Phone: 716-826-3038

Mark J. Schlant
404 Cathedral Place
298 Main Street
Buffalo, NY 14202
Phone: 716-855-3200

Peter R. Scribner
1110 Park Avenue
Rochester, NY 14610
Phone: 585-261-6461

Richard P. Vullo
2000 Winton Road S.
Building 4, Suite 100
Rochester, NY 14618
Phone: 585-262-2320

Mark S. Wallach
169 Delaware Avenue
Buffalo, NY 14202
Phone: 716-852-1835

NORTH CAROLINA

The U.S. Trustee Program does not administer bankruptcy estates in North Carolina at this time. Questions about cases in North Carolina should be addressed to:

The Administrative Office of the U.S. Courts
Bankruptcy Judges Division
1 Columbus Circle, N.E.,
    Suite 4-250
Washington, DC 20544
Phone: 202-502-1900

NORTH DAKOTA

Note: The individuals listed are private parties, not government employees.

Wayne E. Drewes
650 1st Avenue N., Suite 113
P.O. Box 1021
Fargo, ND 58107
E-mail: waynedrewes@earthlink.net
Phone: 701-237-6650

Kip M. Kaler
111 Roberts Street
Fargo, ND 58107
P.O. Box 423
Fargo, ND 58107
Phone: 701-232-8757

Michael L. Wagner
1533 N. 12th Street
Bismarck, ND 58502-2056
P.O. Box 639
Bismarck, ND 58502-2056
Phone: 701-530-9410

NORTHERN MARIANA ISLANDS

Note: The individual listed is a private party, not a government employee.

Robert J. Steffy, Sr.
210 Archbishop Flores Street,
    Suite 100
Hagatna, GU 96910
Phone: 671-477-7829

OHIO

Note: The individuals listed are private parties, not government employees.

TRUSTEE(S) COVERING THE NORTHERN DISTRICT OF OHIO

Farley K. Banks
311 E. Market Street, Suite 201
Lima, OH 45801
Phone: 419-222-9933
Fax: 419-222-9245

Brian Alan Bash
1900 E. 9th Street, Suite 3200
Cleveland, OH 44114
Phone: 216-621-0200

Richard A. Baumgart
Ohio Savings Plaza
1801 E. 9th Street, Suite 1100
Cleveland, OH 44114-3169
Phone: 216-696-6000

Mark A. Beatrice
201 E. Commerce Street,
    Level Two
Youngstown, OH 44503
Phone: 330-743-1171

Kathryn Augusta Belfance
One Cascade Plaza, Suite 900
Akron, OH 44308
Phone: 330-535-0505

Virgil E. Brown, Jr.
2136 Noble Road
Cleveland, OH 44112
Phone: 216-851-3304

Michael Douglas Buzulencia
253 E. Market Street, Third Floor
Warren, OH 44481
Phone: 330-392-8551

D. William Davis
407-A Howard Street
Bridgeport, OH 43912
Phone: 740-635-1217

Elizabeth H. Doucet
895 S. High Street
Columbus, OH 43206
Phone: 614-444-5700

Eileen Kay Field
36 E. 4th Street, Suite 1305
Cincinnati, OH 45202
Phone: 513-684-9000

Thomas James Geygan
805-0 Hosbrook Road, Suite 107
Cincinnati, OH 45236
Phone: 513-791-1673

Eric W. Goering
220 W. Third Street
Cincinnati, OH 45202
Phone: 513-621-0912

Mark Alan Greenberger
105 E. 4th Street, Suite 400
Cincinnati, OH 45202
Phone: 513-721-5151

Clyde C. Hardesty III
1763 Bryn Mawr Circle
Newark, OH 43055
P.O. Box 731
Newark, OH 43058-0731
Phone: 740-344-6567

Donald F. Harker III
One First National Plaza
130 W. 2nd Street, Suite 2103
Dayton, OH 45402
Phone: 937-461-8800

Eleanor E. Haynes-Beavers
399 E. Main Street, Suite 200
Columbus, OH 43215
Phone: 614-221-9500
Fax: 614-621-1115

Thomas Mck. Hazlett
185 W. Main Street
St. Clairsville, OH 43950
Phone: 740-695-9202

Harold Jarnicki
27 N. East Street
Lebanon, OH 45026
Phone: 513-932-5792

Carl E. Juergens
1504 N. Limestone Street
Springfield, OH 45503
Phone: 937-399-8180

Monica V. Kindt
250 E. Fifth Street, Suite 1200
Cincinnati, OH 45202
Phone: 513-333-5245

David Willard Kuhn
Courthouse Annex
612 6th Avenue, Suite A,
Portsmouth, OH 45662
Phone: 740-354-1454

George P. Leicht
202 E. Plane Street
Bethel, OH 45106
Phone: 513-734-4848

William Boyd Logan, Jr.
50 W. Broad Street, Suite 1200
Columbus, OH 43215-3374
Phone: 614-229-4449

Frederick Morris Luper
50 W. Broad Street, #1200
Columbus, OH 43215-3374
Phone: 614-229-4409

Roger E. Luring
314 W. Main Street
Troy, OH 45373
Phone: 937-339-2627

Larry J. McClatchey
65 E. State Street, Suite 1800
Columbus, OH 43215
Phone: 614-462-5463

Henry Edward Menninger, Jr.
2500 Cincinnati Commerce Center
600 Vine Street
Cincinnati, OH 45202
Phone: 513-852-6033

David L. Mikel
210 W. Main Street
Troy, OH 45373
Phone: 937-339-0511

Richard D. Nelson
250 E. Fifth Street, 12th Floor
Cincinnati, OH 45202
Phone: 513-333-5255

Thomas R. Noland
110 N. Main Street,
1520 Fifth Third Center
Dayton, OH 45402-1520
Phone: 937-294-7704

Elliott Polaniecki
9000 Plainfield Road
Cincinnati, OH 45236
Phone: 513-793-5999
Fax: 513-793-4691

Frederick L. Ransier III
52 E. Gay Street
Columbus, OH 43215
P.O. Box 1008
Columbus, OH 43216-1008
Phone: 614-464-8226

Susan L. Rhiel
392 E. Town Street
Columbus, OH 43215
Phone: 614-221-4670
Fax: 614-232-9306

John Paul Rieser
1520 First National Plaza
130 W. 2nd Street
Dayton, OH 45402-1519
Phone: 937-224-4128

Ruth Ann Slone-Stiver
22 Brown Street
Dayton, OH 45401
P.O. Box 3340
Dayton, OH 45401
Phone: 937-222-9687

Norman L. Slutsky
4153-U Crossgate Drive
Cincinnati, OH 45236
Phone: 513-793-5560

Paul H. Spaeth
12 W. Monument Avenue, Suite 100
Dayton, OH 45402-1202
Phone: 937-223-1655

Dennis E. Stegner
111 E. Cecil Street
Springfield, OH 45504
Phone: 937-322-2161

Myron N. Terlecky
392 E. Town Street
Columbus, OH 43215
Phone: 614-221-4670
Fax: 614-232-9306

James R. Warren
34 W. Main Street, Suite 934
Springfield, OH 45502
P.O. Box 706
Springfield, OH 45501
Phone: 937-323-1131

David M. Whittaker
50 W. Broad Street, Suite 1200
Columbus, OH 43215-3374
Phone: 614-221-7663

Lori A. Williams-DeKalb
808 24th Avenue, N.W., Suite 105
Norman, OK 73069
Phone: 405-292-1212
Fax: 405-292-1202

OREGON

Note: The individuals listed are private parties, not government employees.

Candace E. Amborn
P.O. Box 580
Medford, OR 97501-0214
Phone: 541-858-9591

Michael B. Batlan
P.O. Box 3729
Salem, OR 97302
Phone: 503-588-9192

Kenneth S. Eiler
515 N.W. Saltzman Road
PMB 810
Portland, OR 97229
Phone: 503-292-6020

Michael A. Grassmueck
P.O. Box 5248
Portland, OR 97208
E-mail: Magi@spiritone.com
Phone: 503-294-9928

Thomas A. Huntsberger
870 W. Centennial
Springfield, OR 97477
Phone: 541-746-6574

Amy E. Mitchell
P.O. Box 14490
Portland, OR 97293
Phone: 503-827-4480

John Harvey Mitchell
P.O. Box 14490
Portland, OR 97293
Phone: 503-827-4480

Robert K. Morrow
P.O. Box 1328
1515 S.W. 5th Avenue, Suite 600
Portland, OR 97207
E-mail: Robert.Morrow@psinet.com
Phone: 503-227-5120

Thomas M. Renn
P.O. Box 91399
Portland, OR 97291-0399
Phone: 503-645-1497

Robert E. Ridgway
P.O. Box 993
Pendleton, OR 97801
E-mail: rrtrustee@ucinet.com
Phone: 541-276-0124
Fax: 541-276-2959

Eric R. T. Roost
P.O. Box 12060
Eugene, OR 97440
Phone: 541-485-8565

Ronald R. Sticka
P.O. Box 10990
Eugene, OR 97440
Phone: 541-344-0695

David F. Wurst
P.O. Box 610
Medford, OR 97501
Phone: 541-773-6761

PENNSYLVANIA

Note: The individuals listed are private parties, not government employees.

TRUSTEE(S) COVERING THE EASTERN DISTRICT OF PENNSYLVANIA

Terry P. Dershaw
P.O. Box 556
Bryn Athyn, PA 19090-0556
E-mail: TD@IX.NETCOM.COM
Phone: 215-322-0774

David Alan Eisenberg
1132 Hamilton Street, Suite 204
Allentown, PA 18101
Phone: 610-437-1410

Bonnie B. Finkel
P.O. Box 1710
Cherry Hill, NJ 08034-0091
E-mail: finkeltrustee@comcast.net
Phone: 856-216-1278

Howard T. Glassman
One Logan Square, 3rd Floor
Philadelphia, PA 19103
Phone: 215-569-5568

Robert H. Holber
41 E. Front Street
Media, PA 19063-2807
Phone: 610-565-5463

Michael H. Kaliner
312 Oxford Valley Road
Fairless Hills, PA 19030
Phone: 215-946-4342

Marvin Krasny
1650 Arch Street, 22nd Floor
Philadelphia, PA 19103-2097
Phone: 215-977-2096

Lawrence J. Lichtenstein
127 Mews, 404 Kings Highway
Haddonfield, NJ 08033
Phone: 856-428-2433

Arthur P. Liebersohn
924 Cherry Street
Philadelphia, PA 19107
Phone: 215-922-7990

Mary T. Martin
19 Byberry Avenue
Hatboro, PA 19040
Phone: 215-675-6940

Gloria M. Satriale
One McKinley Lane
Chester Springs, PA 19425
Phone: 610-827-4038

Gary F. Seitz
222 Delaware Avenue, Suite 900
P.O. Box 25130
Wilmington, DE 19888-5130
Phone: 302-429-4247
Fax: 302-658-6395

Christine C. Shubert
10 Teaberry Drive
Medford, NJ 0805-5
Phone: 856-983-7735
Fax: 856-983-7736

Barry A. Solodky
28 Penn Square
Lancaster, PA 17603
Phone: 717-299-1100

Wayne R. Walker
Two Penn Center Plaza, Suite 7000
Philadelphia, PA 19102
Phone: 215-972-2528

TRUSTEE(S) COVERING THE MIDDLE DISTRICT OF PENNSYLVANIA

Charles A. Bierbach
113 Fourth Street
Huntington, PA 16652
E-mail: cbierbach@bmzlaw.com
Phone: 814-643-3555

Steven M. Carr
119 E. Market Street
York, PA 17401
E-mail: Carr20@aol.com or
    Steven.Carr@psinet.com
Phone: 717-843-8968

George W. Stevenson
200 Jefferson Avenue, Suite 1113
Memphis, TN 38103
Phone: 901-576-1313

Michael T. Tabor
202 W. Baltimore
P.O. Box 2877
Jackson, TN 38301
Phone: 731-424-3074

Marianna G. Williams
P.O. Box H
Dyersburg, TN 38024
E-mail: marianna@ashleyarnold.com
Phone: 731-285-5074

TEXAS

Note: The individuals listed are private parties, not government employees.

TRUSTEE(S) COVERING THE
EASTERN DISTRICT OF TEXAS

Bob A. Anderson
2110 Horseshoe Lane
Longview, TX 75605
Phone: 903-232-1880

Michelle H. Chow
5207 McKinney Avenue
Dallas, TX 75205
Phone: 214-521-6627

Daniel J. Goldberg
2 Riverway, Suite 700
Houston, TX 77056
Phone: 713-626-1200

Michael J. McNally
400 First Place
(Broadway and Ferguson)
Tyler, TX 75702
Phone: 903-597-6301

Christopher J. Moser
2001 Bryan Street, Suite 1800
Dallas, TX 75201
Phone: 214-880-1805

Linda S. Payne
First National Bank Building,
    Suite 300
Paris, TX 75460
Phone: 903-784-4393

Jason R. Searcy
P.O. Box 3929
119 W. Tyler, #168
Longview, TX 75606
Phone: 903-757-3399

Mark A. Weisbart
5950 Sherry Lane, #222
Dallas, TX 75225
Phone: 214-379-0790

Stephen Joseph Zayler
123 E. Lufkin Avenue
Lufkin, TX 75901
Phone: 936-634-1020

TRUSTEE(S) COVERING THE
NORTHERN DISTRICT OF TEXAS

Shawn K. Brown
1701 River Run Road, Suite 1000
Fort Worth, TX 76107
Phone: 817-348-0777

Donna K. Christie
612 S. Van Buren
Amarillo, TX 79101
Phone: 806-372-4420

James W. Cunningham
6412 Sondra Drive
Dallas, TX 75214
Phone: 214-827-9112

Carey D. Ebert
1236 Southridge Court
Hurst, TX 76053
Phone: 817-268-2468

Marilyn D. Garner
2000 E. Lamar Boulevard, Suite 600
Arlington, TX 76006
Phone: 817-588-3075

Floyd D. Holder, Jr.
3223 S. Loop 289, Suite 420
Lubbock, TX 79423
Phone: 806-763-9296

John H. Litzler
1412 Main Street, 24th Floor
Dallas, TX 75202
Phone: 214-752-0999

Myrtle L. McDonald
P.O. Box 2426
Lubbock, TX 79408-2426
Phone: 806-765-8851

Robert Milbank, Jr.
500 Akard, Suite 3960
Dallas, TX 75201
Phone: 214-880-8771

Jeffrey H. Mims
3102 Oaklawn, Suite 700
Dallas, TX 75219
Phone: 214-522-1678

Harvey L. Morton
P.O. Box 10305
Lubbock, TX 79408
E-mail: hlmortonlaw@aol.com
Phone: 806-762-0570

Robert F. Newhouse
1412 Main Street, Suite 2450
Dallas, TX 75202
E-mail: newhouse46@hotmail.com
Phone: 214-752-0999

Deborah J. Penner
P.O. Box 65166
Lubbock, TX 79464
E-mail: dpenner@epitrustee.com
Phone: 806-794-7163

Diane G. Reed
501 N. College Street
Waxahachie, TX 76165
Phone: 972-923-2244

Kent D. Ries
600 S. Taylor Street, Suite 900
Amarillo, TX 79101
Phone: 806-242-7437

Scott M. Seidel
2500 Renaissance Tower,
    Suite 2500
Dallas, TX 75270
Phone: 214-742-2121

Daniel J. Sherman
509 N. Montclair Avenue
Dallas, TX 75208
Phone: 214-942-5502

John Dee Spicer
6851 N.E. Loop 820, Suite 102
North Richland Hills, TX 76180
Phone: 817-281-3467

Max R. Tarbox
3223 S. Loop 289, Suite 103
Lubbock, TX 79423
Phone: 806-780-5955

Robert Yaquinto, Jr.
509 N. Montclair Avenue
Dallas, TX 75208
Phone: 214-942-5502

TRUSTEE(S) COVERING THE
SOUTHERN DISTRICT OF TEXAS

David J. Askanase
1415 Louisiana, 37th Floor
Houston, TX 77002
Phone: 713-759-0818

Michael D. Boudloche
711 N. Carancahua, Suite 1508
Corpus Christi, TX 78475
Phone: 361-883-5786

Lowell T. Cage
5851 San Felipe, #950
Houston, TX 77057
Phone: 713-789-0500

Ben B. Floyd
700 Louisiana, Suite 4600
Houston, TX 77002-2732
Phone: 713-222-1470

Kenneth Reagan Havis
114 N. 10th Street
Navasota, TX 77868
Phone: 409-825-7982

Joseph M. Hill
5851 San Felipe, Suite 950
Houston, TX 77057
Phone: 713-789-0500

Pamela Gale Johnson
1000 Louisiana, Suite 2000
Houston, TX 77002-5009
Phone: 713-751-1600

Lisa J. Nichols
10637 Leopard
Corpus Christi, TX 78410
Phone: 361-242-2403

William C. Romo
400 N. McColl Road
McAllen, TX 78501
Phone: 956-686-3707

Michael B. Schmidt
711 N. Carancahua, Suite 712
Corpus Christi, TX 78475
Phone: 361-884-6321

W. Steve Smith
2015 Crocker
Houston, TX 77006
Phone: 713-533-1833

Ronald J. Sommers
2800 Post Oak Boulevard, 61st Floor
Houston, TX 77056
Phone: 713-960-0303

George W. Stone
122 W. Ocean Boulevard
Los Fresnos, TX 78566
Phone: 956-233-1610

James E. Studensky
510 North Valley Mills Drive,
   Suite 405
Waco, TX 76710
Phone: 254-772-5350

Rodney Dwayne Tow
10077 Grogans Mill Road, Suite 150
Conroe, TX 77380
Phone: 281-681-9100

Robbye R. Waldron
15150 Middlebrook Drive
Houston, TX 77058
Phone: 713-488-4438

William G. West, Jr.
10601 Grant Road, Suite 222
Houston, TX 77070
Phone: 281-807-7811

Randy W. Williams
333 Clay Street, Suite 3300
Houston, TX 77002-4499
Phone: 713-654-8111

TRUSTEE(S) COVERING THE
WESTERN DISTRICT OF TEXAS

Janet S. Casciato-Northrup
4615 S.W. Freeway, #410
Houston, TX 77027
Phone: 713-666-1105

William A. Frazell
1008 Mopac Circle, Suite 100
Austin, TX 78746
Phone: 512-327-7777

Ronald E. Ingalls
720 Brazos, Suite 1100
Austin, TX 78768-4903
Phone: 512-469-3798

Donald S. Leslie
2731-A Montano Avenue
El Paso, TX 79903
Phone: 915-565-9000

John P. Lowe
318 E. Nopal Street
Uvalde, TX 78801
Phone: 830-278-4471

Marsha Kocurek Milligan
P.O. Box 92408
Austin, TX 78709-2408
Phone: 512-494-1077

Randolph N. Osherow
342 W. Woodlawn, Suite 300
San Antonio, TX 78212-3314
Phone: 210-738-3001

Charles Daniel Roberts
1515 Capitol of Texas Highway,
   Suite 415
Austin, TX 78746
Phone: 512-327-7086

Jose C. Rodriguez
45 N.E Loop 410, Suite 205
San Antonio, TX 78249
Phone: 210-490-1541

Helen G. Schwartz
9901 I.H. 10 West, Suite 770
San Antonio, TX 78230
Phone: 210-699-8086

Johnny W. Thomas, Jr.
1153 E. Commerce
San Antonio, TX 78205
Phone: 210-226-5888

UTAH

Note: The individuals listed are
private parties, not government
employees.

Steven R. Bailey
2454 Washington Boulevard
Ogden, UT 84401
Phone: 801-621-4430

J. Kevin Bird
384 E. 720 South, #201
Orem, UT 84058
Phone: 801-426-4700

Duane H. Gillman
50 W. Broadway, 12th Floor
Salt Lake City, UT 84101
Phone: 801-359-3500

David L. Gladwell
476 W. Heritage Park Boulevard,
   Suite 200
Layton, UT 84041
E-mail: g.david@epitrustee.com
Phone: 801-927-1110

Philip G. Jones
853 W. Center Street
Orem, UT 84057
Phone: 801-224-2119

Gary Evan Jubber
215 S. State Street, 12th Floor,
   Suite 1200
Salt Lake City, UT 84111
Phone: 801-323-2245

Joel T. Marker
10 E. South Temple, Suite 600
Salt Lake City, UT 84133
Phone: 801-521-4135

David L. Miller
Barnes Banking Building #202
849 W. Hill Field Road
Layton, UT 84041
Phone: 801-447-8777

WISCONSIN

Note: The individuals listed are private parties, not government employees.

TRUSTEE(S) COVERING THE EASTERN DISTRICT OF WISCONSIN

Michael F. Dubis
208 E. Main Street
Waterford, WI 53185
Phone: 262-534-6950

Virginia E. George
4421 N. Oakland Avenue, Suite 201
Milwaukee, WI 53211
Phone: 414-332-3211

Glenn O. Givens, Jr.
P.O. Box 511280
Milwaukee, WI 53202
Phone: 414-374-7797

Mary B. Grossman
550 Bay View Road, #D
P.O. Box 418
Mukwonago, WI 53149
Phone: 262-363-5830

Andrew N. Herbach
324 E. Wisconsin Avenue, Suite 1100
Milwaukee, WI 53202
Phone: 414-272-0760

Bruce A. Lanser
Suite Mezzanine 140
205 E. Wisconsin Avenue
Milwaukee, WI 53202
Phone: 414-272-5700

Larry H. Liebzeit
512 W. College Avenue
Appleton, WI 54911
Phone: 920-739-6307

Helen Margaret Ludwig
10150 W. National Avenue, Suite 390
West Allis, WI 53227
Phone: 414-321-0078

Douglas F. Mann
740 N. Plankinton Avenue, Suite 210
Milwaukee, WI 53203
Phone: 414-276-5355

Michael P. Maxwell
633 W. Wisconsin Avenue, 20th Floor
Milwaukee, WI 53203
Phone: 414-224-0300

Neil R. McKloskey
122 N. Madison
P.O. Box 1863
Green Bay, WI 54305-1863
Phone: 920-432-8677

John M. Scaffidi
P.O. Box 11975
Milwaukee, WI 53211
E-mail: JMScaffidi@rsmlaw.com
Phone: 414-963-9303

Paul G. Swanson
107 Church Avenue
P.O. Box 617
Oshkosh, WI 54903-0617
Phone: 920-235-6690

TRUSTEE(S) COVERING THE WESTERN DISTRICT OF WISCONSIN

John M. Cirilli
116 E. Davenport Street
Rhinelander, WI 54501
Phone: 715-369-3443

Peter F. Herrell
21 S. Barstow Street
Eau Claire, WI 54702
Phone: 715-835-6171

Melvyn L. Hoffman
312 S. Third Street
La Crosse, WI 54602-1503
Phone: 608-782-8098

Robert T. Kasdorf
16 N. Carroll Avenue, Suite 500
Madison, WI 53703
Phone: 608-257-1369

Michael E. Kepler
634 W. Main Street, Suite 202
Madison, WI 53703
Phone: 608-257-5424

James W. McNeilly, Jr.
P.O. Box 966
King on 5th
La Crosse, WI 54602-0966
E-mail: jim.mcneilly@ bosshardlaw.com
Phone: 608-782-1469

Randi L. Osberg
402 Graham Avenue
Eau Claire, WI 54702
Phone: 715-834-3425

William J. Rameker
2 E. Mifflin Street
Madison, WI 53701
Phone: 608-257-7181

Claire A. Resop
2 E. Mifflin Street, Suite 800
Madison, WI 53703
Phone: 608-268-5607

Scott F. Shadel
100 S. Main Street
Janesville, WI 53547
Phone: 608-755-8100

Mark Joseph Wittman
223 S. Central Avenue
Marshfield, WI 54449
Phone: 715-387-1388

WYOMING

Note: The individuals listed are private parties, not government employees.

Gary A. Barney
267 Main Street
Lander, WY 82520
Phone: 307-332-4848

Randy L. Royal
P.O. Box 551
524 5th Avenue S.
Greybull, WY 82426
E-mail: rlroyal@tctwest.com
Phone: 307-765-4433

R. Michele Russell
303 N. Broadway
Riverton, WY 82501
Phone: 307-857-1200

Tracy L. Zubrod
400 E. 20th Street
Cheyenne, WY 82001
Phone: 307-778-2557

Chapter 13 Standing Trustees

ALABAMA

The U.S. Trustee Program does not administer bankuptcy estates in Alabama at this time. Questions about cases in Alabama should be addressed to:

The Administrative Office of the U.S. Courts
Bankruptcy Judges Division
1 Columbus Circle, N.E.,
Suite 4-250
Washington, DC 20544
Phone: 202-502-1900

ALASKA

Note: The individual listed is a private party, not a government employee.

Larry D. Compton
400 D Street, Suite 210
Anchorage, AK 99501
E-mail: akchapter13@gci.net
Phone: 907-276-6660
Fax: 907-258-3348

ARIZONA

Note: The individuals listed are private parties, not government employees.

Russell Brown
P.O. Box 33970
Phoenix, AZ 85067-3970
E-mail: trustee@ch13bk.com
Phone: 602-277-8996

Dianne C. Kerns
PMB 413, 7320 N. La Cholla, #154
Tucson, AZ 85741
E-mail: dianne.kerns@dcktrustee
.com
Phone: 520-544-9094

Edward J. Maney
P.O. Box 10434
Phoenix, AZ 85064-0434
E-mail: edward.maney@azbar.org
Phone: 602-277-3776

ARKANSAS

Note: The individuals listed are private parties, not government employees.

TRUSTEE(S) COVERING THE EASTERN DISTRICT OF ARKANSAS

Joyce B. Babin
P.O. Box 8064
Little Rock, AR 72203-8064
E-mail: jbabin@13ark.com
Phone: 501-537-2500

David D. Coop
P.O. Box 5006
North Little Rock, AR 72119
E-mail: dcoop@ddc13.com
Phone: 501-801-5600

Jo-Ann L. Goldman
P.O. Box 22067
Little Rock, AR 72211
E-mail: jgoldman@ark13.com
Phone: 501-537-4400

TRUSTEE(S) COVERING THE WESTERN DISTRICT OF ARKANSAS

Joyce B. Babin
P.O. Box 8064
Little Rock, AR 72203-8064
E-mail: jbabin@13ark.com
Phone: 501-537-2500

David D. Coop
P.O. Box 5006
North Little Rock, AR 72119
E-mail: dcoop@ddc13.com
Phone: 501-801-5600

Jo-Ann L. Goldman
P.O. Box 22067
Little Rock, AR 72211
E-mail: jgoldman@ark13.com
Phone: 501-537-4400

CALIFORNIA

Note: The individuals listed are private parties, not government employees.

TRUSTEE(S) COVERING THE CENTRAL DISTRICT OF CALIFORNIA

Amrane Cohen
770 The City Drive S., Suite 7400
Orange, CA 92868
Phone: 714-621-0200

Nancy K. Curry
606 S. Olive Street, Suite 1850
Los Angeles, CA 90014
Phone: 213-689-3014

Rodney A. Danielson
3435 14th Street, Suite 100
Riverside, CA 92501
Phone: 909-826-8000

Kathy Anderson Dockery
700 S. Flower Street, Suite 1950
Los Angeles, CA 90017
Phone: 213-996-4400

Elizabeth F. Rojas
15301 Ventura Boulevard
Building B, Suite 400
Sherman Oaks, CA 91403
Phone: 818-933-5700

TRUSTEE(S) COVERING THE EASTERN DISTRICT OF CALIFORNIA

M. Nelson Enmark
3446 W. Shaw Avenue
Fresno, CA 93711
E-mail: www.enmark.net/
chapter13/index.html
Phone: 559-277-3995

Russell Dean Greer
1300 K. Street, Suite C
Modesto, CA 95354
P.O. Box 3051
Modesto, CA 95353
E-mail: www.mod13.com
Phone: 209-576-1954

Jan P. Johnson
P.O. Box 1708
Sacramento, CA 95812
E-mail: www.jpj13trustee.com/
homex.html
Phone: 916-856-8036

Lawrence J. Loheit
P.O. Box 2889
Sacramento, CA 95812-1497
E-mail: www.loheit13.com
/index.html
Phone: 916-856-8000

TRUSTEE(S) COVERING THE
NORTHERN DISTRICT OF
CALIFORNIA

Martha G. Bronitsky
P.O. Box 5004
Hayward, CA 94540
E-mail: www.13network.com/
   oakhome.htm
Phone: 510-266-5580

David E. Burchard
P.O. Box 805-9
393 Vintage Park Drive, Suite 150
Foster City, CA 94404
E-mail: www.burchardtrustee
   .com/index.html
Phone: 650-345-7801

Devin Derham-Burk
P.O. Box 50013
Campbell, CA 95150-0013
E-mail: www.13network.com/
   sjohome.htm
Phone: 408-354-4413
Fax: 408-354-5513

Michael H. Meyer
P.O. Box 6609
Santa Rosa, CA 95406-0609
E-mail: www.13network.com/
   snrhome.htm
Phone: 707-544-5500

TRUSTEE(S) COVERING THE
SOUTHERN DISTRICT OF
CALIFORNIA

Thomas H. Billingslea, Jr.
530 "B" Street, Suite 1500
San Diego, CA 92101-4499
Phone: 619-233-7525

David L. Skelton
600 B Street, Suite 2000
San Diego, CA 92101-4587
Phone: 619-338-4006

COLORADO

Note: The individual listed is a
private party, not a government
employee.

Sally Zeman
1888 Sherman Street, #750
Denver, CO 80203
Phone: 303-830-1973

CONNECTICUT

Note: The individual listed is a
private party, not a government
employee.

Molly T. Whiton
10 Columbus Boulevard
Hartford, CT 06106
Phone: 860-278-9410

DISTRICT OF COLUMBIA

Note: The individual listed is a
private party, not a government
employee.

Cynthia Niklas
4545 42nd Street, N.W., Suite. 211
Washington, DC 20016
Phone: 202-362-8500

FLORIDA

Note: The individuals listed are
private parties, not government
employees.

TRUSTEE(S) COVERING THE
MIDDLE DISTRICT OF FLORIDA

Mamie L. Davis
300 W. Adams Street
Jacksonville, FL 32202
Phone: 904-358-9589

Terry E. Smith
P.O. Box 25001
Bradenton, FL 34206
E-mail: chap13@gate.net
Phone: 941-747-4644

Laurie K. Weatherford
P.O. Box 3450
Winter Park, FL 32790
E-mail: lauriew@ch13orl.com
Phone: 407-648-8841

TRUSTEE(S) COVERING THE
NORTHERN DISTRICT OF
FLORIDA

Leigh Annette Hart
P.O. Box 646
Tallahassee, FL 32302
E-mail: ldhtre@earthlink.net
Phone: 904-681-2734

TRUSTEE(S) COVERING THE
SOUTHERN DISTRICT OF
FLORIDA

Nancy N. Herkert
P.O. Box 279806
Miramar, FL 33027-4166
E-mail: nancy@ch13herkert.com
Phone: 954-443-4402

Robin F. Weiner
P.O. Box 559007
Fort Lauderdale, FL 33355-9007
E-mail: robinweiner@hotmail.com
Phone: 954-382-2001

GEORGIA

Note: The individuals listed are
private parties, not government
employees.

TRUSTEE(S) COVERING THE
MIDDLE DISTRICT OF GEORGIA

Camille Hope
111 3rd Street
Macon, GA 31202
E-mail: chope@chapter13macon
   .com
Phone: 912-742-8706

Anne Kristin Smith
1101 Front Avenue, Suite 202
Columbus, GA 31901
E-mail: kristin@ch13trustee.com
Phone: 706-323-4151

TRUSTEE(S) COVERING THE
NORTHERN DISTRICT OF
GEORGIA

James Henry Bone
100 Peachtree Street, Suite 1100
Atlanta, GA 30303
Phone: 404-525-2555

Adam M. Goodman
260 Peachtree Street, N.W.,
   Suite 200
Atlanta, GA 30303
Phone: 678-510-1444
Fax: 678-510-1450

Mary Ida Townson
100 Peachtree Street, Suite 300
Atlanta, GA 30303
Phone: 404-525-1110

Nancy J. Whaley
303 Peachtree Center Avenue,
  Suite 120
Atlanta, GA 30308
Phone: 678-992-1201
Fax: 678-992-1202

TRUSTEE(S) COVERING THE
SOUTHERN DISTRICT OF
GEORGIA

Barnee C. Baxter
P.O. Box 2127
Augusta, GA 30903
E-mail: baxterbarn@aol.com
Phone: 706-724-1039

Sylvia Brown
33 Bull Street, Suite 415
Savannah, GA 31401
Phone: 912-234-5052

Marie Elaina Massey
1608 Newcastle Street
Brunswick, GA 31521
P.O. Box 1717
Brunswick, GA 31521
E-mail: emassey@ch13bwk.com
Phone: 912-466-9787
Fax: 912-466-9755

GUAM

Trustees for chapter 13 bankruptcy
cases are assigned on a case-by-case
basis. For further information,
please contact:

The Office of the U.S. Trustee
1132 Bishop Street, Suite 602
Honolulu, HI 96813-2836
Phone: 808-522-8150

HAWAII

Note: The individual listed is a private party, not a government employee.

Howard M. S. Hu
1132 Bishop Street, Suite 301
Honolulu, HI 96813-2814
Phone: 808-526-3083

IDAHO

Note: The individuals listed are private parties, not government employees.

L. D. Fitzgerald
P.O. Box 6199
Pocatello, ID 83205
E-mail: fitzgeraldld@qwest.net
Phone: 208-233-0500
Fax: 208-233-1339

John H. Krommenhoek
5019 Emerald
Boise, ID 83706
E-mail: jhk713bk@spro.net
Phone: 208-375-1288
Fax: 208-375-5477

Bernie R. Rakozy
824 W. Franklin
Boise, ID 83702
E-mail: bbrakozy@mindspring.net
Phone: 208-343-4474
Fax: 208-343-4494

C. Barry Zimmerman
P.O. Box 1315
Coeur d'Alene, ID 83816-0070
E-mail: cbarryz@my180.net
Phone: 208-664-6100
Fax: 208-664-4737

ILLINOIS

Note: The individuals listed are private parties, not government employees.

TRUSTEE(S) COVERING THE
CENTRAL DISTRICT OF ILLINOIS

Richard A. Bowers
1800 3rd Avenue, Suite 402
Rock Island, IL 61204
Phone: 309-788-9355

Michael Clark
401 Main Street, Suite 1130
Peoria, IL 61602
Phone: 309-674-6137

James R. Geekie
211 N. Central Avenue
Paris, IL 61944
P.O. Box 65
Paris, IL 61944
Phone: 217-465-7681

John H. Germeraad
113 N. Seventh Street
Petersburg, IL 62675
P.O. Box 257
Petersburg, IL 62675
Phone: 217-632-4346

TRUSTEE(S) COVERING THE
NORTHERN DISTRICT OF
ILLINOIS

Marilyn O. Marshall
224 S. Michigan Avenue, Suite 800
Chicago, IL 60604
Phone: 312-431-1300

Lydia S. Meyer
308 W. State Street, Suite 212
Rockford, IL 61105-4127
P.O. Box 14127
Rockford, IL 61105-4127
Phone: 815-968-5354

Glenn B. Stearns
4343 Commerce Court, Suite #120
Lisle, IL 60532
Phone: 630-577-1313

Thomas E. Vaughn
200 S. Michigan Avenue, Suite 1300
Chicago, IL 60603-6398
Phone: 312-294-5900

TRUSTEE(S) COVERING THE
SOUTHERN DISTRICT OF
ILLINOIS

Robert Gene Kearney
104 W. Main Street
Benton, IL 62812
P.O. Box 998
Benton, IL 62812
Phone: 618-435-3001

James W. McRoberts, Jr.
33 Bronze Point, Suite 10
Swansea, IL 62226
Phone: 618-277-0086

INDIANA

Note: The individuals listed are private parties, not government employees.

TRUSTEE(S) COVERING THE
NORTHERN DISTRICT OF INDIANA

Donald M. Aikman
203 W. Wayne Street, Suite 400
Fort Wayne, IN 46802
Phone: 260-422-7062

Paul R. Chael
401 W. 84th Drive, Suite C
Merrillville, IN 46410
Phone: 219-650-4015

Debra L. Miller
100 E. Wayne Street, Suite 210
South Bend, IN 46601
Phone: 574-251-1493

David Rosenthal
P.O. Box 505
Lafayette, IN 47902
E-mail: dar@nlci.com
Phone: 765-742-8248

TRUSTEE(S) COVERING THE
SOUTHERN DISTRICT OF
INDIANA

Joseph M. Black, Jr.
114 W. Tipton Street
Seymour, IN 47274
P.O. Box 846
Seymour, IN 47274
Phone: 812-524-7211

Robert A. Brothers
151 N. Delaware Street, Suite 1400
Indianapolis, IN 46204
Phone: 317-636-1062

Ann M. DeLaney
P.O. Box 441285
Indianapolis, IN 46244
E-mail: ann@trustee13.com
Phone: 317-829-7360

Donald L. Decker
30 N. 7th Street
Terre Haute, IN 47808
P.O. Box 90
Terre Haute, IN 47808
E-mail: ddecker@
 decker13trustee.com
Phone: 812-234-2600

Robert P. Musgrave II
123 N.W. Fourth Street
Evansville, IN 47706-0972
P.O. Box 972
Evansville, IN 47706-0972
Phone: 812-424-3029

IOWA

Note: The individuals listed are
private parties, not government
employees.

TRUSTEE(S) COVERING THE
NORTHERN DISTRICT OF IOWA

Carol F. Dunbar
531 Commercial Street, Suite 500
Waterloo, IA 50701
P.O. Box 1377
Waterloo, IA 50704-1377
E-mail: cfdunbar@cfu.net
Phone: 319-233-6327

TRUSTEE(S) COVERING THE
SOUTHERN DISTRICT OF IOWA

Albert C. Warford
505 5th Avenue, Suite 1020
Des Moines, IA 50309
E-mail: ch13sdia@aol.com
Phone: 515-283-2713

KANSAS

Note: The individuals listed are
private parties, not government
employees.

William H. Griffin
4350 Shawnee Mission Parkway,
 Suite 13
Fairway, KS 66205
Phone: 913-677-1311
Fax: 913-432-7857

Jan Hamilton
507-9 S.W. Jackson Street
Topeka, KS 66601-3527
P.O. Box 3527
Topeka, KS 66601-3527
E-mail: jan.hamilton@
 chapter13trustee.com
Phone: 785-234-1551
Fax: 785-234-0537

Laurie B. Williams
328 N. Main Street, Suite 200
Wichita, KS 67202
Phone: 316-267-1791
Fax: 316-267-0970

KENTUCKY

Note: The individuals listed are
private parties, not government
employees.

TRUSTEE(S) COVERING THE
EASTERN DISTRICT OF
KENTUCKY

Beverly M. Burden
P.O. Box 2204
Lexington, KY 40588-2204
E-mail: bburden@ch13edky.com
Phone: 606-233-1527

TRUSTEE(S) COVERING THE
WESTERN DISTRICT OF
KENTUCKY

William W. Lawrence
200 S. 7th Street
300 Legal Arts Building
Louisville, KY 40202
E-mail: william.lawrence@psinet
 .com
Phone: 502-581-9042

LOUISIANA

Note: The individuals listed are
private parties, not government
employees.

TRUSTEE(S) COVERING THE
EASTERN DISTRICT OF
LOUISIANA

Sterling J. Beaulieu, Jr.
433 Metairie Road, Suite 307
Metairie, AL 70005
Phone: 504-831-1313
TRUSTEE(S) COVERING THE MID-
DLE DISTRICT OF LOUISIANA

Annette C. Crawford
8778 Goodwood Boulevard
Baton Rouge, LA 70896
P.O. Box 64868
Baton Rouge, LA 70806
E-mail: ACRAWFORD@
 ANNETTECRAWFORD.COM
Phone: 504-928-2531

TRUSTEE(S) COVERING THE
WESTERN DISTRICT OF
LOUISIANA

Willie Banks, Jr.
209 Pecan Park Avenue, #A
Baton Rouge, LA 71309-1991
P.O. Box 1991
5615-A Jackson Street
Alexandria, LA 71303
Phone: 318-448-1306

Paul H. Davidson
6007 Financial Plaza, Suite 713
Shreveport, LA 71149-0300
P.O. Box 19300
Shreveport, LA 71129
Phone: 318-687-1300

E. Eugene Hastings
P.O. Box 14839
Monroe, LA 71207
E-mail: geneh@bayou.com
Phone: 318-651-7733
Fax: 318-651-7742

Keith A. Rodriguez
700 St. John Street, Suite 201
Lafayette, LA 70502-3445
P.O. Box 3445
Lafayette, LA 70501
Phone: 337-233-4413

MAINE

Note: The individual listed is a
private party, not a government
employee.

Peter Fessenden
14 Main Street, Suite 307
P.O. Box 429
Brunswick, ME 04011
Phone: 207-725-1300

MARYLAND

Note: The individuals listed are
private parties, not government
employees.

Timothy P. Branigan
1402 Greenview Drive, Suite 506
Laurel, MD 20708
Phone: 301-483-9118

Ellen W. Cosby
300 E. Joppa Road, Suite 409
Baltimore, MD 21286
Phone: 410-825-5923

Joel P. Goldberger
7310 Ritchie Highway, Suite 715
Glen Burnie, MD 21061
Phone: 410-766-9665

Nancy Spencer Grigsby
4201 Mitchellville Road, Suite 401
Bowie, MD 20716
Phone: 301-805-4700

MASSACHUSETTS

Note: The individuals listed are
private parties, not government
employees.

Denise Marie Pappalardo
44 Front Street, Suite 230
Worcester, MA 01608
E-mail: d.pappalardo@ch13worc
  .com
Phone: 508-791-3300

Doreen B. Solomon
180 Canal Street, 6th Floor
Boston, MA 02114
Phone: 617-723-1313

MICHIGAN

Note: The individuals listed are
private parties, not government
employees.

TRUSTEE(S) COVERING THE
EASTERN DISTRICT OF MICHIGAN

Carl L. Bekofske
510 W. Court Street
Flint, MI 48503
Phone: 810-238-4675

Krispen S. Carroll
535 Griswold,
1230 Buhl Building
Southfield, MI 48226
Phone: 313-962-5035

Thomas W. McDonald, Jr.
3126 Davenport Avenue
Saginaw, MI 48602
P.O. Box 6310
Saginaw, MI 48608
E-mail: tom@mcdonaldsag.com
Phone: 989-792-6766

David W. Ruskin
1100 Travelers Tower
26555 Evergreen Road
Southfield, MI 48076
Phone: 248-352-7755

Tammy L. Terry
2100 Buhl Building
535 Griswold
Detroit, MI 48226
Phone: 313-967-9857

TRUSTEE(S) COVERING THE
WESTERN DISTRICT OF MICHIGAN

Mary K. V. Hamlin
415 W. Michigan Avenue
Kalamazoo, MI 49007
Phone: 616-343-0305

Raymond B. Johnson
555 Cascade West Parkway, S.E.
Grand Rapids, MI 49546-2105
Phone: 616-956-9900

Brett N. Rodgers
The Frey Building
300 Ottawa N.W., Suite 210
Grand Rapids, MI 49503
Phone: 616-454-9638

MINNESOTA

Note: The individuals listed are
private parties, not government
employees.

Wayne E. Drewes
650 1st Avenue N., Suite 113
P.O. Box 1021
Fargo, ND 58107
E-mail: waynedrewes@earthlink.net
Phone: 701-237-6650

Michael J. Farrell
P.O. Box 519
Barnesville, MN 56514
E-mail: MFarrell@RRT.net
Phone: 218-354-7356

Jasmine H. Keller
12 S. Sixth Street, Suite 310
Minneapolis, MN 55402
E-mail: jzk@ch13mn.com
Phone: 612-338-7591

NEW YORK

Note: The individuals listed are private parties, not government employees.

TRUSTEE(S) COVERING THE EASTERN DISTRICT OF NEW YORK

Marianne DeRosa
100 Jericho Quadrangle, Suite 208
Jericho, NY 11753
Phone: 516-622-1340

Stuart P. Gelberg
600 Old Country Road, Suite 410
Garden City, NY 11530
Phone: 516-228-4280

Michael J. Macco
135 Pinelawn Road
Melville, NY 11747
Phone: 631-549-7900

TRUSTEE(S) COVERING THE NORTHERN DISTRICT OF NEW YORK

Andrea E. Celli
350 Northern Boulevard
Albany, NY 12204
Phone: 518-449-2043

Mark W. Swimelar
250 S. Clinton Street, 5th Floor
Syracuse, NY 13202
Phone: 315-471-1499

TRUSTEE(S) COVERING THE SOUTHERN DISTRICT OF NEW YORK

Jeffrey L. Sapir
399 Knollwood Road
White Plains, NY 10603
Phone: 914-328-7272

TRUSTEE(S) COVERING THE WESTERN DISTRICT OF NEW YORK

Albert J. Mogavero
110 Pearl Street, 6th Floor
Buffalo, NY 14202
Phone: 716-854-5636

George M. Reiber
3136 S. Winton Road, Suite 206
Rochester, NY 14623
Phone: 585-427-7225

NORTH CAROLINA

The U.S. Trustee Program does not administer bankruptcy estates in North Carolina at this time. Questions about cases in North Carolina should be addressed to:

The Administrative Office of the U.S. Courts
Bankruptcy Judges Division
1 Columbus Circle, N.E., Suite 4-250
Washington, DC 20544
Phone: 202-502-1900

NORTH DAKOTA

Note: The individual listed is a private party, not a government employee.

Wayne E. Drewes
650 1st Avenue N., Suite 113
P.O. Box 1021
Fargo, ND 58107
E-mail: waynedrewes@earthlink.net
Phone: 701-237-6650

NORTHERN MARIANA ISLANDS

Trustees for chapter 13 bankruptcy cases are assigned on a case-by-case basis. For further information, please contact:

The Office of the U.S. Trustee
1132 Bishop Street, Suite 602
Honolulu, HI 96813-2836
Phone: 808-522-8150

OHIO

Note: The individuals listed are private parties, not government employees.

TRUSTEE(S) COVERING THE NORTHERN DISTRICT OF OHIO

Anthony B. DiSalle
501 Toledo Building
316 N. Michigan Street
Toledo, OH 43624
Phone: 419-255-0675

Michael A. Gallo
20 Federal Plaza W., Suite 600
Youngstown, OH 44503
Phone: 330-743-1246

Jerome L. Holub
159 S. Main Street,
Key Building, Suite 930
Akron, OH 44308
Phone: 330-762-6335

Toby L. Rosen
400 W. Tuscarawas, Fourth Floor
Canton, OH 44702
Phone: 330-455-2222

Craig H. Shopneck
BP Tower
200 Public Square, Suite 3860
Cleveland, OH 44114
Phone: 216-621-4268
Fax: 216-621-4806

TRUSTEE(S) COVERING THE SOUTHERN DISTRICT OF OHIO

Margaret A. Burks
36 E. Fourth Street, #700
Cincinnati, OH 45202
Phone: 513-621-4488

Jeffrey M. Kellner
131 N. Ludlow Street, Suite 900
Talbot Tower
Dayton, OH 45402
Phone: 937-222-7600
Fax: 937-222-5694

Frank M. Pees
130 E. Wilson Bridge Road, #200
Worthington, OH 43085
Phone: 614-436-6700

OKLAHOMA

Note: The individuals listed are private parties, not government employees.

TRUSTEE(S) COVERING THE EASTERN DISTRICT OF OKLAHOMA

William Mark Bonney
215 State Street, Suite 404
Muskogee, OK 74401-1548
P.O. Box 1548
Muskogee, OK 74401-1548
Phone: 918-683-3840
Fax: 918-683-3302

VIRGIN ISLANDS

Note: The individual listed is a private party, not a government employee.

Jose Ramon Carrion
500 Tanca Street
Ochoa Building, Suite 501
Old San Juan, PR 00901
Phone: 787-977-3535

VIRGINIA

Note: The individuals listed are private parties, not government employees.

TRUSTEE(S) COVERING THE EASTERN DISTRICT OF VIRGINIA

Robert E. Hyman
1313 E. Main Street, Suite 339
Richmond, VA 23219
Phone: 804-775-0979

George W. Neal
355 Crawford Parkway, Suite 320
Portsmouth, VA 23704
Phone: 757-399-5545

Gerald M. O'Donnell
201 N. Union Street, #120
Alexandria, VA 22314
Phone: 703-836-2226

Frank Santoro
1435 Crossways Boulevard,
   Suite 301
Chesapeake, VA 23320
Phone: 757-333-4000
Fax: 757-333-3434

TRUSTEE(S) COVERING THE WESTERN DISTRICT OF VIRGINIA

Herbert L. Beskin
401 E. Market Street, Suite 202
Charlottesville, VA 22902
Phone: 434-817-9913

Rebecca B. Connelly
36 W. Church Avenue S.W.,
   Suite 400
Roanoke, VA 24011
Phone: 540-342-3774

Jo S. Widener
1 W. Valley Drive
Bristol, VA 24201
Phone: 276-466-4539

WASHINGTON

Note: The individuals listed are private parties, not government employees.

TRUSTEE(S) COVERING THE EASTERN DISTRICT OF WASHINGTON

Daniel H. Brunner
P.O. Box 1513
Spokane, WA 99210
E-mail: ch13trustee@spokane13.org
Phone: 509-747-8481
Fax: 509-623-2126

TRUSTEE(S) COVERING THE WESTERN DISTRICT OF WASHINGTON

K. Michael Fitzgerald
2200 One Union Square
600 University Street
Seattle, WA 98101-4100
E-mail: kmfitzgerald@
   seattlech13.com
Phone: 206-624-5124
Fax: 206-624-5282

Karla L. Forsythe
3305 Main Street, Suite 305
Vancouver, WA 98663
E-mail: karla_ch13_vanc@qwest.net
Phone: 360-993-4400
Fax: 360-993-4659

David M. Howe
P.O. Box 1255
500 Union Street,
525 Logan Building
Tacoma, WA 98401
E-mail: tacomachapter13@qwest
   .net
Phone: 253-572-6603
Fax: 253-627-2978

WEST VIRGINIA

Note: The individuals listed are private parties, not government employees.

TRUSTEE(S) COVERING THE NORTHERN DISTRICT OF WEST VIRGINIA

Helen M. Morris
600 D Street, Suite 1
South Charleston, WV 25303
Phone: 304-744-6730

TRUSTEE(S) COVERING THE SOUTHERN DISTRICT OF WEST VIRGINIA

Helen M. Morris
600 D Street, Suite 1
South Charleston, WV 25303
Phone: 304-744-6730

WISCONSIN

Note: The individuals listed are private parties, not government employees.

TRUSTEE(S) COVERING THE EASTERN DISTRICT OF WISCONSIN

Louis R. Jones
740 N. Plankinton Avenue,
   Suite 400
Milwaukee, WI 53203
E-mail: ljones@
   chapter13milwaukee.com
Phone: 414-271-3943

Thomas King
1012 W. 20th Avenue
P.O. Box 3170
Oshkosh, WI 54903-3170
E-mail: www.ch13oshkosh.com
Phone: 920-231-2150

TRUSTEE(S) COVERING THE WESTERN DISTRICT OF WISCONSIN

William A. Chatterton
324 S. Hamilton Street
Madison, WI 53701
Phone: 608-256-2355

WYOMING

Note: The individual listed is a private party, not a government employee.

Marcus R. Stewart III
P.O. Box 865
2005 Warren Avenue
Cheyenne, WY 82003
E-mail: mrstewart@qwest.net
Phone: 307-778-4115

U.S. Trustee Program Nationwide Office Locator

Executive Office for U.S.
  Trustees—Lawrence A.
  Friedman, Director
20 Massachusetts Avenue, N.W.,
  Room 8000F
Washington, DC 20530
Phone: 202-307-1391
Fax: 202-307-0672

Martha L. Davis,
Principal Deputy Director
20 Massachusetts Avenue, N.W.,
  Room 8000E
Washington, DC 20530
Phone: 202-307-1391
Fax: 202-307-0672

Clifford J. White III,
Deputy Director
20 Massachusetts Avenue, N.W.,
  Room 8000D
Washington, DC 20530
Phone: 202-307-1391
Fax: 202-307-0672

Jeffrey M. Miller,
Associate Director
20 Massachusetts Avenue, N.W.,
  Room 8000G
Washington, DC 20530
Phone: 202-307-1391
Fax: 202-307-0672

Joseph A. Guzinski,
General Counsel
20 Massachusetts Avenue, N.W.,
  Room 8100
Washington, DC 20530
Phone: 202-307-1399
Fax: 202-307-2397

Sara L. Kistler,
Acting Assistant Director for
  Review and Oversight
20 Massachusetts Avenue, N.W.,
  Room 8338
Washington, DC 20530
Phone: 202-307-3698
Fax: 202-307-2185

Santal Manos,
Assistant Director for
  Administration
20 Massachusetts Avenue, N.W.,
  Room 8200
Washington, DC 20530
Phone: 202-307-2759
Fax: 202-307-3960

Sara L. Kistler,
Acting Assistant Director for
  Research and Planning
20 Massachusetts Avenue, N.W.,
  Room 8310
Washington, DC 20530
Phone: 202-307-3698
Fax: 202-616-4576

ALABAMA

The U.S. Trustee Program does not
administer bankruptcy estates in
Alabama at this time. Questions
should be addressed to:

The Administrative Office of the
  U.S. Courts
Bankruptcy Judges Division
1 Columbus Circle, N.E.,
  Suite 4-250
Washington, DC 20544
Phone: 202-502-1900

ALASKA

Antonia K. Hill,
Assistant U.S. Trustee
605 W. Fourth Avenue,
  Suite 258
Anchorage, AK 99501
Phone: 907-271-2604
Fax: 907-271-2610
Go to USTP Region 18 Web site

ARIZONA

Ilene J. Lashinsky,
U.S. Trustee (Region 14)
2929 N. Central Avenue, Room 700
Phoenix, AZ 85012
Phone: 602-640-2100
Fax: 602-640-2217
Go to USTP Region 14 Web site
Elizabeth C. Amorosi,
Assistant U.S. Trustee
2929 N. Central Avenue, Room 700
Phoenix, AZ 85012
Phone: 602-640-2100
Fax: 602-640-2217

ARKANSAS

Charles W. Tucker,
Assistant U.S. Trustee
500 S. Broadway, Suite 201
Little Rock, AR 72201
Phone: 501-324-7357
Fax: 501-324-7388

CALIFORNIA

Steven J. Katzman,
U.S. Trustee (Region 15)
402 W. Broadway, Suite 600
San Diego, CA 92101-8511
Phone: 619-557-5013
Fax: 619-557-6980

John P. Boyl,
Assistant U.S. Trustee
402 W. Broadway, Suite 600
San Diego, CA 92101-8511
Phone: 619-557-5013
Fax: 619-557-5339

Steven J. Katzman,
U.S. Trustee (Region 16)
402 W. Broadway, Suite 600
San Diego, CA 92101-8511
Phone: 619-557-5013
Fax: 619-557-6980

L. Charmayne Mills,
Assistant U.S. Trustee
725 S. Figueroa Street, 26th Floor
Los Angeles, CA 90017
Phone: 213-894-6811
Fax: 213-894-2603

Jill Sturtevent,
Assistant U.S. Trustee
725 S. Figueroa Street, 26th Floor
Los Angeles, CA 90017
Phone: 213-894-6811
Fax: 213-894-2603

Arthur N. Marquis,
Assistant U.S. Trustee
411 W. Fourth Street, Suite 9041
Santa Ana, CA 92701-8000
Phone: 714-338-3400
Fax: 714-338-3421

HAWAII

Gayle J. Lau,
Assistant U.S. Trustee
1132 Bishop Street, Suite 602
Honolulu, HI 96813-2836
Phone: 808-522-8150
Fax: 808-522-8156

IDAHO

Jeffrey G. Howe,
Assistant U.S. Trustee
304 N. Eighth Street, Room 347
Boise, ID 83702
Phone: 208-334-1300
Fax: 208-334-9756

ILLINOIS

Ira Bodenstein,
U.S. Trustee (Region 11)
227 W. Monroe Street, Suite 3350
Chicago, IL 60606
Phone: 312-886-5785
Fax: 312-886-5794

Constantine C. Harvalis,
Assistant U.S. Trustee
227 W. Monroe Street, Suite 3350
Chicago, IL 60606
Phone: 312-886-5785
Fax: 312-886-5794

Sandra T. Rasnak,
Assistant U.S. Trustee
227 W. Monroe Street, Suite 3350
Chicago, IL 60606
Phone: 312-886-5785
Fax: 312-886-5794

James L. Magill,
Assistant U.S. Trustee
401 Main Street, Suite 1100
Peoria, IL 61602
Phone: 309-671-7854
Fax: 309-671-7857

INDIANA

Nancy J. Gargula,
U.S. Trustee (Region 10)
101 W. Ohio Street, Room 1000
Indianapolis, IN 46204
Phone: 317-226-6101
Fax: 317-226-6356

Kevin P. Dempsey,
Assistant U.S. Trustee
101 W. Ohio Street, Room 1000
Indianapolis, IN 46204
Phone: 317-226-6101
Fax: 317-226-6356

Alexander L. Edgar,
Assistant U.S. Trustee
100 E. Wayne Street, Room 555
South Bend, IN 46601
Phone: 219-236-8105
Fax: 219-236-8163

IOWA

Habbo G. Fokkena,
U.S. Trustee (Region 12)
225 Second Street, S.E., Suite 400
Cedar Rapids, IA 52401
Phone: 319-364-2211
Fax: 319-364-7370

Janet G. L. Reasoner,
Assistant U.S. Trustee
225 Second Street, S.E., Suite 400
Cedar Rapids, IA 52401
Phone: 319-364-2211
Fax: 319-364-7370

James L. Snyder,
Assistant U.S. Trustee
210 Walnut Street, Suite 793
Des Moines, IA 50309-2108
Phone: 515-284-4982
Fax: 515-284-4986

KANSAS

Mary E. May,
U.S. Trustee (Region 20)
Epic Center Building
301 N. Main Street, Suite 500
Wichita, KS 67202
Phone: 316-269-6637
Fax: 316-269-6182

Joyce G. Owen,
Assistant U.S. Trustee
Epic Center Building
301 N. Main Street, Suite 500
Wichita, KS 67202
Phone: 316-269-6637
Fax: 316-269-6182

KENTUCKY

John R. Stonitsch,
Assistant U.S. Trustee
100 E. Vine Street, Suite 803
Lexington, KY 40507
Phone: 859-233-2822
Fax: 859-233-2834

Joseph J. Golden,
Assistant U.S. Trustee
601 W. Broadway, Suite 512
Louisville, KY 40202
Phone: 502-582-6000
Fax: 502-582-6147

LOUISIANA

R. Michael Bolen,
U.S. Trustee (Region 5)
400 Poydras Street, Suite 2110
New Orleans, LA 70130
Phone: 504-589-4018
Fax: 504-589-4096

Diana L. Rachal,
Assistant U.S. Trustee
400 Poydras Street, Suite 2110
New Orleans, LA 70130
Phone: 504-589-4018
Fax: 504-589-4096

Frances Hewitt Strange,
Assistant U.S. Trustee
300 Fannin Street, Suite 3196
Shreveport, LA 71101-3079
Phone: 318-676-3456
Fax: 318-676-3212

MAINE

Robert Checkoway,
Assistant U.S. Trustee
537 Congress Street, Suite 303
Portland, ME 04101
Phone: 207-780-3564
Fax: 207-780-3568

MARYLAND

Mark A. Neal,
Acting Assistant U.S. Trustee
300 W. Pratt Street, Suite 350
Baltimore, MD 21201
Phone: 410-962-3910
Fax: 410-962-4278

Julie Mack,
Acting Assistant U.S. Trustee
6305 Ivy Lane, Suite 600
Greenbelt, MD 20770
Phone: 301-344-6216
Fax: 301-344-8431

MASSACHUSETTS

John P. Fitzgerald III,
Assistant U.S. Trustee
10 Causeway Street, Room 1184
Boston, MA 02222-1043
Phone: 617-788-0401
Fax: 617-565-6368

Richard T. King,
Assistant U.S. Trustee
Franklin Square Tower
600 Main Street, Suite 200
Worcester, MA 01608
Phone: 508-793-0555
Fax: 508-793-0558

Guy A. Van Baalen,
Assistant U.S. Trustee
10 Broad Street, Room 105
Utica, NY 13501
Phone: 315-793-8191
Fax: 315-793-8133

NORTH CAROLINA

The U.S. Trustee Program does not administer bankruptcy estates in North Carolina at this time. Questions should be addressed to:

The Administrative Office of the U.S. Courts
Bankruptcy Judges Division
1 Columbus Circle, N.E., Suite 4-250
Washington, DC 20544
Phone: 202-502-1900

NORTH DAKOTA

Bankruptcy estates for North Dakota are administered by the U.S. Trustee's office in Sioux Falls, South Dakota (USTP Region 12).

OHIO

Saul Eisen,
U.S. Trustee (Region 9)
200 Public Square, Suite 20-3300
Cleveland, OH 44114
Phone: 216-522-7800
Fax: 216-522-4988

Daniel M. McDermott,
Assistant U.S. Trustee
200 Public Square, Suite 20-3300
Cleveland, OH 44114
Phone: 216-522-7800
Fax: 216-522-4988

Neal J. Weill,
Assistant U.S. Trustee
36 E. Seventh Street, Suite 2030
Cincinnati, OH 45202
Phone: 513-684-6988
Fax: 513-684-6994

Alexander G. Barkan,
Assistant U.S. Trustee
170 N. High Street, Suite 200
Columbus, OH 43215-2403
Phone: 614-469-7411
Fax: 614-469-7448

OKLAHOMA

Herbert M. Graves,
Assistant U.S. Trustee
215 N.W. Dean A. McGee Avenue, Suite 408
Oklahoma City, OK 73102
Phone: 405-231-5950
Fax: 405-231-5958

Katherine M. Vance,
Assistant U.S. Trustee
224 S. Boulder Avenue, Room 225
Tulsa, OK 74103
Phone: 918-581-6670
Fax: 918-581-6674

OREGON

Gail Geiger,
Assistant U.S. Trustee
211 E. 7th Avenue, Room 285
Eugene, OR 97401
Phone: 541-465-6330
Fax: 541-465-6335

Pamela J. Griffith,
Assistant U.S. Trustee
620 S.W. Main Street, Suite 213
Portland, OR 97205-3026
Phone: 503-326-4000
Fax: 503-326-7658

PENNSYLVANIA

Roberta A. DeAngelis,
Acting U.S. Trustee (Region 3)
601 Walnut Street, Room 950W
Philadelphia, PA 19106
Phone: 215-597-4411
Fax: 215-597-5795

Frederic J. Baker,
Senior Assistant U.S. Trustee
601 Walnut Street, Room 950W
Philadelphia, PA 19106
Phone: 215-597-4411
Fax: 215-597-5795

Anne K. Fiorenza,
Assistant U.S. Trustee
228 Walnut Street, Suite 1190
Harrisburg, PA 17101
Phone: 717-221-4515
Fax: 717-221-4554

Joseph S. Sisca,
Assistant U.S. Trustee
Liberty Center
1001 Liberty Avenue, Suite 970
Pittsburgh, PA 15222
Phone: 412-644-4756
Fax: 412-644-4785

PUERTO RICO

Nancy Pujals,
Assistant U.S. Trustee
Ochoa Building
500 Tanca Street, Suite 301
San Juan, PR 00901-1922
Phone: 787-729-7444
Fax: 787-729-7449

RHODE ISLAND

Leonard J. DePasquale,
Assistant U.S. Trustee
10 Dorrance Street, Suite 910
Providence, RI 02903
Phone: 401-528-5553
Fax: 401-528-5163

SOUTH CAROLINA

W. Clarkson McDow, Jr.
U.S. Trustee (Region 4)
1835 Assembly Street, Suite 953
Columbia, SC 29201
Phone: 803-765-5250
Fax: 803-765-5260

David R. Duncan,
Regional Assistant U.S. Trustee
1835 Assembly Street, Suite 953
Columbia, SC 29201
Phone: 803-765-5250
Fax: 803-765-5260

Joseph F. Buzhardt III,
Assistant U.S. Trustee
1835 Assembly Street, Suite 953
Columbia, SC 29201
Phone: 803-765-5250
Fax: 803-765-5260

SOUTH DAKOTA

Bruce J. Gering,
Assistant U.S. Trustee
230 S. Phillips Avenue, Suite 502
Sioux Falls, SD 57104
Phone: 605-330-4450
Fax: 605-330-4456

WISCONSIN

Sheree G. Dandurand,
Assistant U.S. Trustee
780 Regent Street, Suite 304
Madison, WI 53715
Phone: 608-264-5522
Fax: 608-264-5182

David Asbach,
Assistant U.S. Trustee
517 E. Wisconsin Avenue,
    Room 430
Milwaukee, WI 53202
Phone: 414-297-4499
Fax: 414-297-4478

WYOMING

Michele R. Hankins,
Assistant U.S. Trustee
308 W. 21st Street, Suite 203
Cheyenne, WY 82001
Phone: 307-772-2790
Fax: 307-772-2795

Glossary

adjustment of debt   The reorganization of debt that occurs in a Chapter 13 bankruptcy.

adversary proceeding   A legal action usually initiated by a debtor's creditors to take back their collateral or to formally complain about some aspect of a bankruptcy proceeding.

automatic stay   An action of the court that prohibits a debtor's creditors from calling or writing the debtor and from repossessing or foreclosing on the debtor's property after the debtor has filed for bankruptcy. It also stops lawsuits. The automatic stay takes effect as soon as a Chapter 7 or Chapter 13 bankruptcy petition has been filed with the court. It is over when the court lifts the stay or when the debtor receives a discharge of bankruptcy.

Bankruptcy Code   The federal law that governs the bankruptcy process.

Chapter 7   A bankruptcy process that wipes out most debt. If the debtor has nonexempt property, the trustee will liquidate it and use the sale proceeds to pay off the debtor's creditors. Also called a liquidation bankruptcy.

Chapter 13   A bankruptcy process that allows a debtor to reorganize his debt to keep as many of his or her assets as possible and to make regular payments to his or her creditors over a three- to five-year period of time. Also called a reorganization bankruptcy. A business operated as a sole proprietorship as well as individual consumers can file for this kind of bankruptcy.

collateral   Property used by a debtor to secure or guarantee a debt. If the debtor does not pay the debt according to his or her agreement with the creditor, the creditor is entitled to take the collateral.

confirmation   The formal approval and implementation of a debtor's Chapter 13 bankruptcy plan by the court.

creditor   The person or business to whom a debtor owes money.

creditors' meeting   A meeting during the bankruptcy process at which the bankruptcy trustee questions the debtor about his or her financial affairs. In most consumer bankruptcies, although all of a debtor's creditors are entitled to attend and to question the debtor, if any do show up, it will be the debtor's secured creditors for they will want to know what is going to happen to their collateral. The creditors' meeting usually takes place 40 to 60 days after a bankruptcy begins.

debtor   An individual who owes money.

discharge   The elimination of debt through a Chapter 7 or through a Chapter 13 bankruptcy. Certain kinds of debts, however, cannot be discharged and the debtor will have to pay them.

exempt property   Property that a debtor may keep in a Chapter 7 bankruptcy. The federal bankruptcy code specifies certain exemptions and every state also has its own law that defines additional exemptions. See Appendix D for information regarding the exemptions states offer.

liquidation bankruptcy   Another term for a Chapter 7 bankruptcy.

modification request   The method used by a debtor to change the terms of his or her Chapter 13 plan to accommodate new circumstances in the debtor's life such as a reduction in income or the loss of collateral.

nonexempt property   Property a debtor may lose in a Chapter 7 bankruptcy.

nonpurchase-money lien   A lien placed on property owned by a debtor to secure a loan.

objection to confirmation of the debtor's plan   A legal document filed by a debtor with the bankruptcy court by a debtor's creditor that spells out what the creditor doesn't like or objects to in the debtor's reorganization plan. Usually, the creditor objects to the plan because it wants the debtor to pay it more money in his or her bankruptcy.

perfect a lien   An action that is legally necessary to ensure that a secured creditor's lien attaches to a debtor's collateral.

petition   The legal documents that must be filed to initiate a bankruptcy.

priority debt   One of three categories of debt in a Chapter 7 and a Chapter 13 bankruptcy. This type of debt cannot be wiped out or discharged through bankruptcy. In a Chapter 13 bankruptcy, priority debts must be paid in full over the term of a debtor's reorganization plan.

proof of claim   A document that a creditor must file with the court within a specified period of time after a debtor has filed for bankruptcy for the creditor to try to get paid by the debtor.

purchase-money lien   A lien placed on an asset that a creditor purchases on credit and pays for over time. Examples of property commonly associated with a purchase-money lien include cars, homes, and furniture.

reaffirmation agreement   An agreement between a creditor and a debtor in a Chapter 7 bankruptcy that allows the debtor to continue to make payments on a debt to keep a particular asset.

redemption of property   In a Chapter 7 bankruptcy, a process by which a debtor can keep exempt property worth less than the amount owed on it by paying the full value of the property to a creditor.

reorganization bankruptcy   Another term for a Chapter 13 bankruptcy.

reorganization plan   In a Chapter 13 bankruptcy, a written plan that spells out how a debtor intends to pay as much as possible on his or her debts over a specified period of time, usually three to five years. The plan must be approved by the court.

secured creditor   A creditor whose debt is secured by a lien on the debtor's property. Common examples of secured creditors include auto lenders, mortgage lenders, lenders that make home equity loans or loan money for furniture, etc.

secured debt   Debt secured or collateralized with property such as a car, house, boat, etc. If a debtor defaults on a secured debt, the lender can recover what it is still owed by taking the property.

statement of financial affairs In a Chapter 7 or Chapter 13 bankruptcy, a series of written questions that a debtor must answer so that the court can be sure that the debtor has been completely honest about all his or her assets and has not made any inappropriate financial transactions prior to filing.

trustee In a Chapter 13 bankruptcy, a person who is appointed by the court to review a debtor's reorganization plan, recommend approval or changes to it, receive and distribute the debtor's payments to his or her creditors, and monitor the success of the debtor's reorganization plan. In a Chapter 7 bankruptcy, the trustee takes control of a debtor's nonexempt assets, liquidates them, and distributes the proceeds to creditors.

unsecured creditor A creditor whose debt is not secured by a lien on an asset of the debtor. A credit card company is the most common example of an unsecured creditor. Other examples include a utility company, a doctor or hospital, an ex-spouse who is owed past-due support or maintenance, and so on.

unsecured debt Debt that a debtor does not collateralize with an asset, including credit card debt, doctor and hospital bills, money owed to suppliers, signature loans, etc. Unsecured debts get the lowest priority in a Chapter 13 reorganization plan. Also called uncollateralized debt.

Index